WordPerfect® 6.1

for Windows™
Illustrated

WordPerfect 6.1

for Windows™
Illustrated

Rachel Biheller Bunin

Course TECHNOLOGY

Course Technology, Inc. One Main Street, Cambridge, MA 02142
An International Thomson Publishing Company

I(T)P

Albany • Bonn • Boston • Cincinnati • London • Madrid • Melbourne • Mexico City
New York • Paris • San Francisco • Singapore • Tokyo • Toronto • Washington

WordPerfect 6.1 for Windows — Illustrated is published by Course Technology, Inc.

Managing Editor:	Marjorie Hunt
Series Product Manager:	Nicole Jones Pinard
Product Manager:	Ann Marie Buconjic
Production Editor:	Donna Whiting
Text Designer:	Leslie Hartwell
Cover Designer:	John Gamache

©1995 Course Technology, Inc.
A Division of International Thomson Publishing, Inc.

For more information contact:
Course Technology, Inc.
One Main Street
Cambridge, MA 02142

International Thomson Publishing Europe
Berkshire House 168-173
High Holborn
London WCIV 7AA
England

Thomas Nelson Australia
102 Dodds Street
South Melbourne, 3205
Victoria, Australia

Nelson Canada
1120 Birchmount Road
Scarborough, Ontario
Canada M1K 5G4

International Thomson Editores
Campos Eliseos 385, Piso 7
Col. Polanco
11560 Mexico D.F. Mexico

International Thomson Publishing GmbH
Königswinterer Strasse 418
53227 Bonn
Germany

International Thomson Publishing Asia
211 Henderson Road
#05-10 Henderson Building
Singapore 0315

International Thomson Publishing Japan
Hirakawacho Kyowa Building, 3F
2-2-1 Hirakawacho
Chiyoda-ku, Tokyo 102
Japan

Trademarks

Course Technology and the open book logo are registered trademarks of Course Technology, Inc.

I(T)P   The ITP logo is a trademark under license.

WordPerfect is a registered trademark of Novell, Inc.

Some of the product names in this book have been used for identification purposes only and may be trademarks or registered trademarks of their respective manufacturers and sellers.

Disclaimer

Course Technology, Inc. reserves the right to revise this publication and make changes from time to time in its content without notice.

ISBN 0-7600-3481-8

Printed in the United States of America

10 9 8 7 6 5 4

From the Publisher

At Course Technology, Inc., we believe that technology will transform the way that people teach and learn. We are very excited about bringing you, instructors and students, the most practical and affordable technology-related products available.

The Course Technology Development Process

Our development process is unparalleled in the educational publishing industry. Every product we create goes through an exacting process of design, development, review, and testing.

Reviewers give us direction and insight that shape our manuscripts and bring them up to the latest standards. Every manuscript is quality tested. Students whose backgrounds match the intended audience work through every keystroke, carefully checking for clarity and pointing out errors in logic and sequence. Together with our own technical reviewers, these testers help us ensure that everything that carries our name is as error free and easy to use as possible.

Course Technology Products

We show both *how* and *why* technology is critical to solving problems in the classroom and in whatever field you choose to teach or pursue. Our time-tested, step-by-step instructions provide unparalleled clarity. Examples and applications are chosen and crafted to motivate students.

The Course Technology Team

This book will suit your needs because it was delivered quickly, efficiently, and affordably. In every aspect of business, we rely on a commitment to quality and the use of technology. Every employee contributes to this process. The names of all our employees are listed below: Diana Armington, Tim Ashe, Debora Barrow, Stephen M. Bayle, Ann Marie Buconjic, Jody Buttafoco, Kerry Cannell, Jei Lee Chong, Jim Chrysikos, Barbara Clemens, Susan Collins, John M. Connolly, Stephanie Crayton, Myrna D'Addario, Lisa D'Alessandro, Jodi Davis, Howard S. Diamond, Kathryn Dinovo, Jennifer Dolan, Joseph B. Dougherty, Patti Dowley, Laurie Duncan, Karen Dwyer, MaryJane Dwyer, Kristin Dyer, Chris Elkhill, Don Fabricant, Jane Fraser, Viktor Frengut, Jeff Goding, Laurie Gomes, Eileen Gorham, Catherine Griffin, Jamie Harper, Roslyn Hooley, Marjorie Hunt, Matt Kenslea, Marybeth LaFauci, Susannah Lean, Kim Mai, Margaret Makowski, Tammy Marciano, Elizabeth Martinez, Debbie Masi, Don Maynard, Kathleen McCann, Sarah McLean, Jay McNamara, Mac Mendelsohn, Karla Mitchell, Kim Munsell, Michael Ormsby, Debbie Parlee, Kristin Patrick, Charlie Patsios, Darren Perl, Kevin Phaneuf, George J. Pilla, Nicole Jones Pinard, Nancy Ray, Brian Romer, Laura Sacks, Carla Sharpe, Deborah Shute, Roger Skilling, Jennifer Slivinski, Christine Spillett, Audrey Tortolani, Michelle Tucker, David Upton, Jim Valente, Mark Valentine, Karen Wadsworth, Renee Walkup, Tracy Wells, Donna Whiting, Rob Williams, Janet Wilson, Lisa Yameen.

Preface

Course Technology, Inc. is proud to present this new book in its Illustrated series. *WordPerfect 6.1 for Windows — Illustrated* provides a highly visual, hands-on introduction to WordPerfect. The book is designed as a learning tool for WordPerfect novices but will also be useful as a source for future reference.

Organization and Coverage

WordPerfect 6.1 for Windows — Illustrated contains nine units that cover basic WordPerfect skills. In these units students learn how to plan, create, edit, and format documents. They work with text, graphics, tables, data & form files, and macros to create a variety of documents related to simple business applications.

Approach

WordPerfect 6.1 for Windows — Illustrated distinguishes itself from other textbooks with its highly visual approach to computer instruction.

Lessons: Information Displays

The basic lesson format of this text is the "information display," a two-page lesson that is sharply focused on a specific task. This sharp focus and the precise beginning and end of a lesson make it easy for students to study specific material. Modular lessons are less overwhelming for students, and they provide instructors with more flexibility in planning classes and assigning specific work. The units are modular as well and can be presented in any order.

Each lesson, or "information display," contains the following elements:

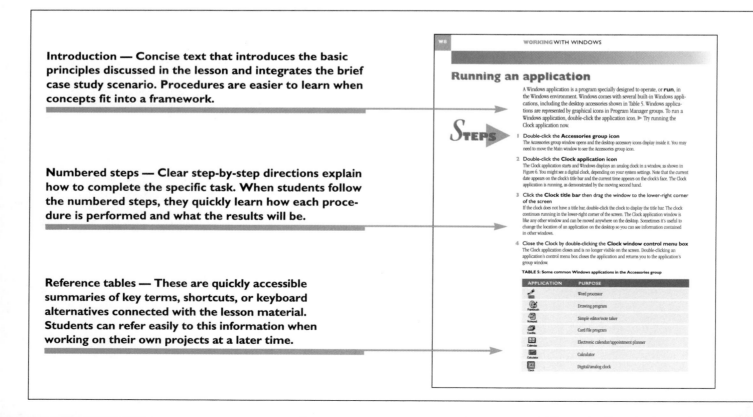

Introduction — Concise text that introduces the basic principles discussed in the lesson and integrates the brief case study scenario. Procedures are easier to learn when concepts fit into a framework.

Numbered steps — Clear step-by-step directions explain how to complete the specific task. When students follow the numbered steps, they quickly learn how each procedure is performed and what the results will be.

Reference tables — These are quickly accessible summaries of key terms, shortcuts, or keyboard alternatives connected with the lesson material. Students can refer easily to this information when working on their own projects at a later time.

Features

WordPerfect 6.1 for Windows — Illustrated is an exceptional textbook because it contains the following features:

- "Read This Before You Begin" Pages — These pages, one for the Windows section and one before Unit 1, provide essential information that both students and instructors need to know before they begin working through the units.

- Real-World Case — The case study used throughout the textbook is designed to be "real-world" in nature and representative of the kinds of activities that students will encounter when working with word-processing software. With a real-world case, the process of solving the problem will be more meaningful to students.

- End of Unit Material — Each unit concludes with a meaningful Concepts Review that tests students' understanding of what they learned in the unit. The Concepts Review is followed by an Applications Review, which provides students with additional hands-on practice of the skills they learned in the unit. The Applications Review is followed by Independent Challenges, which pose case problems for students to solve. The Independent Challenges allow students to learn by exploring, and develop critical thinking skills.

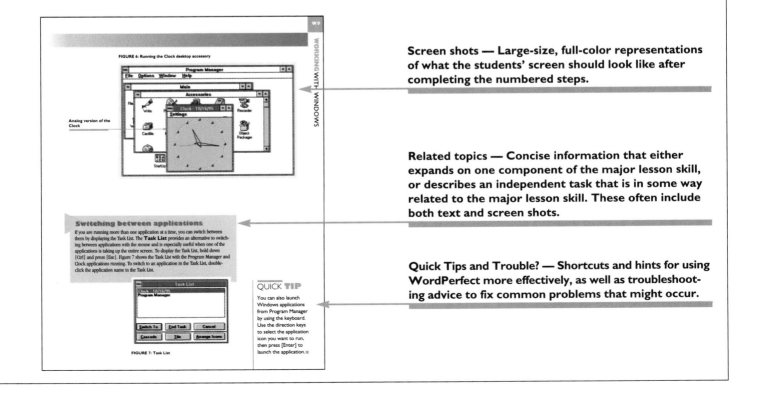

The Student Disk

The Student Disk bundled with the instructor's copy of this book contains all the data files students need to complete the step-by-step lessons.

Adopters of this text are granted the right to post the Student Disk on any standalone computer or network used by students who have purchased this product.

For more information on the Student Disk, see the page in this book called "Read This Before You Begin WordPerfect 6.1."

The Supplements

Instructor's Manual — The Instructor's Manual is quality assurance tested. It includes:

- Solutions to all lessons, Concepts Reviews, Application Reviews, and Independent Challenges
- A disk containing solutions to all of the lessons, Concept Reviews, Application Reviews, and Independent Challenges
- Unit notes, which contain tips from the author about the instructional progression of each lesson
- Extra problems
- Transparency masters of key concepts

Test Bank — The Test Bank contains approximately 50 questions per unit in true/false, multiple choice, and fill-in-the-blank formats, plus two essay questions. Each question has been quality assurance tested by students to achieve clarity and accuracy.

Electronic Test Bank — The Electronic Test Bank allows instructors to edit individual test questions, select questions individually or at random, and print out scrambled versions of the same test to any supported printer.

Acknowledgments

A book of this caliber could not have been realized without the valuable contributions from the many wonderful people at Course Technology who worked on this project. I am grateful to all the members of the development team whose insights and energy facilitated the successful and timely publication of this book. Warm and special thanks go to Ann Marie Buconjic whose excellent organizational skills, delightful sense of humor, keen insights, and strong support made this book a pleasure to write. I especially would like to thank Marjorie Hunt for her vision of this important series and thank Nicole Jones Pinard for her guidance and knowing how to make everything work out just right. Thanks go to Donna Whiting for her superb production editing, and to Nancy Ray for unparalleled excellence in validating this book. Finally, I would like to thank my family, my husband and three wonderful children; their strong support and understanding made this book possible.

Rachel B. Bunin

Brief Contents

Contents

TABLES

Read This Before You Begin Working with Windows

To the Student

The Working with Windows section gives you practice using the main features of Windows, the control program that lets you work easily with your computer and many programs you run. You need a Student Disk to complete this section.

Your instructor might provide you with your own copy of the Student Disk, or might make the Student Disk files available to you over a network in your school's computer lab. See your instructor or technical support person for further information.

To the Instructor

Student Disk

The instructor's copy of this book is bundled with the Student Disk, which contains all the files your students need to complete the step-by-step lessons in this book. Your students will not need the Student Disk files to complete this Working with Windows section, but they will need the Student Disk to create a practice directory called MY_FILES.

If you choose to make the Student Disk files available to students over a network, then be sure to tell students where you want them to create the MY_FILES directory. For more information on the Student Disk, refer to the "Read This Before You Begin WordPerfect 6.1" page.

Screens

This Working with Windows section assumes students will use the default Windows setup. If you want your students' screens to look like those in the figures, set up the Program Manager window to look like Figure 1, and make sure the Clock accessory is in analog mode with the title bar displayed at the top.

Working
WITH WINDOWS

Microsoft Windows 3.1 is the **graphical user interface** (GUI) that works hand in hand with MS-DOS to control the basic operation of your computer and the programs you run on it. Windows is a comprehensive control program that helps you run useful, task-oriented programs known as **applications**. ▶ This introduction will help you to learn basic skills that you can use in all Windows applications. First you'll learn how to start Windows and how to use the mouse in the Windows environment. Next you'll get some hands-on experience with Program Manager, and you'll learn how to work with groups, run an application, resize a window, use menus and dialog boxes, save files, use File Manager, and arrange windows and icons. Then you'll learn how to exit a Windows application and exit Windows itself. ▶

Starting Windows

Windows is started, or **launched**, from MS-DOS with the Win command. Once started, Windows takes over most of the duties of MS-DOS and provides a graphical environment in which you run your applications. Windows has several advantages over MS-DOS. As a graphical interface, it uses meaningful pictures and symbols known as **icons** to replace hard-to-remember commands. Windows lets you run more than one application at a time, so you can run, for example, a word processor and a spreadsheet at the same time and easily share data between them. ▶ Each application is represented in a rectangular space called a **window**. The Windows environment also includes several useful desktop accessories, including Clock and Notepad, which you can use for day-to-day tasks. ▶ Try starting Windows now.

STEPS ▶

I Turn on your computer

The computer displays some technical information as it starts up and tests its circuitry. MS-DOS starts automatically, then displays the **command prompt** (usually C:\>). The command prompt gives you access to MS-DOS commands and applications. If your computer is set up so that it automatically runs Windows when it starts, the command prompt will not display. You can then skip Step 2.

2 Type **win** then press **[Enter]**

This command starts Windows. The screen momentarily goes blank while the computer starts Windows. An hourglass displays, indicating Windows is busy processing a command. Then the Windows Program Manager displays on your screen, as shown in Figure 1. Your screen might look slightly different depending on which applications are installed on your computer.

TABLE I:
Elements of the Windows desktop

DESKTOP ELEMENT	DESCRIPTION
Program Manager	The main control program of Windows. All Windows applications are started from the Program Manager.
Window	A rectangular space framed by a double border on the screen. The Program Manager is framed in a window.
Application icon	The graphic representation of a Windows application.
Title bar	The area directly below the window's top border that displays the name of a window or application.
Sizing buttons	Buttons in the upper-right corner of a window that you can use to minimize or maximize a window.
Menu bar	The area under the title bar on a window. The menu bar provides access to most of an application's commands.
Control menu box	A box in the upper-left corner of each window; provides a menu used to resize, move, maximize, minimize, or close a window. Double-clicking this box closes a window or an application.
Mouse pointer	An arrow indicating the current location of the mouse on the desktop.

FIGURE 1: Program Manager window

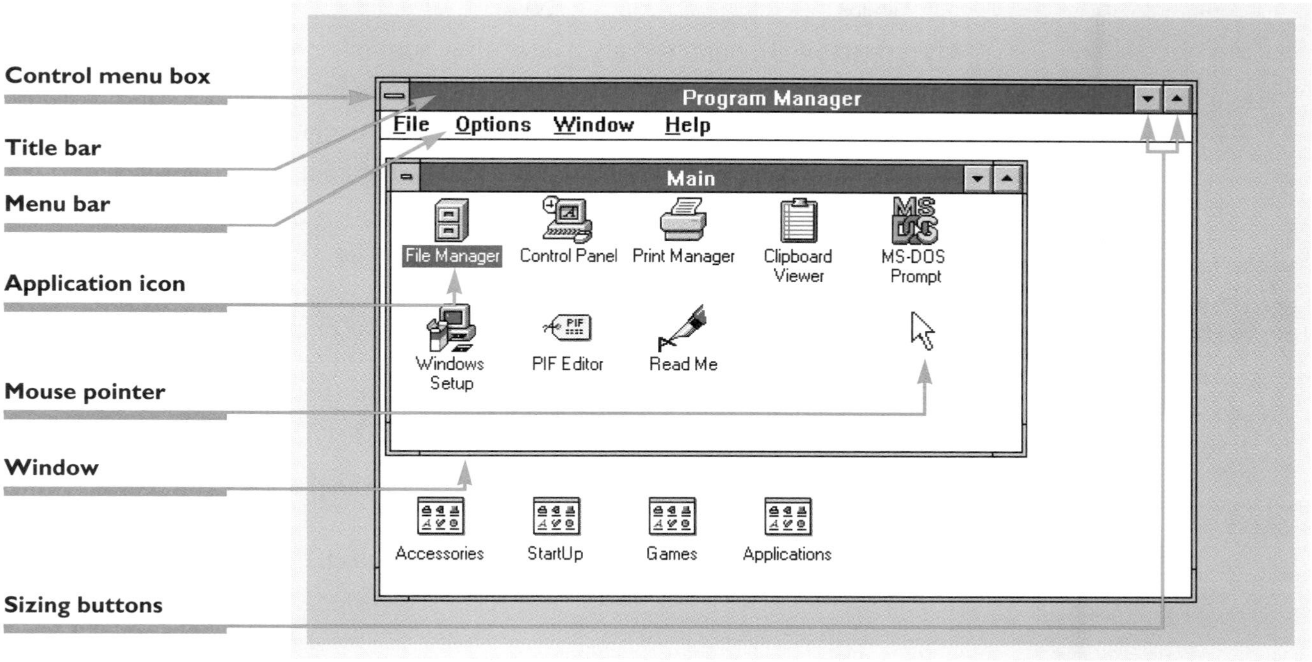

Control menu box

Title bar

Menu bar

Application icon

Mouse pointer

Window

Sizing buttons

The Windows desktop

The entire screen area on the monitor represents the Windows desktop. The **desktop** is an electronic version of a desk that provides workspace for different computing tasks. Windows allows you to customize the desktop to support the way you like to work and to organize the applications you need to run. Use Table 1 to identify the key elements of the desktop, referring to Figure 1 for their locations. Because the Windows desktop can be customized, your desktop might look slightly different.

Using the mouse

The **mouse** is a handheld input device that you roll on your desk to position the mouse pointer on the Windows desktop. When you move the mouse on your desk, the **mouse pointer** on the screen moves in the same direction. The buttons on the mouse are used to select icons and choose commands, and to indicate the work to be done in applications. Table 2 lists the four basic mouse techniques. Table 3 shows some common mouse pointer shapes. ▶ Try using the mouse now.

1 **Locate the mouse pointer** ⬚ **on the Windows desktop and move the mouse across your desk**
Watch how the mouse pointer moves on the Windows desktop in response to your movements. Try moving the mouse pointer in circles, then back and forth in straight lines.

2 **Position the mouse pointer over the Control Panel icon in the Main group window**
Positioning the mouse pointer over an icon is called **pointing**. The Control Panel icon is a graphical representation of the Control Panel application, a special program that controls the operation of the Windows environment. If the Control Panel icon is not visible in the Main group window, point to any other icon. The Program Manager is customizable so the Control Panel could be hidden from view.

3 **Press and release the left mouse button**
Pressing and releasing the mouse button is called **clicking**. When you position the mouse pointer on an icon in Program Manager then click, you **select** the icon. When the Control Panel icon is selected, its title is highlighted, as shown in Figure 2. If you clicked an icon that caused a menu to open, click the icon again to close the menu. You'll learn about menus later. Now practice a mouse skill called **dragging**.

4 **With the icon selected, press and hold the left mouse button and move the mouse down and to the right**
The icon moves with the mouse pointer, as shown in Figure 3. When you release the mouse button, the icon relocates in the group window.

5 **Drag the Control Panel icon back to its original position**

TABLE 2:
Basic mouse techniques

TECHNIQUE	HOW TO DO IT
Pointing	Move the mouse pointer to position it over an item on the desktop.
Clicking	Press and release the mouse button.
Double-clicking	Press and release the mouse button twice quickly.
Dragging	Point at an item, press and hold the mouse button, move the mouse to a new location, then release the mouse button.

FIGURE 2: Selecting an icon

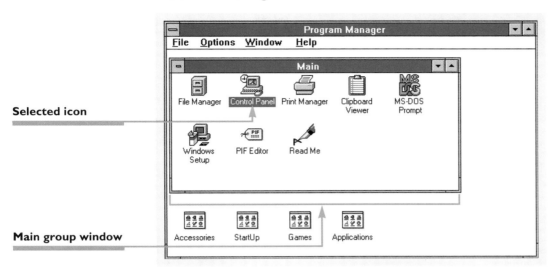

Selected icon

Main group window

FIGURE 3: Dragging an icon

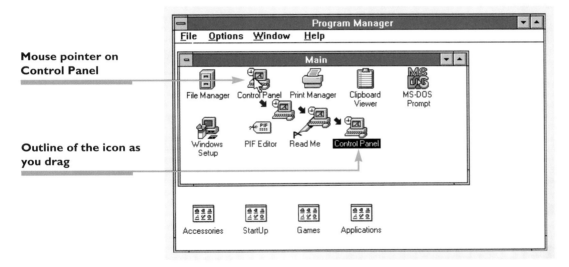

Mouse pointer on
Control Panel

Outline of the icon as
you drag

TABLE 3: Common mouse pointer shapes

SHAPE	USED TO
⮝	Select items, choose commands, start applications, and work in applications.
I	Position mouse pointer for editing or inserting text. This icon is called an insertion point.
⧗	Indicate Windows is busy processing a command.
⟷	Change the size of a window. This icon appears when mouse pointer is on the border of a window.

Using Program Manager groups

In Program Manager, you launch applications and organize your applications into windows called groups. A **group** can appear as an open window or as an icon in the Program Manager window. Each group has a name related to its contents, and you can reorganize the groups to suit your needs. The standard Windows groups are described in Table 4. ▶ Try working with groups now.

1 If necessary, double-click the **Main group icon** to open the Main group window
The Main group icon is usually located at the bottom of the Program Manager window.

2 Double-click the **Accessories group icon**
When you double-click the Accessories group icon, it expands into the Accessories group window, as shown in Figure 4. Now move the Accessories group window to the right.

3 Click the **Accessories group window title bar** and drag the group window to the right
An outline of the window moves to the right with the mouse. When you release the mouse button, the Accessories group window moves to the location you've indicated. Moving a window lets you see what is beneath it. Any window in the Windows environment can be moved with this technique.

4 Click the **title bar** of the Main group window
The Main group window becomes the **active window**, the one you are currently working in. Other windows, including the Accessories group window, are considered background windows. Note that the active window has a highlighted title bar. Program Manager has a highlighted title bar because it is the **active application**.

5 Activate the **Accessories group window** by clicking anywhere in that window
The Accessories group window moves to the foreground again. Now try closing the Accessories group window to an icon.

6 Double-click the **control menu box** in the Accessories group window
When you double-click this box, the Accessories group window shrinks to an icon and the Main group window becomes the active window. Double-clicking the control menu box is the easiest way to close a window or an application.

TABLE 4:
Standard Windows groups

GROUP NAME	CONTENTS
Main	Applications that control how Windows works; the primary Windows group.
Accessories	Useful desktop accessories for day-to-day tasks.
StartUp	Programs that run automatically when Windows is started.
Games	Game programs for Windows.
Applications	Group of applications found on your hard disk.

FIGURE 4: Accessories group expanded into a window

Main group window title bar

Control menu box

Highlighted title bar indicates active window

Accessories group window

Program Manager group icons

Program Manager

File   Options   Window   Help

Main

Accessories

Write   Paintbrush   Terminal   Notepad   Recorder

Cardfile   Calendar   Calculator   Clock   Object Packager

StartUp   Games   Applications

Scroll bars

If a group contains more icons than can be displayed at one time, **scroll bars** appear on the right and/or bottom edges of the window to give you access to the remaining icons, as shown in Figure 5. Vertical or horizontal arrows appear at the ends of the bars. To use scroll bars, click the vertical or horizontal arrows that point in the direction you want the window to scroll or drag the scroll box along the scroll bar. Scroll bars appear whenever there is more information than can fit in a window. You'll see them in many Windows applications.

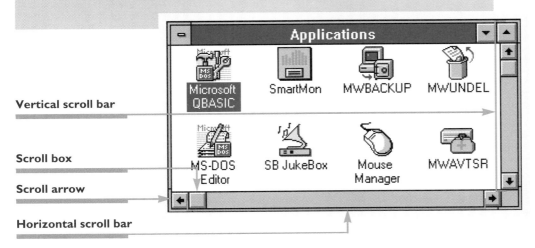

Vertical scroll bar

Scroll box

Scroll arrow

Horizontal scroll bar

Applications

Microsoft QBASIC   SmartMon   MWBACKUP   MWUNDEL

MS-DOS Editor   SB JukeBox   Mouse Manager   MWAVTSR

FIGURE 5: Vertical and horizontal scroll bars on a window

QUICK **TIP**

You can use the direction keys on the keyboard to scroll the contents of the active window. To scroll vertically, press [↑] or [↓]. To scroll horizontally, press [←] or [→].■

Running an application

A Windows application is a program specially designed to operate, or **run**, in the Windows environment. Windows comes with several built-in Windows applications, including the desktop accessories shown in Table 5. Windows applications are represented by graphical icons in Program Manager groups. To run a Windows application, double-click the application icon. ▶ Try running the Clock application now.

I   Double-click the **Accessories group icon**
The Accessories group window opens and the desktop accessory icons display inside it. You may need to move the Main window to see the Accessories group icon.

2   Double-click the **Clock application icon**
The Clock application starts and Windows displays an analog clock in a window, as shown in Figure 6. You might see a digital clock, depending on your system settings. Note that the current date appears on the clock's title bar and the current time appears on the clock's face. The Clock application is running, as demonstrated by the moving second hand.

3   Click the **Clock title bar** then drag the window to the lower-right corner of the screen
If the clock does not have a title bar, double-click the clock to display the title bar. The clock continues running in the lower-right corner of the screen. The Clock application window is like any other window and can be moved anywhere on the desktop. Sometimes it's useful to change the location of an application on the desktop so you can see information contained in other windows.

4   Close the Clock by double-clicking the **Clock window control menu box**
The Clock application closes and is no longer visible on the screen. Double-clicking an application's control menu box closes the application and returns you to the application's group window.

TABLE 5: Some common Windows applications in the Accessories group

APPLICATION	PURPOSE
Write	Word processor
Paintbrush	Drawing program
Notepad	Simple editor/note taker
Cardfile	Card file program
Calendar	Electronic calendar/appointment planner
Calculator	Calculator
Clock	Digital/analog clock

FIGURE 6: Running the Clock desktop accessory

Analog version of the Clock

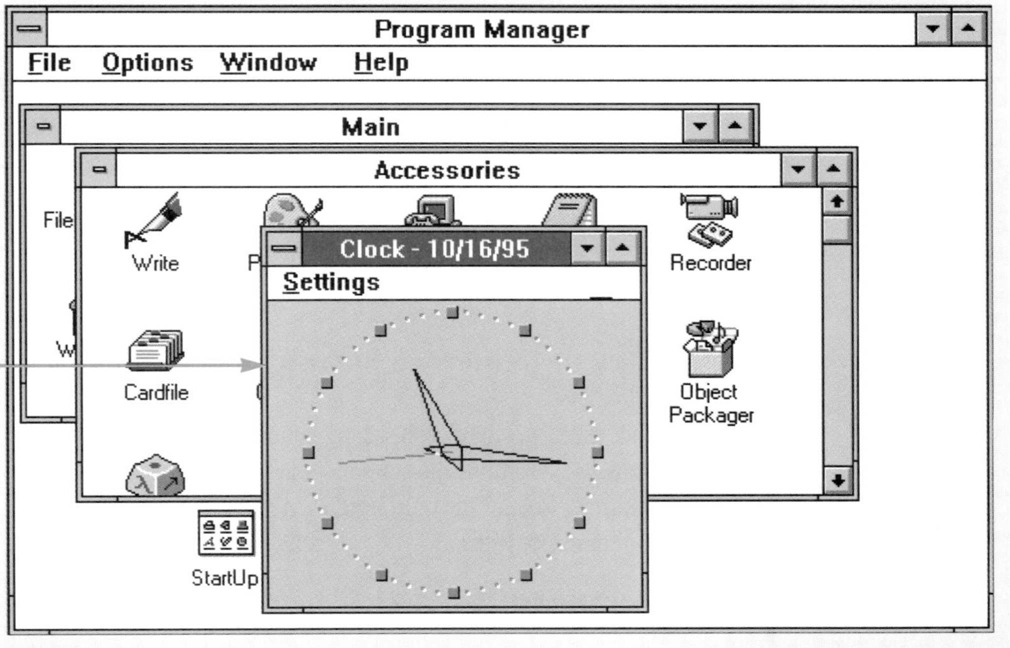

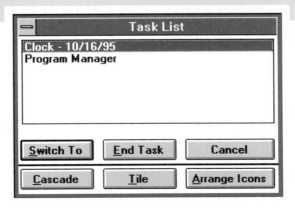

Switching between applications

If you are running more than one application at a time, you can switch between them by displaying the Task List. The **Task List** provides an alternative to switching between applications with the mouse and is especially useful when one of the applications is taking up the entire screen. To display the Task List, hold down [Ctrl] and press [Esc]. Figure 7 shows the Task List with the Program Manager and Clock applications running. To switch to an application in the Task List, double-click the application name in the Task List.

FIGURE 7: Task List

Resizing a window

The Windows desktop can get cluttered with icons and windows if you use lots of applications. Each window is surrounded by a standard border and sizing buttons that allow you to minimize, maximize, and restore windows as needed. The sizing buttons are shown in Table 6. They help you keep the desktop organized. ▶ Try sizing the Clock window now.

1 Double-click the **Clock application icon**
The Clock application restarts.

2 Click the **Minimize button** in the upper-right corner of the Clock window
The Minimize button is the sizing button on the left. When you **minimize** the clock, it shrinks to an icon at the bottom of the screen, as shown in Figure 8. Notice that the Clock icon continues to show the right time, even as an icon. Windows applications continue to run after you minimize them.

3 Double-click the **Clock icon** to restore the Clock window to its original size
The clock is restored to its original size, and the application continues to run.

4 Click the **Maximize button** in the upper-right corner of the Clock window
The Maximize button is the sizing button to the right of the Minimize button. When you **maximize** the clock, it takes up the entire screen, as shown in Figure 9. Although it's unlikely you'll want to maximize this application very often, you'll find the ability to maximize other Windows applications very useful.

5 Click the **Restore button** in the upper-right corner of the Clock window
The Restore button, as shown in Figure 9, is located to the right of the Minimize button *after* an application has been maximized. The Restore button returns an application to its original size.

6 Double-click the **Clock window control menu box** to close the application

TABLE 6:
Buttons for managing windows

BUTTON	PURPOSE
▼	Minimizes an application to an icon on the bottom of the screen.
▲	Maximizes an application to its largest possible size.
⇕	Restores an application, returning it to its original size.

FIGURE 8:
Minimized Clock
application as an icon

Minimize button

Maximize button

Minimized clock with
current time and date

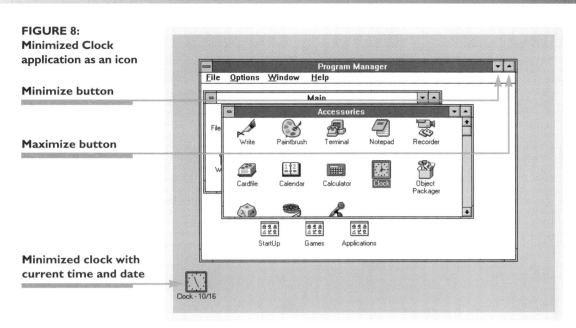

FIGURE 9:
Maximized clock filling
entire screen

Restore button
appears after a window
has been maximized

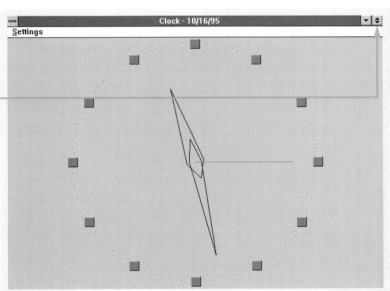

Changing the dimension of a window

The dimension of a window can also be changed, but the window will always be a rectangle. To change the dimension of a window, position the mouse pointer on the window border you want to modify. The mouse pointer changes to ⟨⟷⟩. Drag the border in the direction you want to change. Figure 10 shows the width of the Clock window being increased, which will make the clock face larger.

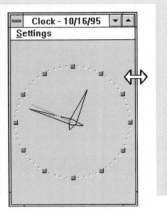

FIGURE 10: Increasing the width of the Clock window

Using menus and dialog boxes

A **menu** is a list of commands that you can use to accomplish certain tasks. Each Windows application has its own set of menus, which are listed on the **menu bar** along the top of the application window. Sometimes when you select a command from a menu, the application needs more information before it can complete the task, in which case a **dialog box** opens, giving you more options. See Table 7 for some of the typical conventions used on menus and dialog boxes. ▶ Try using the Control Panel which lets you customize your Windows desktop.

1 Click the **Main group window** to make it active, then double-click the **Control Panel icon**
Drag other windows out of the way, if necessary. The Control Panel window opens.

2 Click **Settings** on the menu bar
A menu displays listing all the commands that let you adjust different aspects of your desktop. See Table 7.

3 Click **Desktop** to display the Desktop dialog box
This dialog box provides options to customize your desktop. See Figure 11. Next, locate the Screen Saver section of the dialog box. A **screen saver** is a moving pattern that fills your screen after your computer has not been used for a specified amount of time.

4 Click the **Name list arrow** in the Screen Saver section
A list of available screen saver patterns displays.

5 Click the screen saver pattern of your choice, then click **Test**
The Test button is a **command button**. The two most common command buttons are OK and Cancel which you'll see in almost every dialog box. The screen saver pattern you chose displays. It will remain on the screen until you move the mouse or press a key.

6 Move the mouse to exit the screen saver
Next, you'll adjust the cursor blink rate in the Cursor Blink Rate section. The **cursor** is the vertical line that shows you where you are on the screen. See Figure 11.

7 Drag the scroll box all the way to the right of the scroll bar, then click the **left arrow** in the scroll bar a few times
By moving the scroll box between Slow and Fast on the scroll bar, you can adjust the cursor blink rate to suit your needs.

8 Click **OK** to save your changes and close the dialog box
Clicking OK accepts your changes; clicking Cancel rejects your changes. Now you can exit the Control Panel.

9 Double-click the **Control Panel control menu box** to close this window

FIGURE 11:
Desktop dialog box

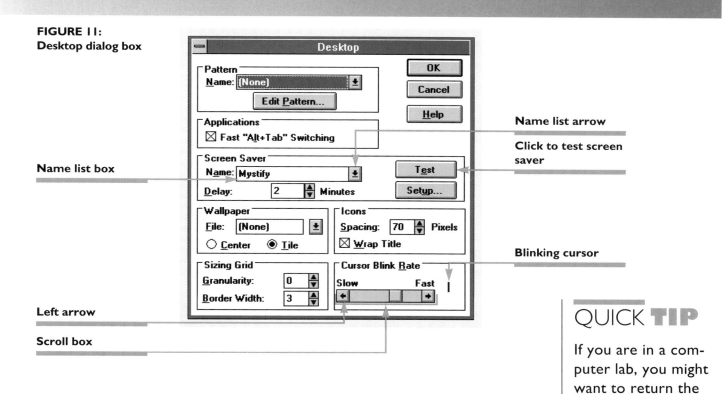

Name list box

Left arrow

Scroll box

Name list arrow

Click to test screen saver

Blinking cursor

QUICK **TIP**

If you are in a computer lab, you might want to return the desktop settings you changed to their original state.■

TABLE 7: Typical items on menus and dialog boxes

ITEM	MEANING	EXAMPLE
Dimmed command	A menu command that is not currently available.	Undo
Ellipsis	Choosing this menu command opens a dialog box that asks for further information.	Paste Special...
Triangle	Clicking this button opens a cascading menu containing an additional list of menu commands.	Axis ▶
Keyboard shortcut	A keyboard alternative for executing a menu command.	Cut Ctrl+X
Underlined letter	Pressing the underlined letter executes this menu command.	Copy Right
Check box	Clicking this square box turns a dialog box option on or off.	☒ Wrap Title
Text box	A box in which you type text.	tours.wk4
Radio button	Clicking this small circle selects a single dialog box option.	◉ Tile
Command button	Clicking this button executes this dialog box command.	OK
List box	A box containing a list of items. To choose an item, click the list arrow, then click the desired item.	c: ms-dos_5

Saving a file

The documents you create using a computer are stored in the computer's random access memory (RAM). **RAM** is temporary storage space that is erased when the computer is turned off. To store a document permanently, you need to save it to a disk. You can either save your work to a 3.5-inch or a 5.25-inch disk that you insert into the disk drive of your computer (i.e., drive A or B), or a hard disk, which is a disk built into the computer (usually drive C). Your instructor has provided you with a Student Disk to use as you proceed through the lessons in this book. This book assumes that you will save all of your files to your Student Disk. Refer to the Read This Before You Begin page immediately preceding this section for more information on your Student Disk. ▶ In this lesson, you'll create a simple document using Notepad, then you will save the document to your Student Disk. **Notepad** is a simple text editor that lets you create memos, record notes, or edit text files. A **text file** is a document containing words, letters, or numbers, but no special computer instructions, such as formatting.

1 Insert your Student Disk into drive A or drive B
Check with your instructor if you aren't sure which drive you should use.

2 Click the **Accessories group window** to activate it

3 Double-click the **Notepad application icon** to start Notepad
The Notepad application starts, and the Notepad window displays. Now, enter some text.

4 Type **Today I started working with Notepad.** then press **[Enter]**
Your screen should look like Figure 12.

5 Click **File** on the Notepad menu bar, then click **Save**
The Save As dialog box displays, as shown in Figure 13. In this dialog box you enter a name for your file and specify where you want to save it.

6 Type **MYNOTES** in the File Name text box
Your entry replaces the highlighted (selected) *.txt. Notepad will automatically add the extension when you click OK. Now you need to specify the drive where your Student Disk is located.

7 Click the **Drives list arrow** to display the drives on your computer, then click **a:** or **b:**, depending on which drive contains your Student Disk
Notice that the list of files that are on your Student Disk displays below the File Name text box.

8 Click **OK**
The Save As dialog box closes and MYNOTES is now saved on your Student Disk.

9 Click **File** on the Notepad menu bar, then click **Exit** to close Notepad

FIGURE 12: Notepad window with text entered

Menu bar

Cursor

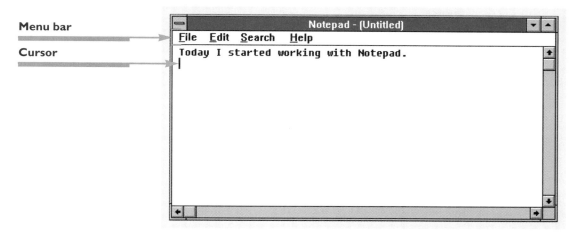

FIGURE 13: Save As dialog box

Highlighted File Name text box

Your list of directories might be different

Drives list arrow

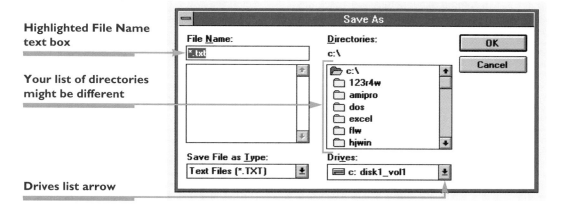

QUICK **TIP**

Save your work often, at least every 15 minutes and before printing.■

Using File Manager

File Manager is an application included with Windows that can help you organize files and directories. A **directory** is like a file folder—it is a part of a disk where you can store a group of related files. For example, you might want to create a directory called PROJECT1 and store all of the files relating to a particular project in that directory. You can use File Manager to create the directory, then move the related files into it.
▶ Use File Manager to create a directory called MY_FILES on your Student Disk and then move the Notepad file you created and saved in the previous lesson into that directory. Make sure your Student Disk is in drive A or drive B before beginning the steps.

1   Double-click the **Main program group icon**, or if it is already open, click the **Main group window** to activate it

2   Double-click the **File Manager application icon** in the Main group window
    File Manager opens to display the directory window, as shown in Figure 14. Your File Manager will contain different files and directories. The directory window is divided by the split bar. The left side of the window displays the structure of the current drive, or the directory tree. The right side of the window displays a list of files in the selected directory. See Table 8 for a description of the various icons used in the directory window. The status bar displays the information about the current drive and directory and other information to help you with file management tasks.

3   Click the **drive icon** that corresponds to the drive containing your Student Disk
    The contents of your Student Disk displays. Now create a directory on this disk.

4   Click **File** on the menu bar, then click **Create Directory**
    The Create Directory dialog box displays listing the current directory, which in this case is the top level directory indicated by the backslash (\). You will type a new directory name in the text box provided. Directory names can have up to 11 characters but cannot include spaces, commas, or backslashes.

5   Type **MY_FILES** in the Name text box, then click **OK**
    You can type in the directory name in either uppercase or lowercase letters. The new directory appears in both sides of the directory window.

6   Press and hold the mouse button to select MYNOTES.TXT, then drag the file into the MY_FILES directory on the left side of the window
    The mouse pointer changes as you drag the file, as shown in Figure 15. Don't worry if you move a file to the wrong place; simply drag it again to the correct location. (You can drag it to the MY_FILES directory in either the left or right side of the window.)

7   Click **Yes** in the Confirm Mouse Operation dialog box
    Notice that the file no longer appears in the list of files. Now check that the file is in the newly created directory.

8   Double-click the **MY_FILES icon**
    The file appears in the list of files. If you want, you can use this directory throughout this book to store the files that you save. Now that you have created a directory and moved a file into it, you can exit File Manager.

9   Double-click the **control menu box** to exit File Manager

FIGURE 14: File Manager

Menu bar

Drive icons

Directory tree

Selected directory

Status bar

Split bar

List of files

Directory window

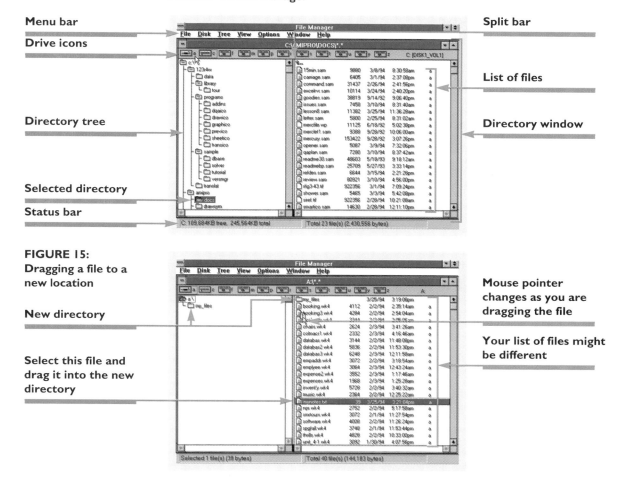

FIGURE 15:
Dragging a file to a new location

New directory

Select this file and drag it into the new directory

Mouse pointer changes as you are dragging the file

Your list of files might be different

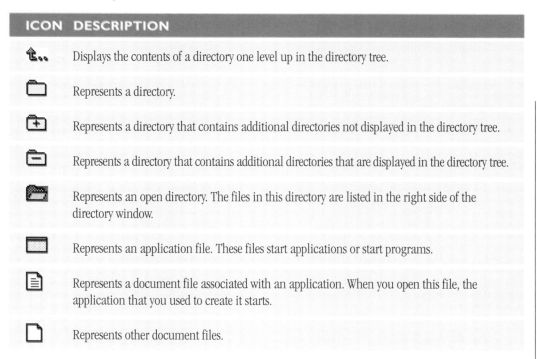

TABLE 8: Directory window icons

ICON	DESCRIPTION
🔼	Displays the contents of a directory one level up in the directory tree.
📁	Represents a directory.
📁+	Represents a directory that contains additional directories not displayed in the directory tree.
📁−	Represents a directory that contains additional directories that are displayed in the directory tree.
📂	Represents an open directory. The files in this directory are listed in the right side of the directory window.
▭	Represents an application file. These files start applications or start programs.
📄	Represents a document file associated with an application. When you open this file, the application that you used to create it starts.
📄	Represents other document files.

QUICK TIP

To select a group of files, click the first file, then press [Shift] and click the last file. To select noncontiguous files (files not next to each other in the file list), click the first file, then press [Ctrl] and click each additional file.

Arranging windows and icons

If your desktop contains many groups that you open regularly, you might find that the open windows clutter your desktop. The Tile and Cascade commands on the Window menu let you view all your open group windows at once in an organized arrangement. You can also use the Window menu to open all the program groups installed on your computer. ▶ Once you are comfortable working with Windows, you might decide to reorganize your group windows. You can easily move an icon from one group window to another by dragging it with the mouse. In the following steps, you'll drag the Clock icon from the Accessories group window to the StartUp group window. The StartUp group window contains programs that automatically start running when you launch Windows.

1   Click the **Program Manager Maximize button** to maximize this window, then click **Window** on the menu bar

The Window menu opens, as shown in Figure 16, displaying the commands Cascade, Tile, and Arrange Icons, followed by a numbered list of the program groups installed on your computer. You might see a check mark next to one of the items, indicating that this program group is the active one. Locate StartUp on the numbered list. If you don't see StartUp, click More Windows at the bottom of the list, then double-click StartUp in the dialog box that displays. If you still can't find StartUp, see your instructor or technical support person for assistance.

2   Click **StartUp**

The StartUp group window opens. Depending on how your computer is set up, you might see some program icons already in this window. At this point, your screen is getting cluttered with three program group windows open (Main, Accessories, and StartUp). Use the Cascade command to arrange them in an orderly way.

3   Click **Window** on the menu bar, then click **Cascade**

The windows display in a layered arrangement, with the title bars of each showing. This formation is neatly organized and shows all your open group windows, but it doesn't allow you to easily drag the Clock icon from the Accessories group window to the StartUp group window. The Tile command arranges the windows so that the contents of all the open windows are visible.

4   Click **Window** on the menu bar, then click **Tile**

The windows are now positioned in an ideal way to copy an icon from one window to another. Before continuing to step 5, locate the Clock icon in the Accessories group window. If you don't see the icon, use the scroll bar to bring it into view.

5   Drag the Clock application icon from the Accessories group window to the StartUp group window

Your screen now looks like Figure 17. The Clock application will automatically start the next time Windows is launched. If you are working on your own computer and want to leave the Clock in the StartUp group, skip Step 6 and continue to the next lesson, "Exiting Windows." If you are working in a computer lab, move the Clock icon back to its original location in the Accessories group window.

6   Drag the Clock application icon from the StartUp group window to the Accessories group window

The Clock icon is now back in the Accessories group.

FIGURE 16:
Window menu

Check mark
indicates the active
program group

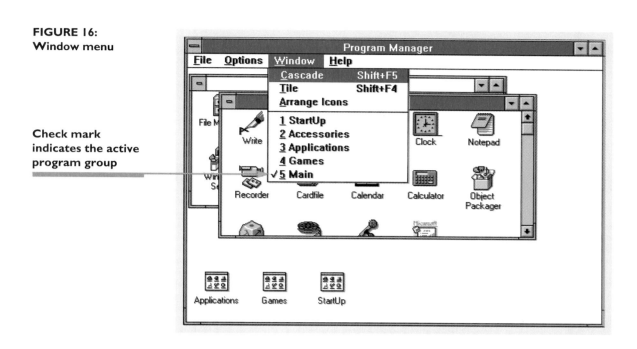

FIGURE 17:
Tiled group windows

StartUp group window
with Clock icon

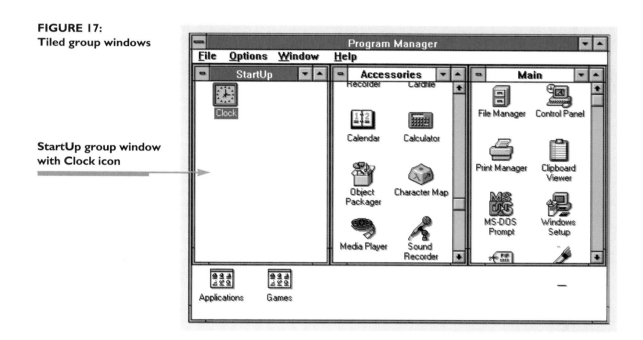

QUICK **TIP**

To move a copy of an
icon from one group
window to another,
hold down [Ctrl] as
you drag the icon.■

Exiting Windows

When you are finished working with Windows, close all the applications you are running and exit Windows. Do not turn off the computer while Windows is running; you could lose important data if you turn off your computer too soon. ▶ Now try closing all your active applications and exiting Windows.

I   **Close any active applications or group windows by double-clicking the control menu boxes of the open windows, one at a time**
The windows close. If you have any unsaved changes in your application, a dialog box displays, asking if you want to save them.

2   **Click File on the Program Manager menu bar**
The File menu displays, as shown in Figure 18.

3   **Click Exit Windows**
Program Manager displays the Exit Windows dialog box, as shown in Figure 19. You have two options at this point: Click OK to exit Windows, or click Cancel to abort the Exit Windows command and return to the Program Manager.

4   **Click OK to exit Windows**
Windows finishes its work and the MS-DOS command prompt appears. You can now safely turn off the computer.

FIGURE 18: Exiting Windows using the File menu

Menu bar

Exit Windows
command

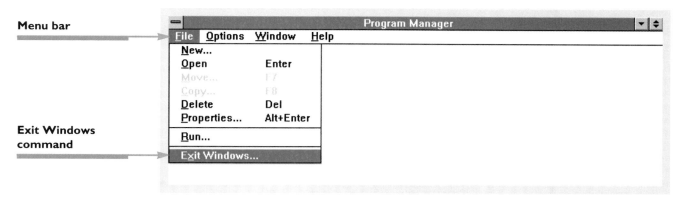

FIGURE 19: Exit Windows dialog box

Exiting Windows with the Program Manager control menu box

You can also exit Windows by double-clicking the control menu box in the upper-left corner of the Program Manager window, as shown in Figure 20. After you double-click the control menu box, you see the Exit Windows dialog box. Click OK to exit Windows.

Double-click the
control menu box

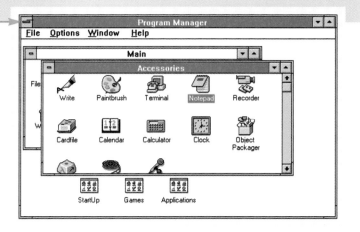

FIGURE 20: Exiting Windows with the Program Manager
control menu box

TROUBLE?

If you do not exit from Windows before turning off the computer, you might lose data from the applications you used while you were running Windows. Always close your applications and exit from Windows before turning off your computer. Do not turn off the computer if you are in a computer lab.■

CONCEPTS REVIEW

Label each of the elements of the Windows screen shown in Figure 21.

1 _____
2 _____
3 _____
4 _____
5 _____
6 _____

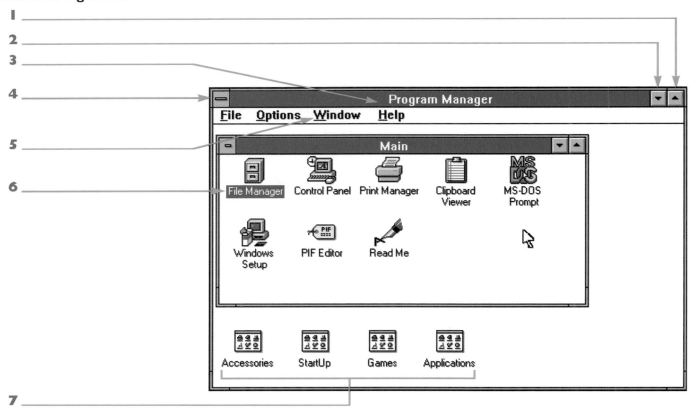

7 _____

FIGURE 21

Match each of the statements with the term it describes.

8 Shrinks an application window to an icon

9 Displays the name of the window or application

10 Serves as a launching pad for all applications

11 Requests more information that you supply before executing command

12 Lets the user point at screen menus and icons

a. Program Manager

b. Dialog box

c. Mouse

d. Title bar

e. Minimize button

Select the best answer from the list of choices.

13 The acronym GUI means:
   a. Grayed user information
   b. Group user icons
   c. Graphical user interface
   d. Group user interconnect

14 The term for starting Windows is:
   a. Prompting
   b. Launching
   c. Applying
   d. Processing

15 The small pictures that represent items such as applications are:

a. Icons

b. Windows

c. Buttons

d. Pointers

16 All of the following are examples of using a mouse, EXCEPT:

a. Clicking the Maximize button

b. Pressing [Enter]

c. Pointing at the control menu box

d. Dragging the Games icon

17 When Windows is busy performing a task, the mouse pointer changes to a(n):

a. Hand

b. Arrow

c. Clock

d. Hourglass

18 The term for moving an item to a new location on the desktop is:

a. Pointing

b. Clicking

c. Dragging

d. Restoring

19 The Clock, Notepad, and Calendar applications in Windows are known as:

a. Menu commands

b. Control panels

c. Sizing buttons

d. Desktop accessories

20 The Maximize button is used to:

a. Return a window to its original size

b. Expand a window to fill the computer screen

c. Scroll slowly through a window

d. Run programs from the main menu

21 What appears if a window contains more information than can be displayed in the window?

a. Program icon

b. Cascading menu

c. Scroll bars

d. Check box

22 A window is active when its title bar is:

a. Highlighted

b. Dimmed

c. Checked

d. Underlined

23 What is the term for changing the dimensions of a window?

a. Selecting

b. Resizing

c. Navigating

d. Scrolling

24 The menu bar provides access to an application's functions through:

a. Icons

b. Scroll bars

c. Commands

d. Control menu box

25 File Manager is a Windows application that lets you:

a. Select a different desktop wallpaper

b. Move a file from one location to another

c. Type entries into a text file

d. Determine what programs begin automatically when you start Windows

26 When your desktop is too cluttered, you can organize it by all the following methods, EXCEPT:

a. Double-clicking the control menu box to close unneeded windows

b. Using the Tile command to view all open group windows

c. Using the Cascade command to open group window title bars

d. Clicking File, clicking Exit Windows, then clicking OK

27 You can exit Windows by double-clicking the:

a. Accessories group icon

b. Program Manager control menu box

c. Main window menu bar

d. Control Panel application

APPLICATIONS
REVIEW

1 Start Windows and identify items on the screen.

a. Turn on the computer, if necessary.

b. At the command prompt, type "WIN," then press [Enter]. After Windows loads, the Program Manager displays.

c. Try to identify as many items on the desktop as you can, without referring to the lesson material. Then compare your results with Figure 1.

2 Minimize and restore the Program Manager window.

a. Click the Minimize button. Notice that the Program Manager window reduces to an icon at the bottom of the screen. Now try restoring the window.

b. Double-click the minimized Program Manager icon. The Program Manager window opens.

c. Practice minimizing and restoring other windows on the desktop.

3 Resize and move the Program Manager window.

a. Click anywhere inside the Program Manager window to activate the window.

b. Move the mouse pointer over the lower-right corner of the Program Manager window. Notice that the mouse pointer changes to a double-ended arrow.

c. Press and hold the mouse button and drag the corner of the window up and to the right until the Program Manager takes up the top third of your screen.

d. Drag the Program Manager title bar to reposition the window at the bottom of the screen.

4 Practice working with menus and dialog boxes.

a. Click Window on the Program Manager menu bar, then click Accessories (if you can't find it in the menu, click More Windows, then double-click it from the list that appears, scrolling if necessary).

b. Double-click the Calculator icon to open the Calculator application.

c. Click numbers and operators as you would on a handheld calculator to perform some simple arithmetic operations, like 22 multiplied by 3.99, to see how much it would cost to take a bus of 22 employees on the way back from a conference to a fast-food place for a quick lunch. (Multiplication is indicated by an asterisk *.)

d. Double-click the Calculator control menu box when you are finished.

5 Practice working with files:

a. Open File Manager from the Main group window.

b. Be sure your Student Disk is in drive A or drive B, then double-click the drive icon containing your Student Disk.

c. Double-click the drive C icon, then choose Tile from the Window menu. The open drive windows display, one above the other. If you have more windows open, double-click their control menu boxes to close them, then choose Tile again.

d. Double-click the c:\ folder icon on the left side of the drive C window, then scroll down the left side of the drive C window using the vertical scroll bar to see the available directories. When you see the Windows folder icon, double-click it to see the directories and files available in the Windows folder.

e. Scroll down the right side of the drive C window using the vertical scroll bar to see the files contained in the Windows folder. If you needed to copy a file from the Windows folder to your Student Disk, you could drag it from the list of files in the drive C window to the drive A window, but don't do so now.

6 Exit Windows.

a. Close any open application by double-clicking the application's control menu box.

b. Double-click the control menu box in the upper-left corner of the Program Manager window. The Exit Windows dialog box displays.

c. Click OK. Windows closes and the DOS command prompt displays.

INDEPENDENT
CHALLENGE

Windows 3.1 provides an on-line tutorial which can help you master essential Windows controls and concepts. The tutorial features interactive lessons that teach you how to use Windows elements such as the mouse, Program Manager, menus, and icons. The tutorial also covers how to use Help.

The tutorial material you should use depends on your level of experience with Windows. Some users might want to review the basics of the Windows work area. Others might want to explore additional Windows topics, such as managing files and customizing windows.

Ask your instructor or technical support person about how to use the Windows tutorial.

WordPerfect 6.1
for Windows™

Read This Before You Begin
WordPerfect 6.1

To the Student

The lessons and exercises in this book feature several WordPerfect document files provided to
your instructor. To complete the step-by-step lessons, Applications Reviews, and Independent
Challenges in this book, you must have a Student Disk. Your instructor will do one of the following: 1) provide you with your own copy of the disk; 2) have you copy it from the network
onto your own floppy disk; or 3) have you copy the lesson files from a network into your own
subdirectory on the network. Always use your own copies of the lesson and exercise files. See
your instructor or technical support person for further information.

Using Your Own Computer

If you are going to work through this book using your own computer, you need a computer
system running Microsoft Windows 3.1, WordPerfect 6.1 for Windows, and a Student Disk.
*You will not be able to complete the step-by-step lessons in this book using your own
computer until you have your own Student Disk.* This book assumes a standard
installation of WordPerfect 6.1 for Windows.

To the Instructor

Bundled with the instructor's copy of this book is the Student Disk. The Student Disk contains
all the files your students need to complete the step-by-step lessons in the units, Applications
Reviews, and Independent Challenges. As an adopter of this text, you are granted the right to
distribute the files on the Student Disk to any student who has purchased a copy of the text.
You are free to post all these files to a network or standalone workstations, or simply provide
copies of the disk to your students. The instructions in this book assume that the students know
which drive and directory contain the Student Disk, so it's important that you provide disk
location information before the students start working through the units. This book also
assumes that WordPerfect is set up using the standard installation.

Using the Student Disk Files

To keep the original files on the Student Disk intact, the instructions in this book for opening
files require two important steps: (1) Open the existing file and (2) Save it as a new file with
a new name. This procedure ensures that the original file will remain unmodified in case the
student wants to redo any lesson or exercise.

To organize their files, students are instructed to save their files to the MY_FILES directory on
their Student Disk that they created in the Working with Windows section.

UNIT 1

OBJECTIVES

▶ Define word pro-
cessing software

▶ Start WordPerfect
6.1 for Windows

▶ View the
WordPerfect
window

▶ Work with the
menu bar and the
Toolbar

▶ Work with the
Power Bar and the
status bar

▶ Get Help

▶ Close a document
and exit
WordPerfect

Getting Started
WITH WORDPERFECT 6.1 FOR WINDOWS

Now that you have learned some of the basics of Microsoft Windows, you are ready to use WordPerfect 6.1 for Windows. The lessons in this unit introduce you to the basic features of WordPerfect. The skills you acquire in this unit will provide the understanding you need to complete the remaining units in this book. ▶ This unit introduces The Write Staff, a company that provides writing services for small business clients. Services include writing marketing materials, sales brochures, and general business correspondence. Jennifer Laina, the owner, has hired you to join her team of promotional writers. Throughout this book, you will learn to use WordPerfect to work with documents that you create for The Write Staff. ▶

Defining word processing software

WordPerfect is a **word processing** software application that enables you to produce a variety of **documents**, including letters, memos, newsletters, and reports, as shown in Figure 1-1. You can use a typewriter to create all of these documents, but WordPerfect makes writing, revising, and printing much easier.
▶ As part of your responsibilities at The Write Staff, you will use WordPerfect 6.1 for Windows to create descriptive text for catalogs, write letters to clients, draft press releases, design advertising copy, send memos to other employees, and prepare written reports.

Some advantages of using a word processing application include the ability to:

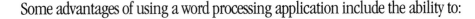

■ **Locate and correct grammatical errors and common spelling mistakes**
WordPerfect provides tools to improve the grammar and vocabulary in your writing as well as to correct any spelling errors.

■ **Move quickly to any point in the document**
WordPerfect provides tools that facilitate working with large documents so that you can access specific sections or words directly.

■ **Rearrange text without having to reenter it**
WordPerfect lets you change text rather than retyping text, making writing more efficient and more enjoyable.

■ **Make editing changes, inserting new text at any location in documents**
WordPerfect lets you enhance your work by adding as much new text anywhere you want in your document.

■ **Make formatting changes to enhance a document's appearance**
WordPerfect has formatting features so you can convey your message not only with words but by the way the words appear on the page.

■ **Align text in rows and columns using tables**
WordPerfect provides Table tools to present your tabular data in the proper format.

■ **Create customized form letters, envelopes, and labels**
WordPerfect has the ability to print in special formats so you can conduct business and personal correspondence in a professional manner.

■ **Add visual interest to your documents by inserting graphics and arranging text in interesting ways**
WordPerfect graphics let a picture be worth more than a thousand words.

■ **Preview a document before printing to see what it will look like**
WordPerfect preview features let you see what you'll get before printing so you save time and paper. Table 1-1 describes some common uses for word processing software.

FIGURE 1-1:
Documents created
with word processing
software

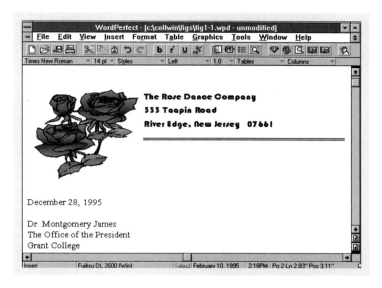

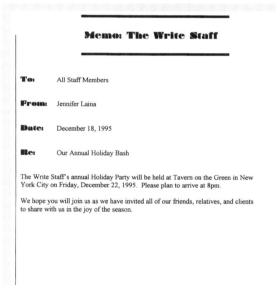

TABLE 1-1: Common uses for word processing software

DOCUMENT TYPE	USE
Letters	Business, personal
Memos	Business interdepartmental correspondence
Reports	Business, schools, government agencies
Manuscripts	Schools, government agencies, publishing
Newsletters	Business, schools, publishing

Starting WordPerfect 6.1 for Windows

In most situations, to use WordPerfect, you must first turn on the computer, access Microsoft Windows from the DOS command prompt, then double-click the WordPerfect applications program group icon. A slightly different procedure might be required for computers on a network and those that use utility programs to enhance Microsoft Windows. ▶ In this lesson, try starting WordPerfect. If you have any problems accessing Windows or starting WordPerfect, consult with the technical support person for assistance.

1   Be sure that the Program Manager is displayed on your computer screen
If the Program Manager is not running, refer to the "Working with Windows" section at the beginning of this book. Locate the WordPerfect applications program group icon. If you have trouble finding it, try clicking Tile or Cascade on the Windows menu.

2   Double-click the WordPerfect applications program group icon
The WordPerfect applications group window opens, and the WordPerfect program icons appear, as shown in Figure 1-2. Your screen might look slightly different; your WordPerfect group window might contain fewer or different icons than those shown.

3   Double-click the WordPerfect 6.1 for Windows program icon
WordPerfect starts and displays the WordPerfect window, as shown in Figure 1-3. You can use this window to create a document.

Compatibility with other WordPerfect versions

If you've created documents with some other version of WordPerfect, you can work on them in WordPerfect 6.1 for Windows. There is no need to spend time recreating existing work. This version recognizes and converts documents created in other versions, whether for DOS or Windows.

FIGURE 1-2: Windows Program Manager with WordPerfect program group icon highlighted

WordPerfect 6.1 for
Windows program
group icon

WordPerfect applica-
tions group window

Applications program
groups

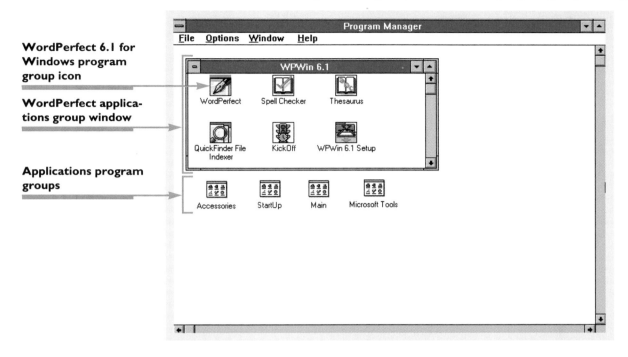

FIGURE 1-3: WordPerfect window

Application title bar

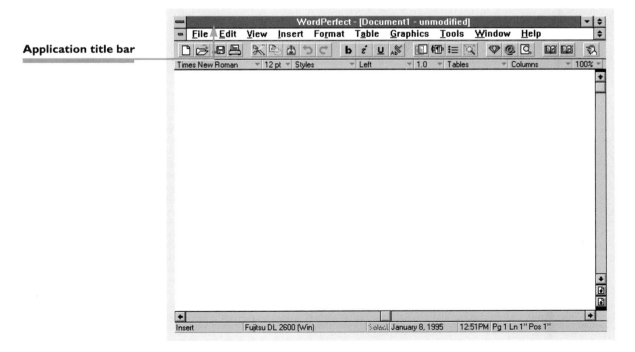

Viewing the WordPerfect window

When you start WordPerfect, you see the WordPerfect window. The items that appear on the WordPerfect window enable you to create, edit, and format documents. If you've used other Windows applications, many of these window elements will be familiar to you. ▶ Familiarize yourself with the WordPerfect window by comparing the descriptions below with Figure 1-4.

■ The **title bar** displays the name of the application—WordPerfect—and the drive, directory path, and name given a document when it is saved and named. Until then, WordPerfect automatically assigns it a name, such as [Document1 - unmodified], which is now showing.

■ The **menu bar** lists the names of the menus that contain WordPerfect commands. Clicking a menu name on the menu bar displays a list of commands from which you can choose.

■ The **Toolbar** provides quick access to frequently used features and to additional Toolbars.

■ The **Power Bar** provides easy access to the most frequently used text editing and text layout features.

■ The **document window** is the area where you type and work. When the mouse pointer is in the document window, it is shaped like an I-beam $\mathcal{I}$. You can open and arrange as many as nine document windows at one time, depending on your computer's available memory. Each window can be maximized, minimized, and sized.

■ The **insertion point** [blinking vertical bar] indicates the position on the screen where text will be inserted.

■ The **scroll bars** on the right side and bottom of the window allow you to move vertically and horizontally through a document by clicking the scroll arrows or dragging the scroll boxes. In addition to the scroll bars, there are Previous Page 🔲 and Next Page 🔲 buttons that you can use for moving quickly through multiple-page documents.

■ The **status bar** displays and accesses information about the document, such as the mode WordPerfect is in, the current printer, the status of Select mode, the current date and time, the page number, line number, and the position of the insertion point in the document window.

■ The **Ruler Bar** allows you to set and move tabs and margins, and to make paragraph adjustments quickly. Unless WordPerfect has been customized, the Ruler Bar does not appear above the document window. You will learn how to display the Ruler Bar in upcoming lessons.

FIGURE I-4: Elements of a WordPerfect window

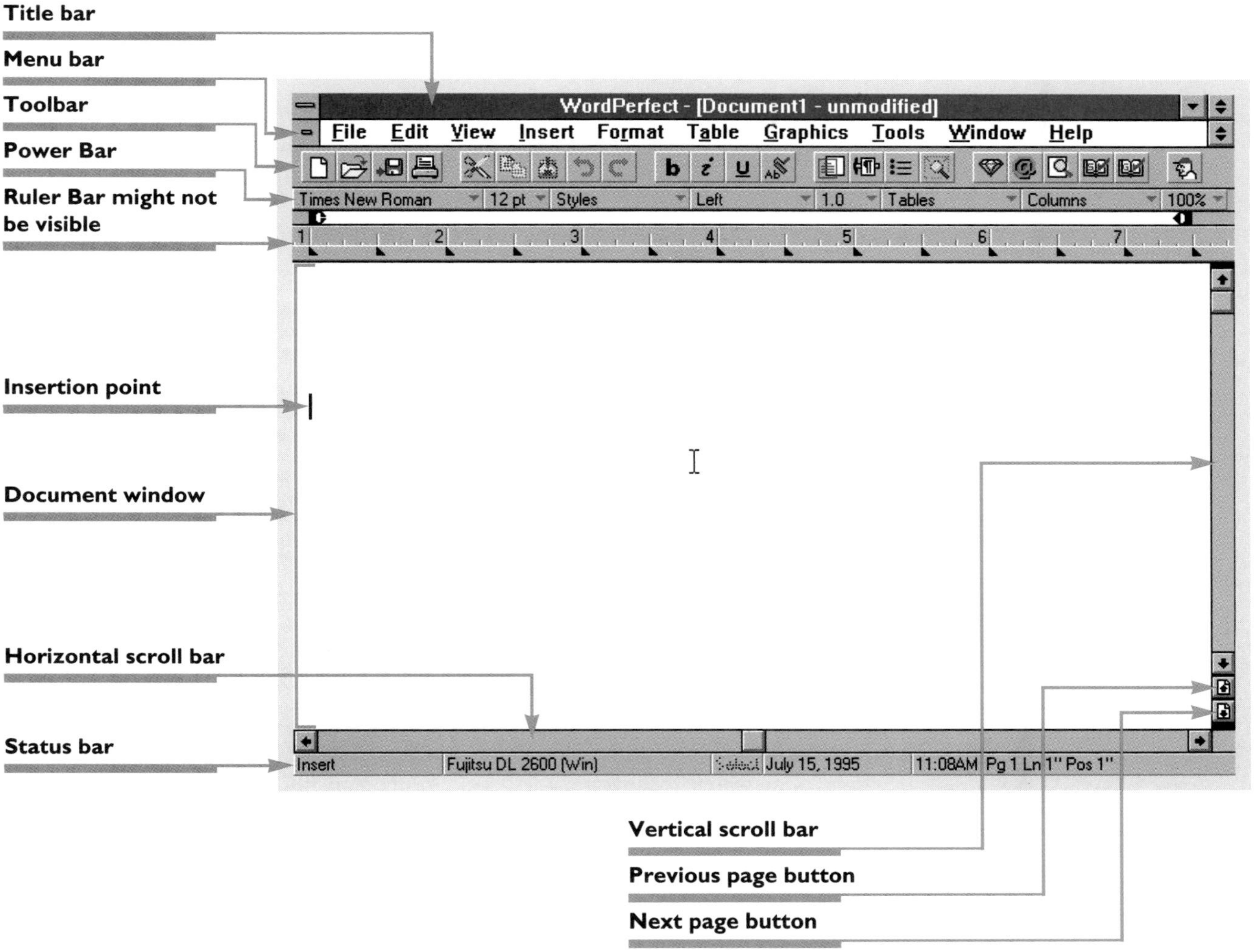

Title bar

Menu bar

Toolbar

Power Bar

Ruler Bar might not
be visible

Insertion point

Document window

Horizontal scroll bar

Status bar

WordPerfect - [Document1 - unmodified]

File   Edit   View   Insert   Format   Table   Graphics   Tools   Window   Help

Times New Roman   12 pt   Styles   Left   1.0   Tables   Columns   100%

Insert   Fujitsu DL 2600 (Win)   Select July 15, 1995   11:08AM Pg 1 Ln 1" Pos 1"

Vertical scroll bar

Previous page button

Next page button

TROUBLE?

If your WordPerfect
window does not fill
the entire screen,
click the Maximize
button ▲.■

Working with the menu bar and the Toolbar

WordPerfect offers many commands and options that allow you to produce professional-looking documents. You can choose most of the commands in WordPerfect by using menus. The **menu bar** is located just below the title bar. You open a menu by clicking the menu name on the menu bar and then choosing a command. The **Toolbar** is a horizontal strip of icons located just below the menu bar. The Toolbar gives you easy access to a variety of commonly used WordPerfect commands. You choose options on the Toolbar by pointing at the icon and clicking the mouse. This is often a fast alternative to clicking open a menu and then choosing a command. To find out how to choose an alternate Toolbar, see the related topic, "Choosing a different Toolbar." ▶ Jennifer wants her writers to include the date the document is created. Because you will be handling some of the letter writing, in this lesson you will learn how to use the Date command on the Insert menu. You will also practice using the Toolbar.

I Place the **insertion point** where you want to insert the date in your document
The **insertion point** is the blinking vertical line where text will appear when you begin typing. Because this is a new document, the insertion point is at the top of the document on page 1.

2 Position the mouse pointer over Insert on the menu bar, then click the **left mouse button**
The Insert menu opens as shown in Figure 1-5.

3 Click **Date**
The arrow after Date indicates a cascading menu, which means another menu with additional options appears to complete the Date command.

4 Click **Date Text**
The current date appears in your document at the insertion point, as shown in Figure 1-6. Note that the date on your screen might be different. Now practice using the Toolbar.

5 Move the mouse pointer slowly across the Toolbar and pause briefly on each button
The WordPerfect default Toolbar is shown in Figure 1-7. When you rest the mouse pointer over a button on the Toolbar, a Help message in the title bar indicates what the button does and provides an alternative keystroke method to complete the command, if applicable. The name of the button is also displayed in a little yellow text box below the button. This is called a **QuickTip**.

6 Position the mouse pointer over the **Undo button** 🔄 on the Toolbar
The Help message at the top of the screen indicates that clicking this button will reverse the last change made to this document.

7 Click 🔄
Because your last action inserted the date, clicking the Undo button removes the date. The date no longer appears in your document.

8 Click the **Redo button** 🔄
Redo undoes the last Undo command. This feature allows you to reverse the action of your last Undo. The date should now appear in its original location in your document.

FIGURE 1-5:
Insert menu

Click to insert
current date

Indicates cascading
menu

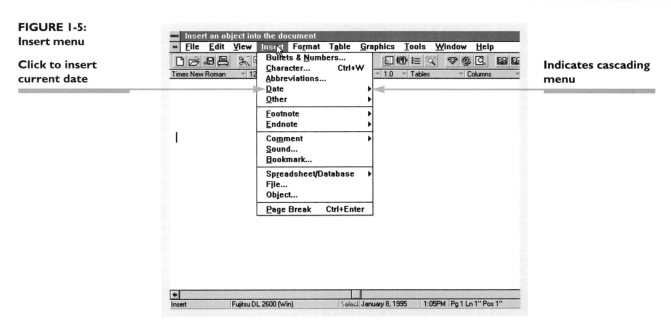

FIGURE 1-6: Current date appears at insertion point

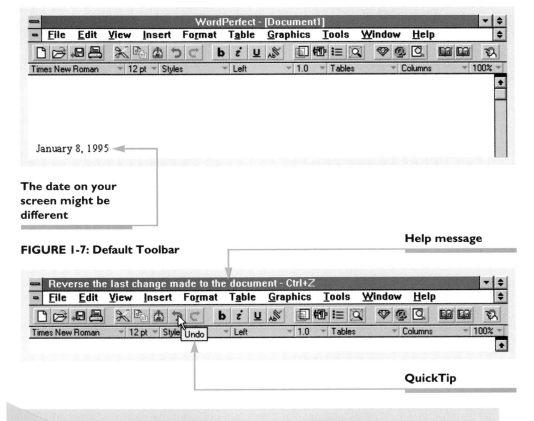

January 8, 1995

The date on your
screen might be
different

Help message

FIGURE 1-7: Default Toolbar

QuickTip

Choosing a different Toolbar

WordPerfect 6.1 for Windows provides 13 predefined Toolbars. You choose a new
Toolbar by clicking the right mouse button while the mouse pointer is anywhere on
the Toolbar. A menu opens, listing the descriptive names of the available Toolbars.
Choose a new Toolbar to replace the current one.

Working with the Power Bar and the status bar

The **Power Bar** is a narrow horizontal strip of buttons directly below the Toolbar near the top of the screen. The Power Bar gives you a quick way to access text and document formatting features that you use most often. The **status bar** is the narrow horizontal strip of buttons at the bottom of your screen. Use the status bar to display and access information about the current document and the state of WordPerfect, such as insertion point position, date, time, selected printer, and status of Select mode. Unlike the Toolbar, which uses icons to represent commands, the Power Bar and the status bar have text descriptions to identify the current setting and function of each button. ▶ Refer to Figure 1-8 and practice using the Power Bar and the status bar to familiarize yourself with these powerful WordPerfect features. For more information on the Power Bar, see the related topic, "Power Bar Options."

1. **Move the mouse pointer slowly across each button on the Power Bar**
   The WordPerfect default settings for the Power Bar are shown in Figure 1-9. When you move the mouse pointer over an item on the Power Bar, a Help message at the top of the screen in the title bar indicates what the button does, and the name of the button is displayed as a QuickTip.

2. **Move the mouse pointer slowly across each button on the status bar**
   When you move the mouse pointer over an item on the status bar, a Help message at the top of the screen in the title bar indicates what the button does.

3. **Click the Justification button on the Power Bar**
   The drop-down list displays the justification options of Left, Right, Center, Full, and All. **Justification** determines how the words are placed on a line in the document. In Unit 4 you will learn how to set and use the different justification options. To learn about the Power Bar, you will select Center justification for the date in your document.

4. **Click Center**
   The date is centered in your document. You can also use the status bar to insert the current date and time in a document. This might be easier than working with the menu bar.

5. **Double-click the current date on the status bar**
   WordPerfect inserts the current date at the insertion point. The date now appears twice.

6. **Double-click the current time on the status bar**
   WordPerfect inserts the current time at the insertion point.

7. **Click Undo** 🔄
   WordPerfect deletes the time that was inserted using the status bar.

8. **Click** 🔄
   WordPerfect deletes the date that was inserted using the status bar.

   These powerful features will be helpful as you create documents for Jennifer Laina as a staff member at The Write Staff.

FIGURE 1-8: Power Bar and the status bar

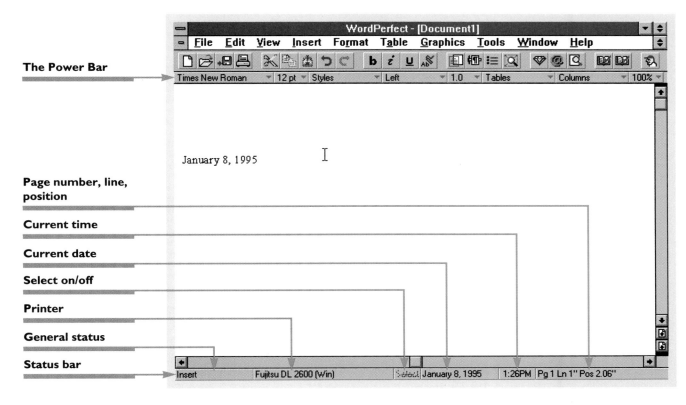

The Power Bar

Page number, line, position

Current time

Current date

Select on/off

Printer

General status

Status bar

FIGURE 1-9: Default Power Bar

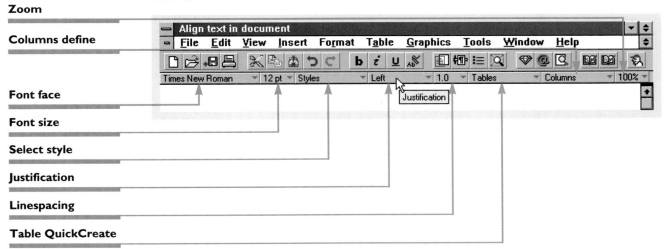

Zoom

Columns define

Font face

Font size

Select style

Justification

Linespacing

Table QuickCreate

Power Bar Options

You can **right-click**, click the right mouse button, on the Power Bar to display a QuickMenu. This menu gives you three options: Edit, Options, and Hide Power Bar. Use Power Bar Options to change the appearance of the Power Bar and to return the Power Bar to its default settings.

Getting Help

WordPerfect comes with an extensive on-line Help system, which gives you definitions, explanations, and useful tips without your having to leave your desk or open a manual. Help information appears in a separate window that you can resize, move, and refer to as you continue to work. To view Help at all times in all documents, see the related topic "Keeping the Help window open." ▶ Use WordPerfect's Help system to find out about working with and displaying different Toolbars.

I Click **Help** on the menu bar, then click **Contents**
The Contents dialog box appears, as shown in Figure 1-10. Table 1-2 provides an explanation of the Help buttons below the Help screen menu bar.

2 Move the mouse pointer over the icons and list of topics
The mouse pointer changes to 🖑. To select a topic, the 🖑 must be pointing to the topic.

3 Click **Using Help** ?
Use the scroll buttons and scroll box to read the entire file. After reading the file, you should be familiar with some of the features in the WordPerfect Help system.

4 Click **Back**
The Contents dialog box appears again. Toolbars is not listed as one of the topics, so you need to choose Search to access an index of topics.

5 Click **Search** 🔍, then type **Toolbar**
Notice as you type each letter, the contents of the list box scroll to match your selection, as shown in Figure 1-11.

6 Click **Show Topics**
A list of related topics appears in the bottom half of the Search dialog box. As you can see, WordPerfect offers a considerable amount of help related to Toolbars.

7 Scroll to display the topic **Toolbar**, click **Toolbar**, then click **Go To**
The Toolbar text appears. Scroll to read the entire file, then you can exit Help.

8 Click **Close** to exit Help and return to your document

TABLE I-2: Help buttons

BUTTON	DESCRIPTION
Contents	Displays the contents of the Help file by subject grouping
Search	Provides a dialog box where you type the feature or command for which you need assistance
Back	Returns you to the previous topic
History	Shows you a list of Help topics that you have recently referred to
Print	Prints a copy of the Help topic
Close	Exits Help and returns you to your document

FIGURE I-10:
Contents dialog box

Help window menu bar

Pointer shape changes
when moved here

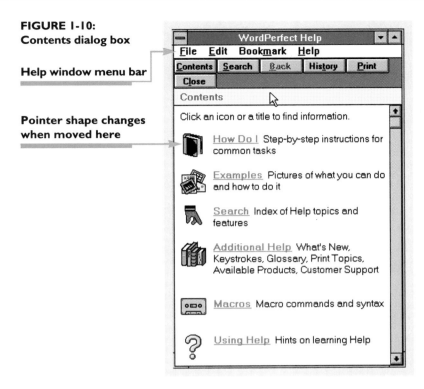

FIGURE I-11:
Search dialog box
in WordPerfect Help

Search topic

List box scrolls

Bottom half of search
dialog box

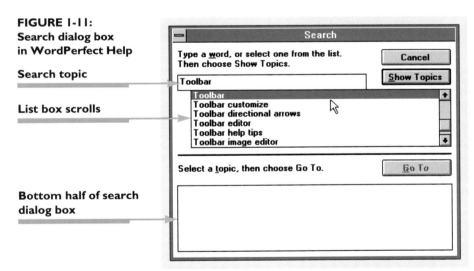

Keeping the Help window open

To make WordPerfect Help appear at all times in all documents, click Help on
the menu bar, click Contents, then click Always on Top in the Help menu of the
WordPerfect Help window. You can size and move the Help window to any area
of the document window and continue to work in your document with the Help
window remaining visible for easy reference.

QUICK **TIP**

Press [F1] to open
WordPerfect Help.■

Closing a document and exiting WordPerfect

When you have finished working on a document, you usually save the document to a disk and then close it. To close a document, use the Close command on the File menu. WordPerfect will always provide a dialog box before closing the document if any new text or revisions have not been saved. This provides you the opportunity to close the document without saving, to save the changes, or to cancel the Close command. When you are finished using WordPerfect, you need to exit the application. To exit WordPerfect, use the Exit command on the File menu. For a comparison of the Close and Exit commands, refer to Table 1-3. ▶ It's the end of the day and you have done a really great job familiarizing yourself with WordPerfect. Before going home, try closing a document and exiting WordPerfect now.

1 Click **File** on the menu bar

The File menu appears. You'll need to click Close, as shown in Figure 1-12.

2 Click **Close**

The Close dialog box appears, asking if you want to save changes to Document1. Because this was only a practice session, there is no need to save the file.

3 Click **No**

The document closes and you can now exit WordPerfect.

4 Click **File** on the menu bar

The File Menu opens. You need to choose Exit. You can exit WordPerfect with many document files open. WordPerfect will close each open document window, one at a time, prompting you to save any changes you have made.

5 Click **Exit**

WordPerfect closes and returns you to the Program Manager.

FIGURE 1-12: File menu with Close highlighted

**Click to close
document**

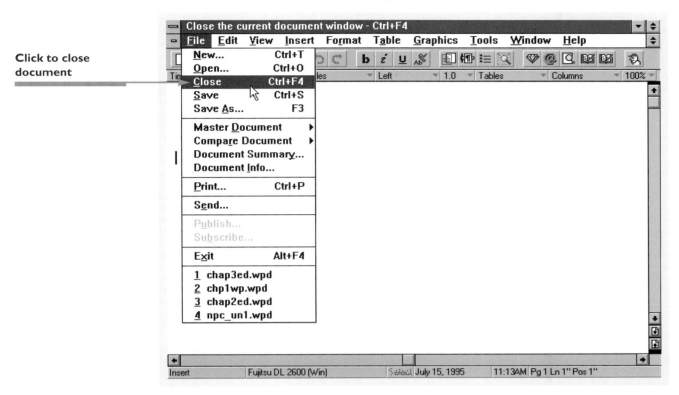

TABLE 1-3: Close and Exit commands

ACTION	RESULT
Closing a file	Puts away a file; leaves WordPerfect running
Exiting WordPerfect	Closes any open files and also closes the WordPerfect application

QUICK **TIP**

Double-clicking the document control menu box  next to the menu bar closes the document. Clicking Exit on the File menu or double-clicking the application control menu box ☐ in the title bar exits WordPerfect.■

CONCEPTSREVIEW

**Label each element of the WordPerfect
window shown in Figure 1-13.**

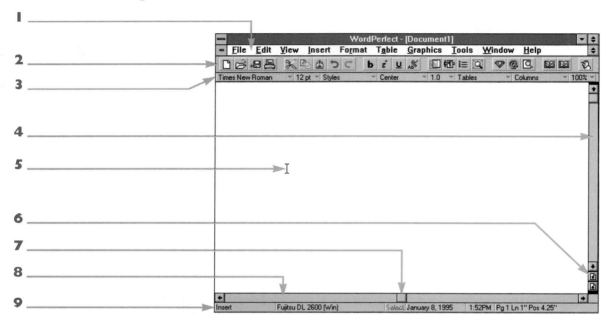

FIGURE 1-13

Match each statement with the term it describes.

10 Shows the name of the current document

11 Brief descriptions of Toolbar features

12 Shows date and time, page, line, and vertical and horizontal positions of the insertion point

13 Double-click to exit WordPerfect and close all the documents

14 Lists the menus that contain WordPerfect commands

a. Status bar

b. QuickTips

c. Application control box

d. Menu bar

e. Title bar

Select the best answer from the list of choices.

15 The WordPerfect menu command that removes all open documents from the screen is

a. Close

b. Exit

c. Cancel

d. Minimize

16 To reverse the last action, you can do any of the following except

a. Click Edit on the menu bar, then click Redo

b. Click Edit on the menu bar, then click Undo

c. Press [Alt][Z]

d. Click Undo on the Toolbar

17 To access the Help system you

a. Click Help on the menu bar, then click Help now

b. Click Tools on the menu bar, then click Help

c. Press [F2]

d. Click Help on the menu bar, then click Contents

18 Word processing software can be used to create all of the following except

a. Documents

b. Reports

c. Letters

d. Sound

19 To insert the current date in a document at the insertion point you

a. Click the date on the status bar

b. Click Insert on the menu bar, then click Date, then Date Text

c. Click Format on the menu bar, then click Date, then Date Text

d. Click Tools on the menu bar, then click Date, then Date Text

20 If you position the mouse pointer on a button in the Toolbar, you see

a. A brief description of the button on the title bar and a QuickTip below the button

b. A QuickTip on the title bar

c. Nothing

d. A Toolbar button tip on the status bar

APPLICATIONS
REVIEW

1 Start WordPerfect.

a. Turn on the computer if necessary.

b. If necessary, at the DOS prompt, launch Windows.

c. Double-click the WordPerfect group icon.

d. Launch WordPerfect to display the default WordPerfect window.

2 Explore the WordPerfect application window.

a. Try to identify as many items in the WordPerfect window as you can without referring to the lesson material.

b. On a notepad, write down all the items you can identify, then compare your notes with Figure 1-4.

3 Practice using the menu bar.

a. Move the mouse pointer to the menu bar.

b. On your notepad, write down all the menu items.

c. Click File on the menu bar, but do not release the mouse button.

d. Drag the mouse pointer to New, but do not release the mouse button. Notice that a description of the New command appears in the title bar.

e. Continue dragging the mouse pointer down the File menu so that you can review the brief description of each command on the title bar.

f. Leave the menu on the screen, but don't execute a command.

g. Open the Format menu.

h. Drag through the commands and review their descriptions in the title bar.

i. Drag the mouse pointer to Paragraph. Continue reviewing other commands on the menu bar in the same manner.

4 Practice using the Toolbar.

a. Move the mouse pointer to the New Blank Document button on the Toolbar.

b. Write the description of the New Blank Document button on your notepad.

c. Move the mouse pointer to other buttons so that you can become familiar with them. Write the brief description of each button as it appears in the title bar.

d. Move the mouse pointer to anywhere on the Toolbar. Press and hold down the right mouse button. Write down the items on the menu. Pick three of these Toolbar names, and write down what functions each of these Toolbars might have. Also notice that the Toolbar named "WordPerfect" has a check mark next to it. This is the standard Toolbar used by WordPerfect, which WordPerfect is currently using.

e. Move the mouse pointer outside the menu, then click the left mouse button. The menu closes without changing the Toolbar.

5 Practice using the Power Bar and the status bar.

a. Move the mouse pointer to the Font Face button, which is the leftmost button on the Power Bar.

b. Read the description of the Font Face button on the title bar.

c. Point at other Power Bar buttons so that you can become familiar with them. Write down the name in the QuickTip and the brief description of each button as they appear in the title bar.

d. Look closely at the Zoom button, which is the last Power Bar button on the right. The description of this button in the title bar is "Zoom document in or out." Click this button. Notice that 100% is highlighted. Click outside the menu.

e. Right-click anywhere on the Power Bar. Click Options. Review the Power Bar Options dialog box as shown in Figure 1-14. Click Cancel.

f. Move the mouse pointer to the status bar.

g. Look closely at the description of each button in the title bar.

h. Watch the time on the time display for a minute. Notice how it changes to reflect the current time.

i. Right-click anywhere on the status bar. Click Preferences. Review the Status Bar Preferences dialog box, as shown in Figure 1-15. Click Cancel.

6 Explore WordPerfect Help.

a. Click Help on the menu bar.

b. Click Search for Help On. The Search dialog box appears on the screen.

c. Identify the buttons that appear in the Search dialog box.

d. Click the down arrow on the list box scroll bar to view possible word choices.

e. Select a word from the list box.

f. Click Show Topics. The various topics related to the selection appear.

g. Choose a topic to read by clicking it.

h. Click Go To. The Help file that you chose appears in the Help window.

i. Read the Help screen. Click any additional topics that appear at the bottom of the file.

j. Read the additional topics.

k. Click Close to exit Help.

7 Close the document and exit WordPerfect.

a. Click File on the menu bar, then click Close. You do not want to save this document.

b. Click No. The dialog box closes.

c. Close any other documents you have opened.

d. Exit WordPerfect by using the File menu.

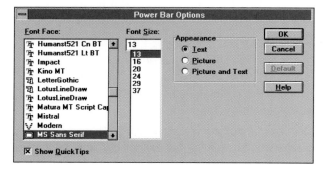

FIGURE 1-14

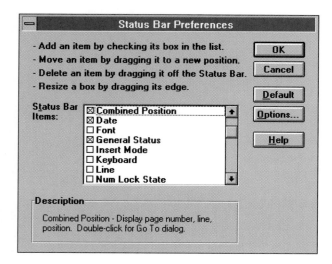

FIGURE 1-15

INDEPENDENT
CHALLENGE 1

WordPerfect provides Coaches and a Tutorial as interactive on-line Help for many of the available features. Coaches give detailed instructions on how to draw borders around a page or around a paragraph, how to insert headers or footers, and so on. The Tutorial provides interactive, step-by-step sessions on how to get started with WordPerfect and how to use selected WordPerfect features.

To complete this independent challenge:

1 Click Help on the Menu bar, then click Tutorial. Work through Lesson 1 of the on-line Tutorial to review the concepts of creating a document. If the Tutorial covers information you don't understand, don't worry. You'll learn more about creating a document in the next unit of this book.

2 Click Coaches on the Help menu. Double-click Borders-Page in the list of items.

3 Follow the Coach on how to create a border on a page in WordPerfect. Then click Quit to exit Help.

INDEPENDENT
CHALLENGE 2

WordPerfect provides you with powerful tools to create and edit documents. Without even realizing it, in your daily life you come across many documents that have been created using powerful word processors. These might include your daily newspaper, the college newsletter, an item received in the mail advertising a new product, or any business correspondence.

To complete this independent challenge:

1 Gather together four different documents that you have recently received.

2 Identify each as either a letter, newsletter, brochure, or whatever category you determine appropriate.

3 Circle two elements in each that could not have been done easily with a regular typewriter.

4 For each document, write a brief paragraph explaining how word processing made the creation of the document easier.

UNIT 2

▶ Plan a document

▶ Enter text

▶ Move around
a document

▶ Select text

▶ Insert, delete, and
correct text

▶ Save a document

▶ Cut, copy, and paste
text

▶ Print a document

Creating
A DOCUMENT

ow that you are familiar with the WordPerfect window, menus, Toolbar buttons, Power Bar, and the status bar, you are ready to create your own document. To create a document, you must first plan it, then you enter text in the document window. Once you create a document, you can add, delete, or copy and move text, then save and print the document. In this unit, you will work through your second day on the job at The Write Staff. ▶ The owner, Jennifer Laina, has asked you to write an upbeat and informative welcoming note to all new employees to help you get started writing and printing documents using WordPerfect. ▶

Planning a document

Planning a document before you write it improves the quality of your writing, makes your document more attractive and readable, and saves you time and effort. You can divide your planning into four parts: content, organization, style, and format. Begin by determining what you want to say in the document, that is, the content. Next, organize the information so that your ideas appear in a logical and coherent sequence. After you have settled on the content and organization, you can begin writing, using a tone that satisfies your purpose and meets the needs of your audience. For example, a promotional piece for The Write Staff should use a different tone from a letter to the corporate office. Last, you should make your document visually appealing, using WordPerfect's formatting features. ▶ The Write Staff needs a general welcoming letter to give to all new employees to introduce them to the company and its policies. Begin your first job assignment by planning the document.

1 Choose the information to include in the document.
Jennifer leaves a note for you outlining the structure of the company, some basic guidelines for working at The Write Staff, and general company policies as shown in Figure 2-1. This is the information you need to include in the document.

2 Decide how you will organize the information.
Because you want new employees to feel welcome and comfortable at The Write Staff, make sure to mention names to help with introductions. You want to be brief because people might want to post this memo on their bulletin boards to use as a reference. However, you also want to make sure you include all of the information Jennifer provided.

3 Pick the tone you will use.
You want The Write Staff to sound like a fun, exciting, and cutting-edge place to work; use a lively, positive tone to help the new people relax and feel good about their new jobs.

4 Think about how you want your document to look.
Jennifer wants this document to be friendly and informal. This must be a single-page document. WordPerfect's default format settings are perfect for this document. Table 2-1 shows these WordPerfect default format settings. You will learn more about these settings throughout the book.

5 Write down your ideas.
Write out some initial, motivating sentences to introduce the company, and draw a sample format for your document.

FIGURE 2-1: Jennifer's note

The Write Staff
Jennifer Laina, Owner and Chief Writer
Emily Caitlin, Chief Financial Officer
Michael Benjamin, Director, Graphics Department
David Chu, Writer
Arianna Quintana, Writer
Erica Brennan, Writer
(your name), Writer

Office Procedures
All documents must be organized on disks by job number
Print all copies on the laser printer
Requests for graphics made through the Graphics Department

Company Policies
All writing done using WordPerfect 6.1 for Windows
Be professional and polite with clients
Have fun and write creatively
No smoking in the office

TABLE 2-1: Some WordPerfect default format settings

FORMAT OPTION	SETTING
Top margin	1 inch
Bottom margin	1 inch
Justification	Left
Linespacing	1.0 (single)
Paper size	8.5" × 11"
Tabs	Every 0.5"
Page numbering	None
Widow/Orphan	Off

Entering text

Once you have planned your document, you are ready to begin entering text. When you start WordPerfect, the application opens an empty document window. You begin entering text at the insertion point in the first line. You will learn how to use the Show command to identify the basic symbols for space, tab, and hard returns in your document. ▶ Using the information Jennifer provided and the planning you did in the previous lesson, you are ready to begin entering the text for the welcoming letter.

1 **Start Windows and WordPerfect using the same method as in Unit 1**
This starts WordPerfect and opens the document window. Near the upper-left corner, the insertion point appears as a blinking vertical bar. Table 2-2 lists some of WordPerfect's basic key functions to help you enter text. This is where the text you type will appear.

2 **Type the following text; when you reach the end of a line, keep typing**
Welcome to The Write Staff! We are so happy to have you as a member of our team of professional writers! You'll find our offices here at One Main Street to be sunny and bright. Frazzle's Diner down the block has a superb lunch special. If you like dining outdoors, you may bag a lunch and eat on our beautiful cedar deck.
Text automatically wraps, or moves, to the next line. This is called **word wrap**. Press [Enter] only at the end of the paragraph to generate a hard return and force a new line. To understand the difference between soft returns and hard returns, read the related topic, "Soft and hard returns." Use the Backspace key to correct any errors you make as you type.

3 **Click View on the menu bar, then click Show ¶**
Notice that a symbol appears at each space in the paragraph and wherever you press [Enter]. The Show ¶ command makes it easy to see if you've pressed [Spacebar] or [Enter] too many times. These symbols do not appear when a document is printed. Clicking Show ¶ again turns the command off.

4 **Press [Enter] twice to create a blank line between paragraphs**
Notice the ¶ symbol that appears when you press [Enter].

5 **Type the new text as shown in Figure 2-2, and press [Enter] at the end of each line**
The first few lines will have scrolled off the screen and out of the document window, as shown in Figure 2-3.

6 **Press [Enter]**
Notice that the insertion point is repositioned to the blank line below the paragraph.

TABLE 2-2: Basic key functions

KEY	ACTION
[Spacebar]	Press once between words and sentences to leave a space
[Enter]	Press at the end of a paragraph or when you want text to begin a new line; when pressed more than once, creates blank lines
[Backspace]	Press to correct any character you mistype; deletes text to the left of the insertion point
[Delete]	Press to delete text to the right of the insertion point

FIGURE 2-2:
Text to be typed into the document

Here are some things you should know about The Write Staff—
Your coworkers are:
Jennifer Laina, Owner and Chief Writer
Emily Caitlin, Chief Financial Officer
Michael Benjamin, Director, Graphics Department
David Chu, Writer
Arianna Quintana, Writer
Erica Brennan, Writer
(your name), Writer

Some basic office procedures include these quick rules:
All documents must be organized on disks by job number
Print all copies on the laser printer
Requests for graphics are made through the Graphics Department

And, of course, we have some company policies:
Write all documents using WordPerfect 6.1 for Windows
Be professional and polite with clients
Have fun and write creatively
No smoking in the office

FIGURE 2-3:
Document with text and symbols

First lines not visible

Space

Hard returns

Insertion point

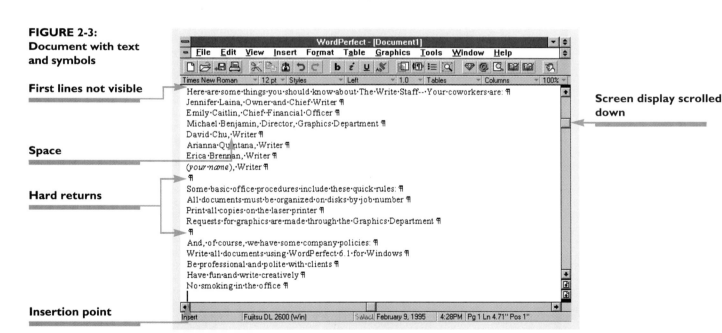

Screen display scrolled down

Soft and hard returns

When lines of text you type wrap automatically, a hidden symbol called a **soft return** is placed at the end of a line of type. When you end a paragraph by pressing [Enter], a **hard return** is placed at that point in the text and a new line is generated. Hard returns can be deleted with the Backspace key. You cannot delete soft returns.

Moving around a document

In WordPerfect you can move around documents using both the keyboard and the mouse. Table 2-3 lists a few of the many keyboard shortcuts available for moving around the document. See the related topic, "Using the Go To dialog box," for another navigation method. ▶ Practice moving around the document using both the mouse and the keyboard. You will need these navigation skills when you edit, delete, and insert text as you create more complex documents.

1 Press **[Ctrl][Home]**
   The document scrolls and the insertion point moves to the beginning of the document.

2 Position the I in between the two "zz"s in the word "Frazzle's," then click the **left mouse button**
   Clicking the mouse when the pointer is shaped like I moves the insertion point to the new location. Any text that you edit, insert, or delete will occur here.

3 Drag the **scroll box** until the first paragraph scrolls out of view, as shown in Figure 2-4
   You can no longer see the insertion point. However, if you entered text now, it would appear at the insertion point, and your screen would reposition the text so you could see it again.

4 Press **[↓]** three times
   The insertion point moves to the first line of the second paragraph, after the word "Here."

5 Press **[Home]**
   The insertion point moves to the beginning of that line.

6 Press **[↓]**, then press **[Ctrl][→]**
   The insertion point moves down one line and over one word and should be at the "L" in "Laina," as shown in Figure 2-5. When you press [Ctrl] at the same time as the right or left arrow keys, the insertion point moves right or left one word.

7 Press **[End]**
   The insertion point moves to the end of the line.

8 Move the insertion point to the beginning of the document

TABLE 2-3: Shortcut navigation keys

KEY	ACTION
[↑], [↓], [←], [→]	Moves insertion point up one line, down one line, left one character, and right one character
[Home]	Moves insertion point to the beginning of a line
[End]	Moves insertion point to the end of a line
[PgUp]	Moves insertion point to previous page in a multiple-page document
[PgDn]	Moves insertion point to next page in a multiple-page document
[Ctrl][Home]	Moves insertion point to beginning of a document
[Ctrl][End]	Moves insertion point to end of a document

FIGURE 2-4:
Document with insertion point at new location

Insertion point out of view

Scroll bar showing position of document

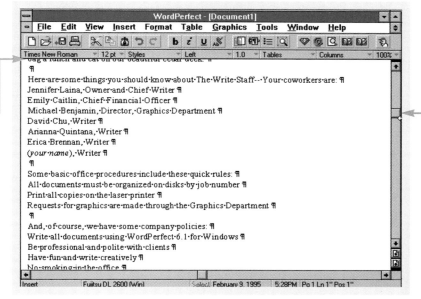

FIGURE 2-5:
Document with insertion point at "Laina"

Insertion point

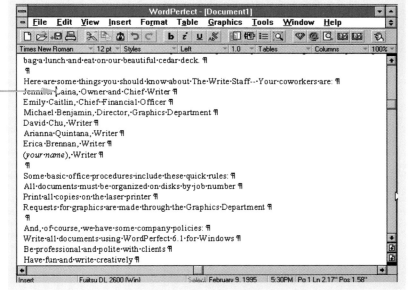

Using the Go To dialog box

If you want to move to a specific location in your document, press [Ctrl][G].
The **Go To dialog box** appears. You can also access the Go To dialog box by
choosing Go To on the Edit menu or double-clicking the Position item on the far
right corner of the status bar. Choose where you want to position the insertion
point, then click OK.

Selecting text

Selecting text is an essential word processing skill because you must select text in order to work with it. There are many options for selecting text in WordPerfect. You can use the Select command on the Edit menu, or use **QuickSelect** to select text by clicking. You can also click and drag the mouse over the text to highlight it. You can select a letter, a word or words, a sentence or several sentences, one or more paragraphs, or an entire document. Once text is selected, you can format it (change its appearance), cut it, copy it, or move it. ▶ You are going to try to learn the many ways to select text so you can be prepared to work efficiently on your documents.

1 **Starting with the insertion point at the beginning of the first paragraph, click and drag the mouse to the end of the paragraph, then release the mouse button**
As you drag the mouse, the text is highlighted, as shown in Figure 2-6. The characters are light and the selected area is dark. When you reach the point where you want to end selecting text, release the mouse button. You can deselect text by selecting other text or clicking outside the selected area.

2 **Press [Ctrl][Home], then press [Ctrl][→] eight times to move the insertion point to the middle of the first line**

3 **Click Edit on the menu bar, click Select, then click Paragraph**
You can select an entire paragraph from anywhere within the paragraph using Select.

4 **Position the insertion point at the top of the document and click once**
The paragraph is no longer selected.

5 **Position the insertion point on any word in the second sentence of the first paragraph**

6 **Click Edit on the menu bar, click Select, then click Sentence**
The sentence is selected. You can select Paragraph, Page, or All in this manner. Choosing All selects the entire document.

7 **Position the insertion point on the word "offices" in the third sentence of the first paragraph**
Now try using QuickSelect.

8 **Double-click to select the word, then triple-click to select the sentence**
Practice using QuickSelect by double-, triple-, and quadruple-clicking to select text. Refer to Table 2-4 for a summary of QuickSelect and the many ways to select text.

9 **Position the insertion point before the word "Diner;" click and drag the mouse across four characters to the "e" to select the word "Dine"**
Selecting characters and words takes practice. Continue selecting and deselecting characters and words until you are comfortable selecting small amounts of text.

FIGURE 2-6: First paragraph selected by dragging mouse

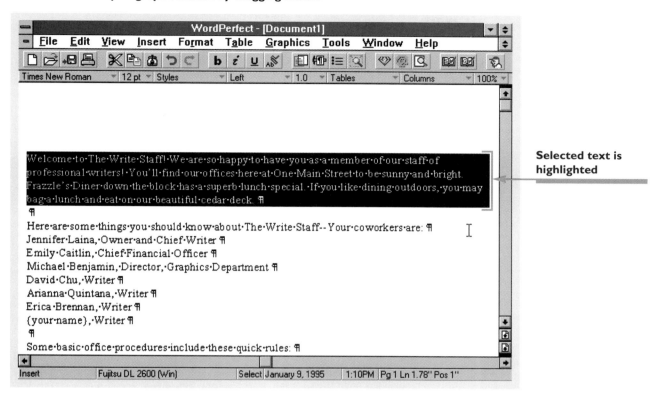

Selected text is highlighted

TABLE 2-4: Selecting text using QuickSelect

TO SELECT	WITH A MOUSE	USING QUICKSELECT
Character	Click and drag across the letter, or use [Alt] and drag across the letter	N/A
Word	Click and drag across the word	Double-click on the word
Sentence	Click and drag across the sentence	Triple-click anywhere in, or next to, the sentence
Paragraph	Click and drag across the paragraph	Click four times anywhere in, or next to, the paragraph

Inserting, deleting, and correcting text

You might need to change the contents of a document or make corrections to existing text. WordPerfect's correcting tools allow you to save time and energy by deleting portions of text, adding new text, or correcting text. Table 2-5 lists methods of changing or correcting text in documents. ▶ At The Write Staff, as in many businesses, most documents go through many revisions before a final version can be released to the client. Emily Caitlin reviewed your first draft and marked a few words that need changing. Figure 2-7 shows you the changes you must make to your document.

1 Position the insertion point in the blank space to the left of the word "Main" in the first paragraph of text, then press **[Delete]** four times
   The word "Main" is deleted.

2 Position the insertion point on the word "Street," double-click to select the word, then press **[Delete]**
   The word "Street" is deleted.

3 Type **Maple Avenue** at the insertion point
   The correct address is now written in the document. The leftmost item on the status bar at the bottom of the document window indicates that WordPerfect is in Insert mode as shown in Figure 2-8. **Insert mode** allows you to type additional text without deleting or writing over the existing text. The existing text moves to the right as you type and automatically wraps to the next line.

4 Position the insertion point after the word "Diner" in the first paragraph
   The correct name of the restaurant is actually Frazzle's Restaurant.

5 Press **[Backspace]** five times to erase "Diner," then type **Restaurant**

6 Double-click **[Insert]** on the status bar
   The status bar displays "Typeover" in place of "Insert." This status bar item is called a **toggle button** because it switches WordPerfect back and forth between two modes: Insert and Typeover. In **Typeover mode**, you "type over," or replace, existing text when making a correction.

7 Position the insertion point after the "e" in "Brennan" in the list of names
   You only need to replace the "nna" with "mmi" to correct the spelling of Erica's name.

8 Type **mmi**
   Notice that character for character, "Bremmin" replaces "Brennan."

9 Double-click **Typeover** on the status bar
   Switching to Insert mode after replacing the characters or words needed allows you to continue adding text without deleting anything else. Compare your document with Figure 2-9.

TABLE 2-5:
Ways to correct text

METHOD	ACTION
Delete key	Deletes a character to the right of the insertion point
Backspace key	Deletes a character to the left of the insertion point
Typeover mode	Replaces existing text with new text
Insert mode	Adds to existing text
Undo button	Reverses your last action

FIGURE 2-7:
Emily's notes for editing the document

Actually called Frazzle's Restaurant

Use Maple Avenue address

Erica's last name is Bremmin

FIGURE 2-8: Status bar item indicating Insert mode

Double-click here to toggle between Insert and Typeover mode

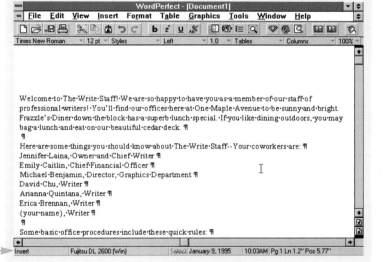

FIGURE 2-9:
All corrections made to document

Corrected word

Typeover

Replaced text

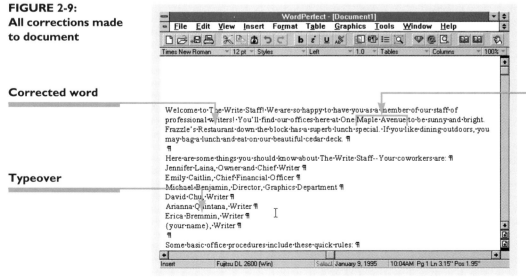

QUICK **TIP**

You can also press the Insert key on your keyboard to toggle between Insert and Typeover mode.■

Saving a document

As you enter text in a document, the text is kept in the computer's random access memory (RAM). To store the document permanently, you must save it to a file on a disk. It's good practice to save often so you don't lose your work. You should save your work frequently and before printing. Refer to Table 2-6 for tips on when to use the two Save commands that are available on the File menu. To learn how to further protect your document, see the related topic, "Setting timed backup." ▶ At The Write Staff, documents are routinely saved and given descriptive names to facilitate retrieval. Often the client wants a copy of the work on disk. Saved documents can be shared among the staff, parts can be used in new documents, and most important, you can continue to work on your document another day. You have done a lot of work and don't want to risk losing it; save the document you created.

1 Click **File** on the menu bar, then click **Save As**
The Save As dialog box appears, as shown in Figure 2-10. To save a newly created document, you must first name the document. Use descriptive filenames to convey the contents of the document. In WordPerfect you can use filenames consisting of one to eight characters, which can include letters, numbers, and most symbols, but no spaces.

2 Type **WELCOME1** in the Filename text box
WELCOME1 replaces the default *.* in the Filename text box. You can type filenames in either uppercase or lowercase, but they are converted to lowercase by WordPerfect.

3 Click the **Drives list arrow**, then click **a:** or **b:** to select the drive where your Student Disk is located
Check to see that a formatted disk is in the selected drive. If you created the MY_FILES directory, save your file there. If you do not have a MY_FILES directory on your Student Disk, skip Step 4 and continue with Step 5 to save the file to the a:\ directory on your Student Disk.

4 Double-click the **my_files** directory in the Directories list box
The drive and directory path where the file will be saved appears just below the Save As dialog box title bar.

5 Click **OK**
This saves a copy of the document as a file named WELCOME1.WPD. The default file extension .WPD is assigned automatically. The Save As dialog box closes and the filename, WELCOME1.WPD, appears in the document window title bar. You realize that you forgot to include the date in the first line of your document, so you'll need to insert it now.

6 Press **[Ctrl][Home]**
The insertion point moves to the beginning of the document.

7 Double-click the **Date** on the status bar, then press **[Enter]**
The current date appears in your document. Now you need to save the document, or file, again.

8 Click the **Save button** 🖫 on the Toolbar
This saves the changes to your already named file. (You could have chosen Save on the File menu or pressed [Ctrl][S] as well.)

Current drive and directory path where file will be saved

FIGURE 2-10: Save As dialog box

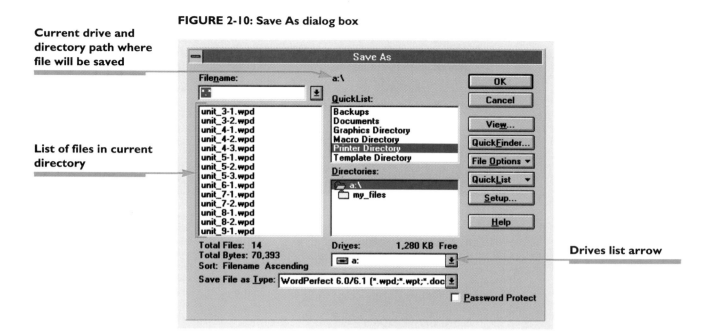

List of files in current directory

Drives list arrow

Setting timed backup

WordPerfect offers a Timed Document Backup option that automatically makes a copy of the document you're working on every 10 minutes. Choose Preferences on the Edit menu, double-click the File icon, then click Documents/Backup. To change the directory of the backup file and the time interval, type the path names you want in the Default Directory and Backup Directory text boxes, then select Timed Document Backup every, and specify a time interval. To guard against accidentally replacing work that you did not intend to replace, select Original Document Backup. Note that this is not a substitute for saving your work regularly.

TABLE 2-6: Save commands

COMMAND	DESCRIPTION	WHEN TO USE
Save	Saves a named file	To save any changes to the original file quickly and easily
Save As	Saves document to a file; asks for filename	To save the document for the first time, to change the file's name, location, application format; useful for making backup copies.

QUICK TIP

If you can't remember the name of your document, click the Drives list arrow, then click the drive where your documents are stored. Use the Filename list shown in Figure 2-10 to view the list of files by drive, then click the file you want to use.■

Cutting, copying, and pasting text

There are two ways to move or copy text from one location in your document to another in WordPerfect. You can use the **Clipboard**, a temporary storage place in the computer's memory, or you can drag text using the mouse. In this lesson, you will use the Clipboard. By placing text on the Clipboard using either the Cut or Copy commands, you can paste the text as many times as you want anywhere in the document. You can also find these commands on the Edit menu. ▶ Jennifer wants you to add a short phone list at the bottom of the document. Practice using Cut, Copy, and Paste to make the changes.

1 Position the mouse pointer at the "J" in "Jennifer" in the name list, and drag the mouse to the end of the name list as shown in Figure 2-11
Instead of retyping the names in the list, you will copy the names to the bottom of the document. Note that before you can cut or copy you must select the text.

2 Click the **Copy button** 📋 on the Toolbar
This copies the selected text to the Clipboard and leaves the selected text in place. You can now paste this text anywhere in your document.

3 Press **[Ctrl][End]** to position the insertion point at the end of the document, then press **[Enter]**
This is where you want to paste the copied text.

4 Click the **Paste button** 📋 on the Toolbar
The copied list of names appears in the document. Now you realize that the procedures really should come at the end of the document. Move the text using the Cut and Paste buttons.

5 Select the four lines of procedures (make sure to include the ¶ on the fifth line as shown in Figure 2-12), then click the **Cut button** ✂ on the Toolbar
The selected text is cut from the document and placed on the Clipboard and the text moves up to fill the space. Because you want to move it, not delete it, you now need to paste it from the Clipboard to a new location in your document. See the related topic, "Delete vs. cut," for more information.

6 Press **[Ctrl][End]** to position the insertion point at the end of the document, press **[Enter]**, then click 📋
The list of office procedures is moved to the end of the document.

7 Press **[Enter]** and type **Phone List:** above the copied list of names, then delete the position titles (Owner and Chief Writer, for example) following everyone's last name and replace it with these phone extensions:

Jennifer	Emily	Michael	David	Arianna	Erica	your name
x2402	**x2401**	**x2305**	**x2409**	**x2306**	**x2408**	**x2500**

Your screen should now look like Figure 2-13. Remember to save your changes.

FIGURE 2-11:
Selecting the text to be copied

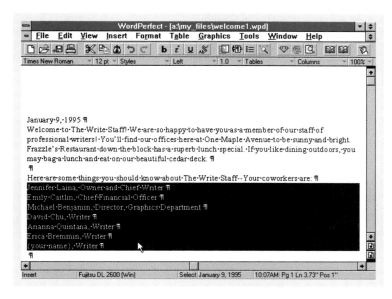

FIGURE 2-12:
Text to move using Cut and Paste

Selected text ⟶

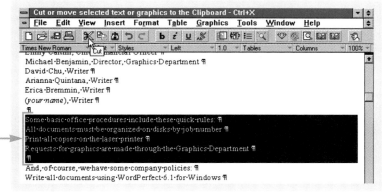

FIGURE 2-13:
Screen with phone list

Copied and pasted list with added phone extensions ⟶

Text that was cut and pasted ⟶

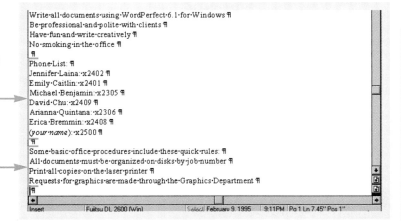

Delete vs. cut

Pressing [Delete] is not the same as using the Cut command. The Cut command places the selected text temporarily on the Clipboard after removing it from the document. Pressing [Delete] removes the text permanently; the text is not available for pasting.

Printing a document

Printing a completed document provides a paper copy to read, to send to others, or to file. You might also want to print a document that is not complete so that you can review it or work on it when you're not at a computer. It's a good idea to save your document immediately before printing. Table 2-7 provides some guidelines for printing a document. ▶ You are pleased with the final outcome of this welcoming document and believe it will be very helpful to all the new employees at The Write Staff. Use the following steps to print a paper copy of your one-page document.

1 Check the printer
Make sure the printer is on, has paper, and is on-line. Before printing, check to see how the document will look when printed. For example, if you add several paragraphs to your document, you might want to check that it still fits on one page. WordPerfect provides a method for viewing a full page of the document before printing it.

2 Click the Page/Zoom Full button 🔍 **on the Toolbar**
Your screen should look like Figure 2-14. The Page/Zoom Full button appears depressed. The words on the screen are hard to read, but the relationship between the text and the page is easy to see. The percentage Zoom displayed on the Power Bar will differ depending on your computer system. See the related topic, "Previewing a document," for more options.

Now that you've seen how your document will print, you can change the view back and print the document.

3 Click 🔍
Your view is back to 100%. Be sure to save before you print your document.

4 Click the Save button 💾 **on the Toolbar**

5 Click the Print button 🖨 **on the Toolbar**
The Print dialog box appears, as shown in Figure 2-15. If necessary, click Full Document, set Number of Copies to 1 and Print Quality to High, using the buttons and lists.

6 Click Print in the Print dialog box
The document is sent to the printer.

7 Click File on the menu bar, then click Exit
All open documents are closed, and you exit WordPerfect.

TABLE 2-7: Document printing guidelines

BEFORE YOU PRINT	COMMENT
Check the printer	Make sure the printer is on and on-line, that it has paper, and there are no error messages or warning signals
Check the printer selection	Click File on the menu bar, then click Select Printer to make sure the correct printer is selected
Preview the document	Review the document before printing to make sure it is set up correctly

FIGURE 2-14:
Viewing the full page

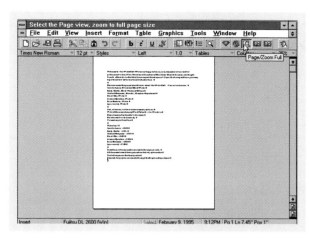

FIGURE 2-15:
Print dialog box

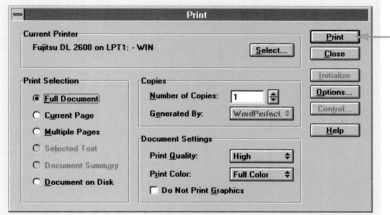

**Click here to print if
settings are correct**

Previewing a document

You can also use the Zoom command from the View menu to see how your document will look when it's printed. When you click Zoom, the Zoom dialog box shown in Figure 2-16 appears. If you work on the document in Page View, 100% appears on the button, indicating that the document is in actual size. If you choose a percentage less than 100, the size of your document is reduced, making more of it visible. If you choose a percentage greater than 100, the size of your document is enlarged, showing greater detail but making less of it visible.

FIGURE: 2-16:
Zoom dialog box

QUICK **TIP**

Press [Ctrl][P] to open the Print dialog box.■

TROUBLE?

If you send a file to print and the printer is off-line, an error message appears on the screen, notifying you of the problem.■

CONCEPTSREVIEW

Label each element of the WordPerfect document window shown in Figure 2-17.

1 _____
2 _____
3 _____
4 _____
5 _____
6 _____
7 _____
8 _____
9 _____

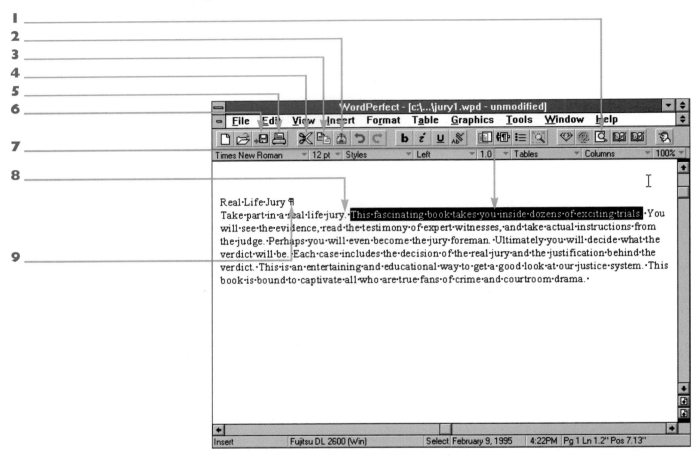

FIGURE 2-17

Match each action with its associated key.

10 Moves the insertion point to the beginning of the document

11 Moves the insertion point to the beginning of the line

12 Deletes a character to the left of the insertion point

13 Deletes a character to the right of the insertion point

14 Saves the current document

15 Opens the Go To dialog box

16 Moves the insertion point to the end of the line

a. [Backspace]

b. [Ctrl][G]

c. [Ctrl][Home]

d. [Del]

e. [Home]

f. [Ctrl][S]

g. [End]

Select the best answer from the list of choices.

17 Which of the following document names will WordPerfect accept?

a. MY_FILE.WP

b. DOCUMENT.WPD

c. MYDOCUMENT.WPD

d. UNIT2.1.WPDOC

18 Which of the following items is NOT an option you can choose from the Print dialog box?

a. Full Document

b. Number of Copies

c. Hard Page Break

d. Print Quality

19 Which commands would you use to copy a sentence to another paragraph in your document?

a. Cut, Copy, Paste

b. Copy, Paste

c. Paste, Copy

d. Move, Copy

20 Which commands would you use to move a paragraph to another page in your document?

a. Move, Paste

b. Cut, Paste

c. Paste, Move

d. Copy, Move

21 If you position the mouse pointer on a word and triple-click the mouse

a. You select the word

b. You select the page

c. You select the paragraph

d. You select the sentence

APPLICATIONS
REVIEW

1 Plan a document.

a. Think about and write down notes on how a greeting card company might plan its advertising copy.

b. Determine the tone of the text and write down notes.

c. Decide what important facts would have to be included in the text.

d. Sketch out how you might want it to look.

2 Enter text for a simple document and save the document.

a. Type the following text exactly as shown below, including errors:

Holiday Gliter. You'll find lots of fun uses for this totally outrageous holiday glitter. Sprinkle on greeting cards or use it to decorate a table top. Packed in a handy 3" plastic tube. Pre-inflated "Happy Valentine's Day" Balloon Assortment. Includes 48 4" clear, round red and white confetti. Each assortment rests on a 7" cup and stick decorated with an "I Love You" banner. Stand included.

b. Save the document as GLITTER.WPD to the MY_FILES directory on your Student Disk.

3 Move around the document.

a. Position the insertion point at the beginning of the document.

b. Position the insertion point at the end of the first line.

c. Position the insertion point at the end of the document.

4 Make corrections to the current document.

a. Change the word "Gliter" to "Glitter."

b. The word "Pre-inflated" should begin a new paragraph. Insert a blank line between the paragraphs.

c. Position the insertion point at the end of the word "round," and insert the words "balloons with."

d. Click View on the menu bar, then click Show ¶ to check for extra spaces in the document. It's up to you if you want to click Show ¶ again to turn this feature off.

e. Save the corrected document with the same filename.

5 Cut, Copy, and Paste text in the document.

a. Make the last sentence the first sentence.

b. Insert a date at the end of the document.

c. Copy the date to the top of the document.

6 Print the current document.

a. Use Zoom to examine the document before printing. The document on the screen will look like the printed version.

b. Print one copy of the full document with the print quality set to High.

7 Change the document filename.

a. Open the Save As dialog box.

b. Save the file with the name SAMPLE.WPD. Notice that two copies of the document now exist (SAMPLE.WPD and GLITTER.WPD).

c. Close the dialog box. Notice that the filename at the top of the window is now SAMPLE.WPD.

8 Exit WordPerfect.

a. Close the document and end the WordPerfect session (Click File on the menu bar, then click Exit).

b. If the document has been changed since the last save, make sure to save it before exiting.

INDEPENDENT
CHALLENGE 1

You are a product manager for Lawn Tools, Inc., a company that designs and manufactures lawn mowers and trimmers. For the past 24 months, you have been developing a new, low-cost, environmentally safe push mower called the SwiftBlade. You are confident that the new product has significant market potential, but you must get final approval from the Corporate Products Group before beginning production.

Write a memo to the Corporate Products Group in which you explain that the SwiftBlade is ready for production but needs final corporate approval. Point out in the memo that you conducted a market study that showed consumers were very interested in the SwiftBlade because it is quiet and light. Explain that the suggested retail price of $198 makes it attractive to new home buyers.

To complete this independent challenge:

1 Make a list of the ideas you want to present to the Corporate Products Group in your memo.

2 Make a rough sketch of how you would like the memo to look on paper.

3 Remember to include a standard memo heading, like the one shown here:

Memo To:	Corporate Products Group
From:	{your name}
Date:	{current date}
Subject:	SwiftBlade product proposal

4 Use WordPerfect to create the document.

5 Carefully review the document and use the WordPerfect editing features to correct any errors.

6 Save the document as LAWNTOOL.WPD.

7 Print the completed document.

8 Submit any preliminary notes or sketches and the completed memo.

INDEPENDENT
CHALLENGE 2

The Morning StarLight cereal company has asked you to write a short description of their new Colorful StarLight cereal. This description will be inserted on the side panel of the box. It should be very exciting and interesting text that promotes this new low-fat kids' cereal. The cereal clusters are in the shape of stars, and they glow when milk is poured on them.

To complete this independent challenge:

1 Make a list of the ideas you want to include in the copy.

2 Make a rough sketch of how you would like text to look on the cereal box.

3 Remember to include all the important and fun facts that would make kids want to buy and eat this breakfast cereal.

4 Use WordPerfect to create the document.

5 Include your name and the current date at the top of the document.

6 Carefully review the document and use the WordPerfect editing features to correct any errors.

7 Save the document as STARL1.WPD.

8 Print the completed document.

9 Submit any preliminary notes or sketches and the completed memo.

UNIT 3

OBJECTIVES

▶ Open an existing document

▶ Use Spell Check

▶ Find and replace text

▶ Use the Thesaurus

▶ Use Grammatik

▶ Set Display Preferences

▶ Use Reveal Codes

Editing
A DOCUMENT

After creating a first draft of a document, you learned how to edit it to make sure the text is free of errors and well organized by copying, cutting, and moving sections of text. In this unit, you will learn to further improve your document by using WordPerfect's proofreading tools. For example, you can check for spelling and typographical errors using the Spell Checker, you can find and replace text, you can find a synonym or antonym for a particular word using the Thesaurus, or you can check for grammatical mistakes using Grammatik. There are also various display options in WordPerfect that help you edit your document. ▶ At The Write Staff, you edit the documents that you create. In this unit, you'll find errors in grammar and style and make corrections to a letter written by the owner of the company, Jennifer, to promote her catalog writing department. ▶

Opening an existing document

You can use the **Open** command to open an existing document you have previously saved on a hard disk or a floppy disk. When you open an existing document, a new window opens in your work area, displaying the document in it. To prevent any accidental changes to the original document, now, and throughout this book, you will save it with a new name. This makes a copy of the document in which you can make changes, leaving the original unaltered so that you can repeat a lesson.

▶ The Write Staff is trying to expand the department that specializes in writing services for clients in the catalog shopping business. Jennifer Laina has asked you to do a final edit on a letter that she is sending out to prospective clients. This letter is to a company that sells upscale clothing through a catalog.

1   **Launch WordPerfect, then click the Open button 🖼 on the Toolbar**
The Open File dialog box appears, as shown in Figure 3-1. Note that the Open File dialog box looks very similar to the Save As dialog box in the previous lesson. For more information on directory dialog boxes, see the related topic, "Using directory dialog boxes," on the next page.

2   **Click the appropriate drive and directory for your Student Disk**
If you do not have a copy of the Student Disk, ask your instructor or technical support person which drive and directory contains your student data files. You need these files to work through the units in this book.

3   **Click unit_3-1.wpd**
Your file should be listed in the Filename list box. You might have to scroll to find it. If the file you want to open does not appear in the Filename list box, make sure you are looking at the correct drive and/or directory.

4   **Click OK**
UNIT_3-1.WPD opens and appears in the document window, as shown in Figure 3-2. This is the letter you will work on in this unit.

5   **Click File on the menu bar, then click Save As**
The Save As dialog box appears. You need to save this file with a new name in the MY_FILES directory on your Student Disk to preserve the original file. If you do not have a MY_FILES directory, skip Step 6 and continue with Step 7.

6   **Click my_files in the Directories list box**

7   **Type CLOTHES1 in the Filename text box, then click OK**
The UNIT3-1.WPD file is saved with a new name, CLOTHES1.WPD. The original document is automatically closed. You will continue working with the document called CLOTHES1.WPD.

8   **If you prefer to work with the symbols displayed on your screen as you did in the last unit, click View on the menu bar, then click Show ¶**
The screens in this unit do not display the symbols. It is strictly a matter of personal preference whether you use them. You will learn how to set the Display Preferences for many different options later in this unit.

FIGURE 3-1: Open File dialog box

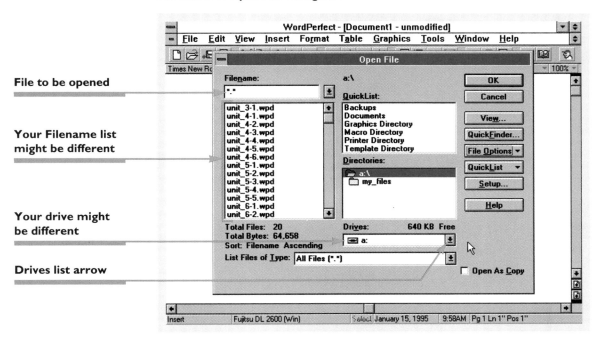

File to be opened

Your Filename list
might be different

Your drive might
be different

Drives list arrow

FIGURE 3-2: UNIT_3-1.WPD document in the WordPerfect window

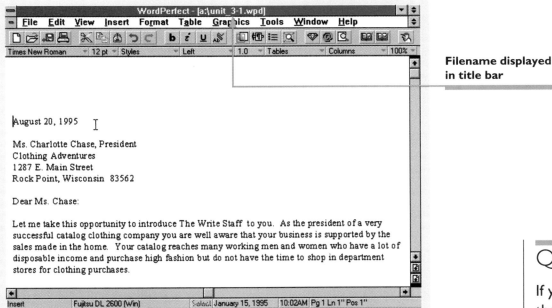

Filename displayed
in title bar

Using directory dialog boxes

Directory dialog boxes are useful in file management; they allow you to open, save,
name, find, view, copy, rename, move, delete, or print files. You can also create or
remove directories. Directory dialog boxes appear whenever you use a retrieve,
open, or save command.

QUICK **TIP**

If you try to open a file
that was created using
an application other
than WordPerfect 6.1,
choose OK in the
Convert File Format
message box that
appears to convert the
file to WordPerfect 6.1
format.■

Using Spell Check

The WordPerfect **Spell Checker** assists you in creating professional quality documents by checking for misspelled words, duplicate words, words containing numbers, or irregular capitalization by noting words not contained in its main dictionary. However, if you need to add a word that is not in the main dictionary, refer to the related topic, "Creating supplemental dictionaries." As the writer, you ultimately decide whether the word is correct or should be changed. ▶ Now, using the Spell Checker, check Jennifer's letter for possible spelling errors before mailing it out to the potential client. From this point on, you should spell check all of your documents before printing.

1 Click **Tools** on the menu bar, then click **Spell Check**, or click the **Spell Checker button** 🔤
The Spell Checker dialog box appears, as shown in Figure 3-3. Table 3-1 explains the Spell Checker dialog box buttons. The Spell Checker looks at each word, but it stops and shows only words it does not recognize. The Spell Checker does not stop on correctly spelled words that are used incorrectly in a sentence. The first misspelled word found is "competative." The suggested spelling is displayed in the Replace With text box. You can choose the word in the Replace With text box, choose a word from the Suggestions list, or manually make corrections in the Replace With text box.

2 Click **Replace** to choose the word in the Replace With text box
"Competative" is replaced with "competitive," and the Spell Checker continues looking for the next spelling error or repeated word. The next misspelled word found is "infrormation."

3 Click **Replace** to choose the word "information" in the Replace With text box
The next word the Spell Checker stops on is a duplicate word. You need to delete "to."

4 Click **Replace** to replace "to to" with "to"
Continue spell checking the document using Figure 3-4 as your guide until the Spell Checker finds the word "Laina." This word is not in the dictionary so the Spell Checker suggests correctly spelled words that are similar. Laina is a proper noun and is spelled correctly.

5 Click **Skip Always**
After the last correction, a dialog box appears letting you know that the Spell Check is completed.

6 Click **Yes** in the dialog box
This closes the Spell Checker and the corrected document appears.

7 Click the **Save button** 🖫 on the Toolbar to save all spelling changes

Creating supplemental dictionaries

You can create an additional, or supplemental, dictionary to include words and phrases that aren't in WordPerfect's main dictionary. Click Add in the Spell Checker dialog box to add a word to a dictionary. When checking for spelling errors, the Spell Checker will search both the main and supplemental dictionaries and will skip any word you have added. You can use supplemental dictionaries for abbreviations or people's names you use often.

FIGURE 3-3: Spell Checker dialog box

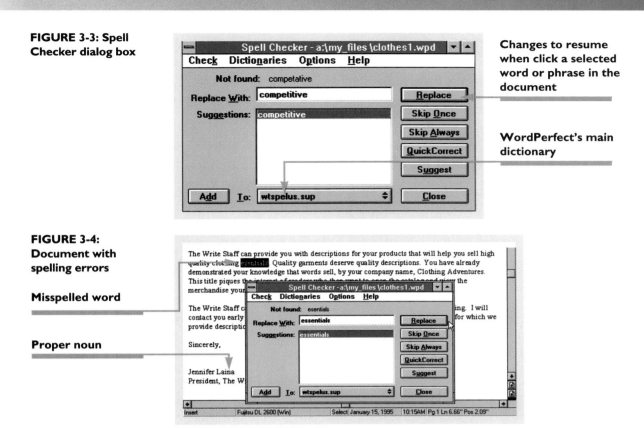

Changes to resume when click a selected word or phrase in the document

WordPerfect's main dictionary

FIGURE 3-4: Document with spelling errors

Misspelled word

Proper noun

TABLE 3-1 Spell Checker dialog box command buttons

COMMAND BUTTONS	ACTION
Replace	Replaces the word with selected spelling suggestion
Resume	Lets you continue an incomplete Spell Check
Skip Once	Skips one occurrence of the word during the current Spell Check
Skip Always	Skips every occurrence of the word during the current Spell Check
Add	Adds the word to the dictionary
Suggest	Displays additional correctly spelled alternatives
QuickCorrect	Replaces the word or phrase with the text specified in the Replace With text box and adds the word or phrase to the QuickCorrect Dictionary
Close	Exits Spell Checker

Finding and replacing text

Sometimes the changes you need to make in a document occur more than once. For example, if you want to change the word "wonderful" to "fabulous," you could read the document looking for each occurrence and then make the change. But in a very large document, it would be easy to overlook one or two instances. With the **Find and Replace** feature in WordPerfect, each occurrence of the text you want to replace is identified. Then you can choose to replace that occurrence or skip it and go on to the next occurrence. You also have the option to replace all occurrences at once, without verifying each one. Table 3-2 lists these options in more detail. ▶ David Chu, a colleague, ran into your office at the last minute to tell you that the name of the company is actually "Clothing Adventure," not "Clothing Adventures." You use Find and Replace to make this change in the letter.

1 Click **[Ctrl][Home]** to position the insertion point at the beginning of the document
This starts the search at the top of the letter.

2 Click **Edit** on the menu bar, then click **Find and Replace**
The Find and Replace Text dialog box appears, as shown in Figure 3-5. You type the text you want to find in the Find text box. If you wish, you can also press [F2] to make the dialog box appear.

The default Find button that appears is the Find Next button. You can choose the other direction by opening the Direction menu in the Find and Replace dialog box. Find Next searches forward and Find Prev searches backward in your document. Now enter the search text, which is the text you want the Spell Checker to search for.

3 Type **Adventures** in the Find text box, then press **[Tab]**
The cursor moves to the Replace With text box.

4 Type **Adventure** in the Replace With text box, then click **Find Next**
The Spell Checker searches for the first occurrence of the word "Adventures" and highlights the one in the address. You want to change this occurrence from "Adventures" to "Adventure."

5 Click **Replace**
This replaces "Adventures" with "Adventure" and moves to the next occurrence of the search text.

6 Click **Replace All** in the Find and Replace Text dialog box to replace the remaining occurrences
The Not Found dialog box appears when the entire document has been searched and there are no additional occurrences of the search text.

7 Click **OK** in the Not Found dialog box, then click **Close** to return to the document
Scroll through the letter and compare it with Figure 3-6. Check to see that the changes have been made.

8 Click the **Save button** 🖫
Remember to save your work often.

Determines direction
of the search

FIGURE 3-5: Find and Replace Text dialog box

Text to search for

Replacement text

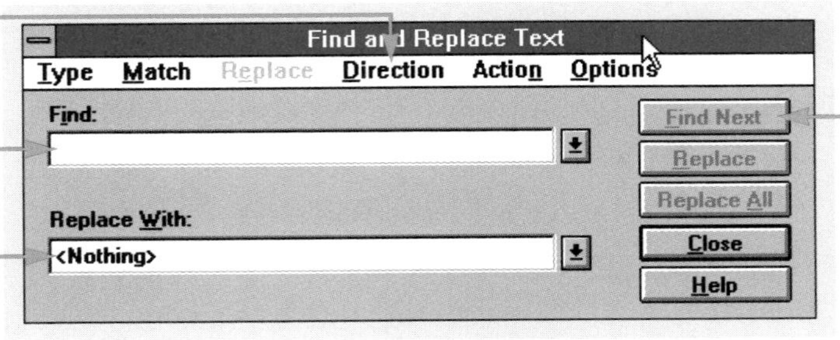

Default search button

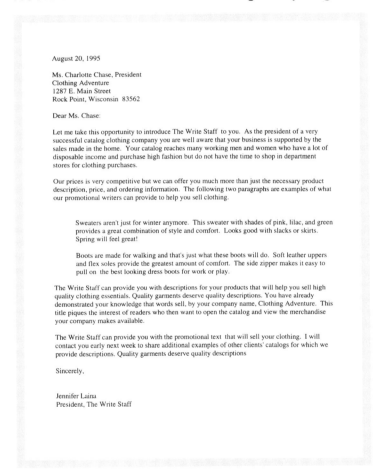

FIGURE 3-6: CLOTHES1.WPD after finding and replacing text

TABLE 3-2: Find and Replace Text dialog box options

SEARCH OPTIONS	ACTION
Find	Finds all occurrences of the search text
Replace	Replaces the first occurrence of the search text and continues to look for the search text; if found again, prompts user to replace or skip
Replace All	Replaces all occurrences of the search text

Using the Thesaurus

The WordPerfect Thesaurus offers you a list of alternative words so you can add variety to your documents. It includes both synonyms, words with like meanings, and antonyms, words with opposite meanings. The words that you look up using the Thesaurus are called **headwords**. Table 3-3 lists and defines various Thesaurus terms. Use the Thesaurus to substitute a word with the same type of word, that is, replace a verb with a verb or a noun with a noun. ▶ After reading Jennifer's letter several times, you don't like the use of the word "products" in the second to last paragraph. Use the Thesaurus to find a synonym to use as a substitute word.

1 Double-click **products** in the first sentence of the fifth paragraph
The word "products" is highlighted. You want to find a synonym for this word.

2 Click **Tools** on the menu bar, then click **Thesaurus**
The Thesaurus dialog box appears, as shown in Figure 3-7. The word "products" appears in the text box, and replacement options appear in the list box.

3 Click ▼ to scroll through the options in the list box
A list of synonyms for "products" appears, followed by a list of antonyms.

4 Click ▲ to scroll back through the options
"Merchandise" seems like a good alternative word to use. "Merchandise" is also bulleted, which indicates it is a headword. You can click a headword to display other references, which are grouped by nouns (n), verbs (v), adjectives (a), and antonyms (ant).

5 Double-click **merchandise**
A list of synonyms appears for the noun "merchandise," as well as for the verb "merchandise" in the adjacent list boxes. The noun is the word you choose to use.

6 Click **Replace**
The Thesaurus dialog box closes, and the word "merchandise" replaces "products" in the document. Compare your document with Figure 3-8. Reread the sentence to ensure that the word change enhances the sentence and conveys the meaning you wanted.

7 Click the **Save button** 🖫 to save your document with the change

TABLE 3-3: Thesaurus terms

TERM	DEFINITIONS
Headword	Bulleted word that can be looked up in the Thesaurus
Reference	Abbreviation that identifies type of words, such as noun (n), verb (v), adjective (a), and antonym (ant)
Subgroup	Words that correspond to different meanings of a headword

FIGURE 3-7: Thesaurus dialog box

Headword

Subgroup

Replacement options

Word that will replace
the headword

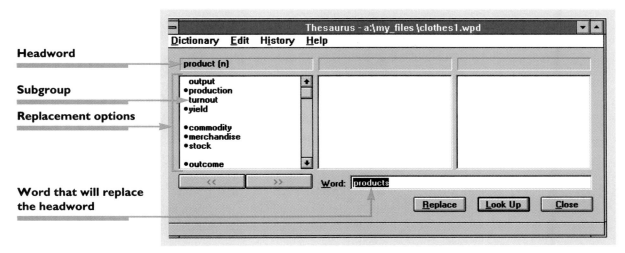

FIGURE 3-8: Document with word change

Products changed
to merchandise

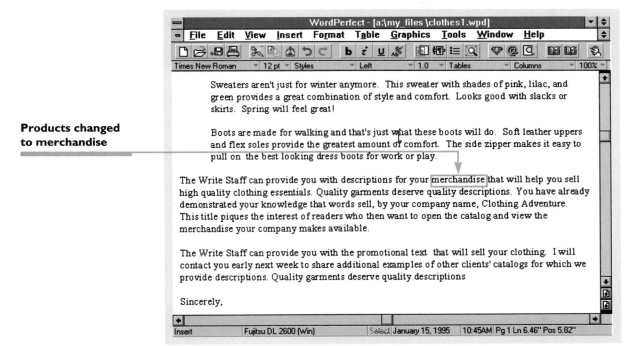

QUICK **TIP**

Press [Alt][F1] to
open the Thesaurus
dialog box.■

Using Grammatik

Grammatik (rhymes with dramatic) enables you to review your documents for grammatical errors such as mistakes in punctuation, sentence fragments, or agreement. When Grammatik locates an error, you can review an explanation of the corresponding grammar rule and select a correction from a list of alternatives. Table 3-4 lists the Grammatik dialog box options. ▶ You are not sure if all the grammar is correct in the letter. Because you want the letter to represent The Write Staff in the best light, use Grammatik to check for any grammatical errors.

1 Click the **Grammatik button** 🔲 on the Toolbar
You don't have to press [Ctrl][Home] to position the insertion point at the top of the document; unless you select text, Grammatik always begins at the top of a document. This ensures that Grammatik checks the entire document for grammatical errors. The Grammatik dialog box appears, as shown in Figure 3-9. Grammatik begins its work immediately. You have several options for choosing the checking style that is appropriate for your document. Use the style most appropriate for this document.

2 Click the **Checking Style down list arrow**, click **Informal Memo or Letter**
The first phrase Grammatik stops on is "prices is." Grammatik has detected an error in the number agreement. Read the description in the New Sentence and Subject/Verb Agreement text boxes. Assume you don't understand why Grammatik flagged this error.

3 Position the mouse pointer on the green dotted word **subject** so the pointer changes to a ⌖⑦
If you don't understand the definition of the underlined word in the suggested replacement text box, you can get help by clicking on it.

4 Click **subject**
The Help window opens, as shown in Figure 3-10. After reading the Help text, you agree that "are" is the correct verb and the sentence needs to be corrected.

5 Click **Close** to close Help, click **prices are** in the Replacements text box, and then click **Replace**
The next word Grammatik stops on is "provide you with." Grammatik displays the grammar rule and suggests a replacement sentence. You are not sure if you agree that "provide you with" is a bit wordy.

6 Click **provide you with**, read the replacement sentence, click **gives you**, read the replacement sentence, click **Skip Once**
You choose to ignore those suggestions and stick with Jennifer's original wording. Grammatik continues to check the document.

7 Click **Skip Once** for the rest of the words Grammatik stops on
Notice that it stops on more than grammatical errors. Depending on your document and the selected Style, among the many things Grammatik flags are errors in punctuation, passive tense, and how many times you start a sentence with "The." When Grammatik is finished, it displays a dialog box asking if you want to close.

8 Click **Yes**, then press **[Ctrl][Home]**

9 Save the changes you have made to CLOTHES1.WPD

FIGURE 3-9:
Grammatik dialog box

Offers alternative
words or phrases

Displays the sentence
using the suggested
replacement phrase
or word

Displays the grammar
rule class Grammatik
assigns to the error

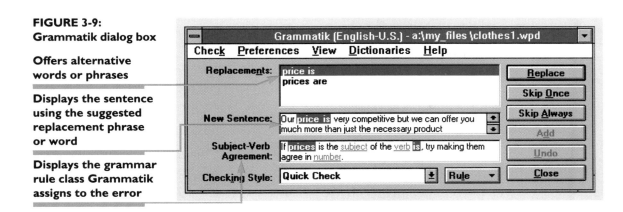

FIGURE 3-10:
Explanation of
grammar rule with
suggested replacement

Click here to open
Help Window

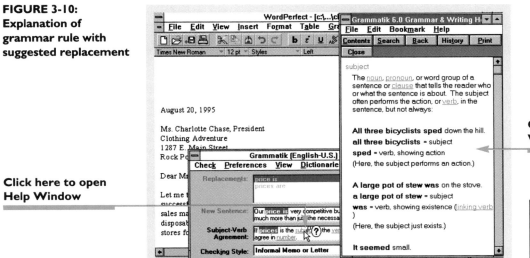

Grammatik Help
Window

QUICK **TIP**

While using
Grammatik, you can
edit text manually by
placing the insertion
point in the document
window, clicking,
typing in the new text,
then clicking Resume.■

TABLE 3-4: Grammatik dialog box command buttons

COMMAND BUTTONS	ACTION
Replace	Replaces highlighted error with new word and goes to the next error
Skip	Ignores the highlighted error and goes to the next error
Next Sentence	Skips all remaining errors in the current sentence and goes to first error in next sentence
Ignore Phrase/Word	Ignores a specific word or phrase for the rest of the proofreading session
Add	Adds word to Grammatik dictionary
Resume	Rechecks from the current sentence onward

Setting Display Preferences

WordPerfect contains many preset options, or **defaults**, which accommodate most users. This book assumes that the settings on your computer match WordPerfect's default settings unless otherwise specified. Now that you know how to execute commands and use dialog boxes, you can check, and change, if necessary, your computer's settings to meet your personal style of working for all documents. ▶ After working on several documents for The Write Staff, you are developing your own preferences for how you like your screen to display text and features. You are familiar with the Show feature; Table 3-5 lists some other common features you might want to customize as you continue to work on your own.

I Click **View** on the menu bar
A check mark in front of a menu command means that it is in effect. Make sure the following commands have check marks: Page, Toolbar, Power Bar, status bar, and Graphics. The check mark ensures that these options appear on your screen. If they are not checked, click them to check them. You might also have Show ¶ checked. See Figure 3-11.

2 Choose **Preferences** on the Edit menu
The Preferences dialog box appears, as shown in Figure 3-12. Notice that the Preferences dialog box looks different from other WordPerfect dialog boxes. It contains a group of icons, rather than a list of options, that represent the different categories of options you can select to use as default settings.

3 Double-click the **Display icon** 🖥
Use Display Preferences to change options for the document window and to set options for Reveal Codes, Ruler Bar, Merge, and Zoom; you will learn more about these options in upcoming units. Next, check that the default Toolbar appears on your screen.

4 Click **Cancel** to close the Display Preferences dialog box, then double-click the **Toolbar icon** 🖿 in the Preferences dialog box
The Toolbar Preferences dialog box opens, as shown in Figure 3-13. 6.1 WordPerfect should be highlighted. If it is not highlighted, be sure to select it.

5 Click **Select**, then double-click the **control menu box** in the Preferences dialog box
The Toolbar Preferences dialog box and the Preferences dialog box close.

6 Click **View** on the menu bar, then click **Ruler Bar**
The Ruler Bar appears below the Power Bar and continues to appear until you remove it. You will learn more about the Ruler Bar in Unit 4.

7 Click **View** on the menu bar, then click **Ruler Bar**
The Ruler Bar disappears.

FIGURE 3-11:
View menu with
default settings

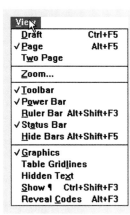

FIGURE 3-12:
Preferences dialog box

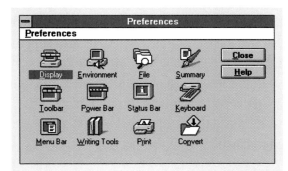

FIGURE 3-13: Toolbar
Preferences dialog box

Default Toolbar called
6.1 WordPerfect

TABLE 3-5: Features you can customize

FEATURE	COMMON CHANGES
Display (Preferences)	Change the look of the default document window
Menus	Add, delete, or move items on menu bar
Toolbar	Change the text and/or graphics that appear on buttons
Power Bar	Edit/customize items frequently used in word processing tasks
Status bar	Change information displayed about documents

Using Reveal Codes

Codes determine how your document looks on the screen and how it will appear on paper. A code is inserted in the document almost every time you use a WordPerfect feature. You cannot see these codes in a normal document window. While the Show ¶ command displays a limited number of key symbols, **Reveal Codes** displays all the codes that are in the document and helps you determine why your document is treating text in certain ways you might not understand. Reveal Codes divides the document window into two parts split by a divider line. The top part is your normal editing window. The lower part displays the same text as in the upper part but includes all the document's codes. See Table 3-6 for an explanation of common codes. Reveal Codes is available through the View menu on the menu bar, through Display Preferences on the Edit menu, and by dragging the small bars above and below the vertical scroll bar to where you want Reveal Codes to begin. ▶ After completing a trial printout run of Jennifer's letter, you found that the letter prints with an extra blank page. Scrolling through the document does not reveal why WordPerfect would add the extra page. Use Reveal Codes to identify all the codes in the letter and make the letter only one page.

1   Press **[Ctrl][Home]** to position the insertion point at the top of the document

2   Click **View** on the menu bar, then click **Reveal Codes**
Your screen splits into two windows, revealing the codes in your document. Refer to Figure 3-14. Notice the location of the insertion point.

You could also drag either of the small bars on the vertical scroll bar as shown in Figure 3-15 to display the Reveal Codes window.

3   Position the mouse pointer in the text window, click ⊞ until the second paragraph appears, and click the word **competitive**
The Reveal Codes screen scrolls to display the corresponding text, and the red insertion point moves to the new location in the Reveal Codes window. The code [SRt] identifies a soft return and [HRt] identifies a hard return. Please note that you cannot delete the [SRt] soft return code in WordPerfect. Only [HRt] codes at the end of lines can be deleted. Hyphenate a word or delete text to change its position.

4   Position the mouse pointer on the divider line; when the cursor shape changes to a ⇕, drag the line up until it is directly under the first paragraph
You can adjust the ratio of the normal text to Reveal Codes text by dragging the dividing line to any desired position.

5   Position the mouse pointer in the Reveal Codes window and double-click to select the word **disposable**
The Select code appears to identify the selected text. Now you have a good understanding of Reveal Codes and can look for the code that is generating the extra page.

FIGURE 3-14: Document displaying Reveal Codes

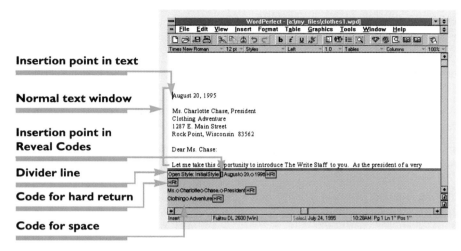

Insertion point in text

Normal text window

Insertion point in Reveal Codes

Divider line

Code for hard return

Code for space

FIGURE 3-15: Displaying Reveal Codes from the vertical scroll bar

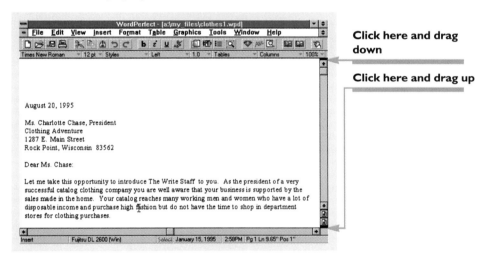

Click here and drag down

Click here and drag up

TABLE 3-6: Some common codes in Reveal Codes

CODE	MEANING
[SRt]	Soft return
[HRt]	Hard return
[HPg]	Hard page
[SPg]	Soft page
◇	Space

QUICK **TIP**

To locate codes in your document, click Match, then Codes in the Find and Replace dialog box.■

Using Reveal Codes, continued

There are extra codes at the bottom of the document. You can see how those extra hard returns made the document go to a second page. You will learn about multiple-page documents in later lessons. For now, you have to get rid of those extra codes.

6 Press **[Ctrl][End]** to position the insertion point at the end of the document

7 Position the mouse pointer on the last **[HRt]**; when your cursor shape is ⟨⟩, drag the code up into the normal text area
See Figure 3-16. Dragging the codes off the Reveal Codes window deletes them.

8 Drag each of the extra hard returns into the normal text area to delete them; leave only one [HRt] below the word **President**
The document now fits on one page. The final codes at the bottom of the document should look like Figure 3-17.

9 Click the **Save button** 🖳 to save your document
Save and print the letter.

10 Click the **Print button** 🖨, then click **Print**
Jennifer is very pleased with the final letter. She is confident The Write Staff will receive positive response and get the account.

FIGURE 3-16: Dragging the codes to delete them

Drag into text area and release mouse button

Code moved from here

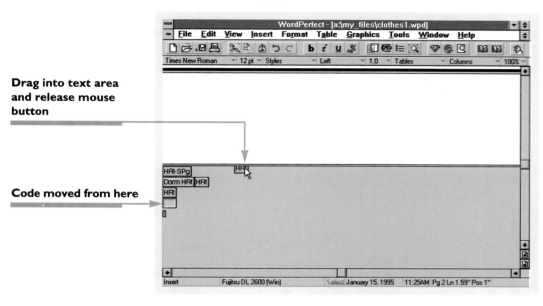

FIGURE 3-17: Final codes

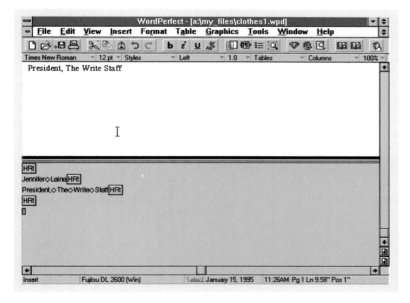

CONCEPTSREVIEW

Label each element of the WordPerfect window shown in Figure 3-18.

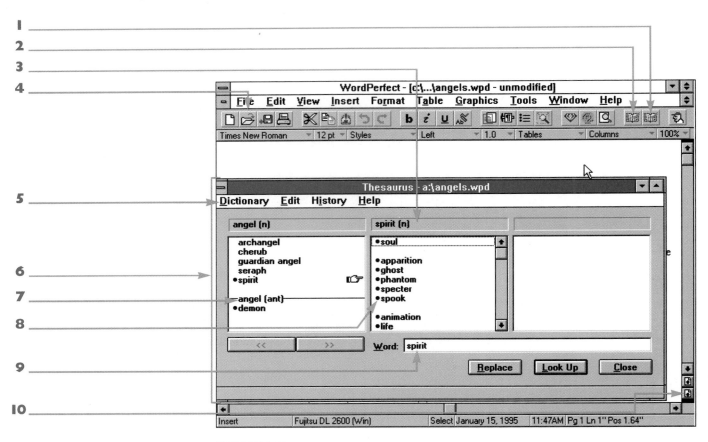

FIGURE 3-18

Match each statement with the term it describes.

11 A temporary storage area in the computer's memory

12 A WordPerfect feature that informs you of irregular capitalization

13 A WordPerfect feature that lets you replace a word in the text with a synonym

14 A personalized list of abbreviations or commonly used jargon

15 A WordPerfect feature that checks documents for errors in writing style

a. Thesaurus

b. Clipboard

c. Supplemental dictionary

d. Spell Checker

e. Grammatik

Select the best answer from the list of choices.

16 How many documents can you open at a time in WordPerfect?

a. 2

b. 1

c. 9

d. 100

17 Which of these cannot be displayed or hidden using the View menu?

a. Power Bar

b. Status bar

c. Toolbar

d. Menu bar

18 Which tool will identify the word "two" as misspelled when the correct word should be "too"?

a. Spell Checker

b. Grammatik

c. Thesaurus

d. All of the above

19 The changes you make in Display Preferences remain in effect until

a. You open a new document

b. You save a document and exit WordPerfect

c. You change them again

d. You reset the options on the View menu

20 You can hide Reveal Codes by

a. Choosing Reveal Codes on the View menu

b. Right-clicking in Reveal Codes and then choosing Hide Reveal Codes

c. Dragging the divider to the bottom of the window

d. All of the above

APPLICATIONS
REVIEW

1 Open and save an existing document.

a. Open UNIT_3-2.WPD.

b. Enter the current date and your name in the first line.

c. Save the file as CLIENT.WPD to the MY_FILES directory on your Student Disk.

2 Use the Spell Checker.

a. Spell check CLIENT.WPD from the beginning of the document.

b. In the address at the beginning of the document, skip words that WordPerfect doesn't recognize.

c. Remove duplicate words.

d. Replace misspelled words with the appropriate suggested words.

3 Use the Find and Replace feature.

a. Open the Find and Replace Text dialog box.

b. Replace each occurrence of "flowers" with "flowering plants."

c. Replace each occurrence of "clients" with "customers."

4 Use the Thesaurus.

a. Move the insertion point to the word "jealousy" in the first paragraph.

b. Open the Thesaurus dialog box.

c. Replace "jealousy" with a synonym such as "envy."

5 Use Grammatik.

a. Open the Grammatik dialog box.

b. Decide whether to skip or replace the words or phrases Grammatik identifies as errors.

6 Set Display Preferences.

a. Open the Display Preferences dialog box.

b. Review the options for the Toolbars.

c. Select an unfamiliar Toolbar and see how it differs from the default.

d. Set the Toolbar back to WordPerfect 6.1.

7 Use Reveal Codes.

a. Display Reveal Codes.

b. Drag the window up to display Reveal Codes in more than half the screen.

c. Identify four different codes and write them on a notepad.

d. Hide Reveal Codes using any method other than dragging the window.

8 Save and print your work.

a. Save your work to disk.

b. Print a copy of CLIENT.WPD.

INDEPENDENT
CHALLENGE 1

You are the assistant manager of Ocean Breeze Book Store. One of your responsibilities is to respond to customer complaints, comments, and questions.

A customer, Teresa Alvarez, of 888 Manzana Street, La Jolla, CA 92122, has recently written to compliment the store on its excellent service. Write a letter to Ms. Alvarez, thanking her for her kind letter and telling her about the Ocean Breeze Book Store philosophy.

To complete this independent challenge:

1 Type the letter using the standard letter format, beginning with the current date, an inside address, and salutation.

2 In the first paragraph of the letter, thank Ms. Alvarez for her kind remarks about Ocean Breeze Book Store.

3 In the second paragraph, tell her that the bookstore's philosophy is summarized in two words, "quality service."

4 In the third paragraph, list the company goals: (1) a clean, attractive, well-organized sales room; (2) a large inventory of quality books and magazines; and (3) knowledgeable, enthusiastic employees.

5 In the final paragraph, explain that through quality service, Ocean Breeze Book Store maintains loyal customers, benefits from volume sales, and gives customers the best prices in the industry.

6 At the end of the letter, include a cordial closing (such as "Sincerely yours") and your signature block.

7 Save the letter as OBBS_DFT.WPD. Print the document.

8 Review the document and change all occurrences of "Ocean Breeze Book Store" to "Ocean Breeze Bookstore."

9 Use the Spell Checker to check the spelling of your document.

10 Use the Thesaurus to replace the first occurrence of "customers" with "clients."

11 Use Grammatik to check the grammar in your document.

12 Save your final letter as OBBS_LET.WPD. Print the document.

INDEPENDENT
CHALLENGE 2

The local elementary school is conducting a writing contest for all aspiring writers in your community. They want to select the best short story on recycling. The winner of the contest will get to go to the school and read the story as part of a presentation to the fifth grade on Ecology. Conservation and the benefits of recycling are very important to your town. The Mayor is trying to raise the awareness of your community.

Your story is about a huge monster who is created out of trash and rises out of the landfill. It turns out he is a good monster and wants to tell all the people to recycle more. Be sure to discuss the philosophy of recycling and all the benefits.

To complete this independent challenge:

1 Type the story as a short one-page document.

2 Name the monster Gargantutrash and have it live in Trashville.

3 Give some background on his family and his "roots." Describe how he looks and use his name and the town name several times in this paragraph.

4 In the second paragraph, mention his message about recycling glass, paper, and plastics. Describe how his life is full of trash.

5 Be sure to mention the monster's good mission and his message to all the children and future generations.

6 At the end of the story, include a happy ending about how people recycle more and Trashville is cleaned up.

7 Make sure to include your name and current date in the document.

8 Save the story as TRASHMAN.WPD. Print the document.

9 Use Find and Replace to change the monster's name to Trashman.

10 Use the Spell Checker to check the spelling of your document. Be careful not to change the name of the monster.

11 Use the Thesaurus to replace the first occurrence of "trash" with "garbage."

12 Use Grammatik to check the grammar in your document.

13 Use Reveal Codes to be sure the document doesn't have any extra codes that would generate unwanted pages.

14 Save your final story as TRASHMN2.WPD. Print the document.

UNIT 4

OBJECTIVES

▶ Choose fonts and sizes

▶ Change the appearance of text

▶ Set margins and line spacing

▶ Align text and use justification

▶ Set tabs

▶ Indent paragraphs

▶ Use QuickFormat

Formatting
A DOCUMENT

Once you create a document, you can format it to improve its appearance. You can format the text by making it bold, italic, or underlined, and choosing fonts and point sizes. You can format the layout by changing the margins, setting tabs, indenting paragraphs, and changing the spacing between lines and paragraphs. ▶ In this unit, you'll format a press release announcing the grand opening of a new branch of a chain of stores, Audiosyncracies, an upscale electronics boutique with locations in fashionable malls. The chain is a very valuable client; The Write Staff has been writing their promotional material and business correspondence for years. To announce the new store, The Write Staff was hired to write the press release for the client to make it look professional, exciting, and polished. ▶

Choosing fonts and sizes

Fonts, or typefaces, refer to the style of letters and numbers. Each font can be produced in several sizes. The size of a font is called its **point size**. Using different fonts and point sizes can improve a document's appearance and readability. You can change the font for an entire document or for any part of it. When you select text and choose a formatting option, the formatting affects only the selected text. If you do not select text, the formatting affects either the word, paragraph, or page after the insertion point, depending on the kind of formatting you choose. The Power Bar provides both a Font button and Font Size button to change fonts and point sizes, or you can use the Format menu to make these changes. Table 4-1 lists some common fonts and shows examples. ▶ Erica, a co-worker, wrote, edited, and proofread the document but did not have time to complete the job. She asked you to put the finishing touches on it. Use fonts to highlight the important words and make the release look interesting.

1   Open the file UNIT_4-1.WPD and save it to the MY_FILES directory on your Student Disk as PRESREL1.WPD

2   Press ⬇ to scroll to the end of the document, then press **[Ctrl][Home]** to position the insertion point at the beginning of the document
    The first thing you notice when you look at Erica's document is that she used the same font, Times New Roman 12 pt, for all the text. Refer to the Power Bar to identify the font and point size. See Figure 4-1.

3   Click `Times New Roman ▾` on the Power Bar
    A list of available fonts appears, as shown in Figure 4-2. Your list might differ, depending on your computer system. While Times New Roman is a very readable font, you want something with a little more style. The font Arial is at or near the top of the list.

4   Click **Arial**
    The current font and the text after the insertion point change to Arial. Next, you decide that the first line, or heading, of the document should be in a sharper font so that it stands out and catches the reader's attention.

5   Triple-click the word **Press** to select the first line, click the **Font button** on the Power Bar, scroll the list, and click **Engravers Bold**
    This changes the font for the selected text to Engravers Bold. If this font is not available, choose one that is similar.

6   Click the **Font Size button** `12 pt ▾` on the Power Bar, then click **18**
    This increases the point size of the letters in the line. See the continuation of this lesson to learn how to use the format menu.

FIGURE 4-1:
PRESREL1.WPD

Font and point size
on the Power Bar

Click to display list
of font faces

Click to display font
size list

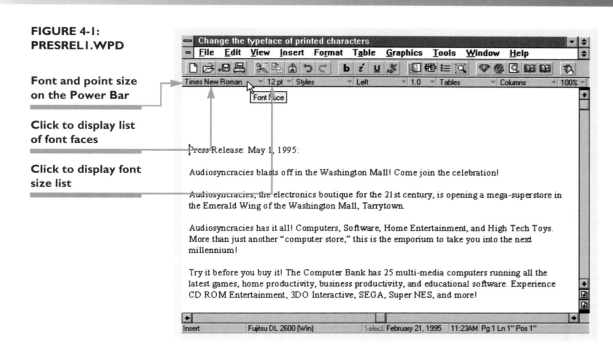

FIGURE 4-2: Font list

Most recently used
fonts

Your list may differ
slightly

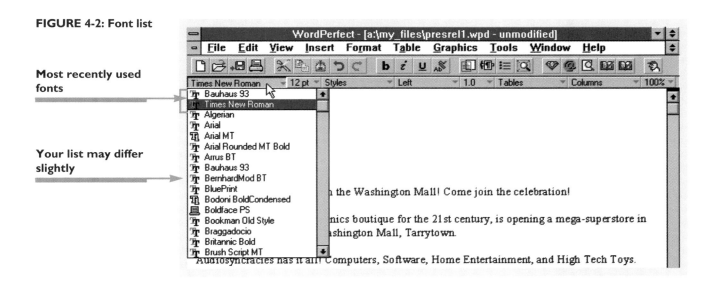

TABLE 4-1: Commonly used fonts

FONT	EXAMPLE
Arial	The Write Staff
Times New Roman	The Write Staff
Courier New	The Write Staff
Script MT	*The Write Staff*

Choosing fonts and sizes, continued

Erica wants the name of the store, Audiosyncracies, to be in a special font but would like to view an example before you make the change. Use the Format menu to do this.

7 Double-click the first occurrence of the word **Audiosyncracies** on the second line
Audiosyncracies is selected.

8 Click **Format** on the menu bar, then click **Font**
The Font dialog box opens, as shown in Figure 4-3. Notice that an example of the font and size appears in this dialog box, allowing you to preview the font before you close the dialog box.

9 Scroll the font face list, click **Century Gothic** in the Font Face list box, click **13** in the Font Size list box, then click **OK**

10 Use either the Font dialog box on the Format menu or Power Bar buttons to change the five other occurrences of the word "Audiosyncracies" to Century Gothic, 13 pt, and remember to save your changes
Notice that the most recently used font faces remain at the top of the list on the Font button on the Power Bar. Your document should now look like Figure 4-4.

FIGURE 4-3:
Font dialog box

Click here to select font

Click here to select size

Selected font and size

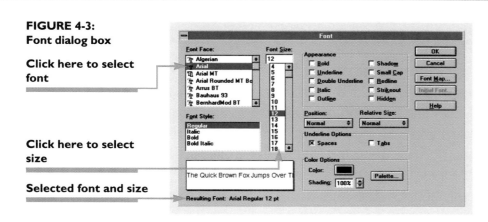

FIGURE 4-4:
Press release after font and sizes changes

Press Release: May 1, 1995:

Audiosyncracies blasts off in the Washington Mall! Come join the celebration!

Audiosyncracies, the electronics boutique for the 21st century, is opening a mega-superstore in the Emerald Wing of the Washington Mall, Tarrytown.

Audiosyncracies has it all! Computers, Software, Home Entertainment, and High Tech Toys. More than just another "computer store," this is the emporium to take you into the next millennium!

Try it before you buy it! The Computer Bank has 25 multi-media computers running all the latest games, home productivity, business productivity, and educational software. Experience CD ROM Entertainment, 3DO Interactive, SEGA, Super NES, and more!

Let your ears and eyes do the walkin'! Audiosyncracies' home-entertainment listening booths offer the latest in digital audio and video components! Experience laser disks, CDs, digital video and more! Enjoy a preview and relax in our lavish showroom.

Play and Play!!! Audiosyncracies The ToyROOM -- will make you a kid again! All the high-tech quality toys for you to play and experience. Be the first kid on your block to bring home the hottest in technotoys!

Take five! A Cup and a Byte, our way cool coffee bar is the place to meet and greet all your fellow techno buddies while enjoying a cafe latte, cappuccino, or espresso and a light healthy snack.

Grand Opening attractions:
Free software for the first 100 guests through our doors on Monday, June 1, 1995
Enter our great Technology Giveaway! Prizes include:
10 Laserdisc players
10 Pentium computers
and hundreds of other prizes.

Everyday discounts:
Books - 10% off publisher's list for hardcover
Computer Software - 20 % off list price
Computer Hardware - Our best buys on new technology

Audiosyncracies: 58 Emerald Wing - Washington Mall, Tarrytown, NY
Store hours: Monday-Saturday: 9am-10pm Sunday: 11am-5pm
Phone: 914-555-0101   FAX: 914-555-1010

QUICK **TIP**

After you select text, press [F9] to open the Font dialog box.

Changing the appearance of text

Character **formats** such as **bold**, *italics*, and <u>underline</u> add emphasis and make a document easier to read. You can apply character formats to single characters, words, lines, and whole documents. Table 4-2 shows some common WordPerfect character formats. To apply character formats, you first select the text you want to format, then use the menu commands or Toolbar buttons to select a formatting option. For more formatting options, see the related topic, "Additional font and format changes." ▶ The writers at The Write Staff use character formats to draw the reader's attention to product names, pricing strategies, and important facts. Michael Benjamin, the Graphics Director, advised you to try using character formats to enhance the document for Audiosyncracies.

1   Press **[Ctrl][Home]**, press **[↓]**, then click the **Underline button** 🆄 on the Power Bar

Notice that 🆄 is indented on the Power Bar. This indicates that the underline format is on.

2   Type **For General Release:** and press **[Enter]**

"For General Release:" is underlined. 🆄 is still pressed. Compare your screen with Figure 4-5. If you accidentally format the wrong character or word, you can remove the format by selecting the same text again, then clicking the format button again. Click the button once to turn the formatting on; click it again to turn it off.

3   Click 🆄, then position the insertion point at the beginning of the third paragraph, click **Edit** on the menu bar, click **Select**, then click **Sentence**

The sentence "Audiosyncracies has it all!" is selected.

4   Click the **Italics button** 𝑖 on the Power Bar

"Audiosyncracies has it all!" is now italicized for emphasis.

5   Repeat Steps 3 and 4 to add italics to the first sentences of the next four paragraphs so that "Try it before you buy it!," "Let your ears and eyes do the walkin'!," "Play and Play!!!," and "Take five!" are all in italics

6   Select the last line in the document, then click the **Bold button** 🅱 on the Power Bar

The phone and fax numbers for Audiosyncracies are now bold. Figure 4-6 shows the document with formatting changes.

TABLE 4-2:
Character formats

7   Click the **Save button** 💾 to save your changes to PRESREL1.WPD

CHARACTER FORMATS	SAMPLE TEXT
Bold	**Audiosyncracies**
Italics	*Audiosyncracies*
Underline	<u>Audiosyncracies</u>
Double-underline	<u>Audiosyncracies</u>

FIGURE 4-5:
"For General Release:" is underlined

Underline button pressed

Your heading may differ slightly

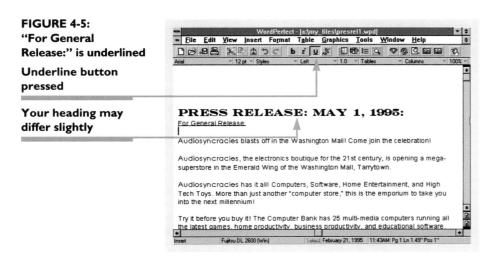

FIGURE 4-6:
Document after changing appearance of text

Press Release: May 1, 1995:
For General Release:

Audiosyncracies blasts off in the Washington Mall! Come join the celebration!

Audiosyncracies, the electronics boutique for the 21st century, is opening a mega-superstore in the Emerald Wing of the Washington Mall, Tarrytown.

Audiosyncracies has it all! Computers, Software, Home Entertainment, and High Tech Toys. More than just another "computer store," this is the emporium to take you into the next millennium!

Try it before you buy it! The Computer Bank has 25 multi-media computers running all the latest games, home productivity, business productivity, and educational software. Experience CD ROM Entertainment, 3DO Interactive, SEGA, Super NES, and more!

Let your ears and eyes do the walkin'! Audiosyncracies' home-entertainment listening booths offer the latest in digital audio and video components! Experience laser disks, CDs, digital video and more! Enjoy a preview and relax in our lavish showroom.

Play and Play!!! Audiosyncracies The ToyROOM -- will make you a kid again! All the high-tech quality toys for you to play and experience. Be the first kid on your block to bring home the hottest in technotoys!

Take five! A Cup and a Byte, our way cool coffee bar is the place to meet and greet all your fellow techno buddies while enjoying a cafe latte, cappuccino, or espresso and a light healthy snack.

Grand Opening attractions:
Free software for the first 100 guests through our doors on Monday, June 1, 1995
Enter our great Technology Giveaway! Prizes include:
10 Laserdisc players
10 Pentium computers
and hundreds of other prizes.

Everyday discounts:
Books - 10% off publisher's list for hardcover
Computer Software - 20 % off list price
Computer Hardware - Our best buys on new technology

Audiosyncracies: 58 Emerald Wing - Washington Mall, Tarrytown, NY
Store hours: Monday-Saturday: 9am-10pm   Sunday: 11am-5pm
Phone: 914-555-0101   FAX: 914-555-1010

Additional font and format changes

If you choose the Font option on the Format menu (or press [F9]), to display the Font dialog box, you can test various formatting options, such as **strikeout**, **shadow**, **double-underline**, and even **colored** text. Because you will see an example of each selected font and appearance change, you might wish to do this when using an unfamiliar font or trying combinations of different formatting options. This way you can choose a font, size, and/or format before entering new text or changing existing text.

QUICK TIP

Text can have multiple formats. Select the text to be formatted, then click **b** *i* **u** in any combination.■

TROUBLE?

If you are unsure of the font, size, or format of text, select it, then look at the Power Bar or press [F9] to display the Font dialog box. The formats will be checked or displayed.■

Setting margins and line spacing

Two formatting options that change the appearance of your entire document are margins and line spacing. **Margins** are the boundaries which enable you to have white space around the edges of the document. **Line spacing** is the amount of space between lines of text. WordPerfect's default setting for margins is one inch around all sides of the page. The default setting for line spacing is single-spaced. ▶ The client, Audiosyncracies, requested that the margins and line spacing in the press release adhere to the Washington Mall media space requirements. All press releases must be single-spaced and have 1½" margins. However, when editing the document, double-spacing makes it easier to read and correct any errors. Try changing these formats and printing the document.

1 Click **View** on the menu bar, then click **Ruler Bar**
The Ruler Bar appears just below the Power Bar. Figure 4-7 shows the margin markers for this document on the Ruler Bar. To change the margins using the Ruler Bar, you first place the insertion point in the paragraph or page where you want margin changes to take place.

2 Press **[Ctrl][Home]** to position the insertion point to the left of the first line of text in the document

3 Click and drag the **left margin marker** on the Ruler Bar to the 1½" mark, then click and drag the **right margin marker** to the 7" mark
This resets the margins for the entire document or up to a point in the document where a different margin is set. To set the top and bottom margins, use the Margins dialog box.

4 Click **Format** on the menu bar, then click **Margins**
The Margins dialog box opens as shown in Figure 4-8. You can specify right, left, top, or bottom margins in this dialog box.

5 Double-click the **Top text box**, type **1.5**, double-click the **Bottom text box**, type **1.5**, then click **OK**
The right, left, top, and bottom margins are now set to 1½". Next, you will change the paragraph spacing from single to double to make the document easy to read before printing. The insertion point should still be at the top of the document.

6 Click the **Line Spacing button** ▭1.0▾ on the Power Bar, then click **2.0**
The document is now double-spaced, as shown in Figure 4-9, making it easy to read and edit. Now use the Format menu to set line spacing back to single-spacing before printing.

7 Click **Format**, click **Line**, then click **Spacing**
The Line Spacing dialog box opens. Notice how representation of the document in the dialog box displays the effect of changing line spacing. Change the spacing back to single.

8 Type **1**, then click **OK**
The press release is now single-spaced again. Finally, save PRESREL1.WPD, then print the document.

9 Click the **Save button** ▣, click the **Print button** ▤ on the Power Bar to display the Print dialog box, then click **Print**
The document is printed. Review the document to see the many changes you have made to it in this unit and check for errors.

FIGURE 4-7: Ruler Bar with margin markers

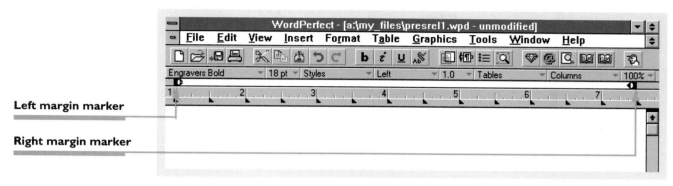

Left margin marker

Right margin marker

FIGURE 4-8: Margins dialog box

Click arrows to
increase or decrease
margin settings

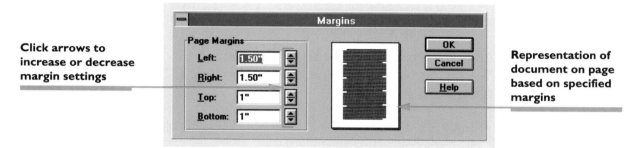

Representation of
document on page
based on specified
margins

FIGURE 4-9: Press release with wider margins and double-spacing

Power Bar indicates
double-spacing

Margin markers at
new location

More white space
in margins

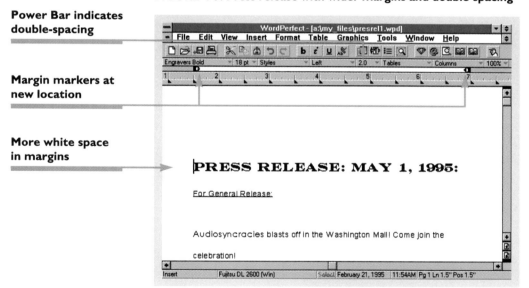

QUICK TIP

If you're printing your
document on three-
hole paper, or if you
need to put the docu-
ment in a binder, set
the left margin to 2"
or 2.5". This gives you
enough room for the
three holes and still
provides an appropri-
ate left margin.■

TROUBLE?

If you drag the indent
marker by mistake,
click and drag it to its
original location and
start again with the
left margin marker.■

Aligning text and using justification

There are several ways to align, or line up, text in your WordPerfect documents. Justification aligns text on the right or left margins, along both margins, or centered between the margins. If you want to change the alignment of a single line of text, you can use the Line and then Flush Right or Center commands on the Format menu. For other options, use the Justification command on the Format menu, the Justification button on the Power Bar, or the Format Toolbar, as described in Table 4-3. ▶ The Write Staff uses a combination of centered and flush-right formats. Michael asks you to center the heading, full-justify the text, and change the justification of the section on prizes. You will change the Toolbar to have a more appropriate selection of tools to format the PRESREL1.WPD document.

1 Position the mouse pointer on the Toolbar, right-click, then click **Format**
The Format Toolbar replaces the default 6.1 WordPerfect Toolbar. Refer to Table 4-3 as you identify the new buttons.

2 Press **[Ctrl][Home]**, click **Format** on the menu bar, click **Line**, then click **Center**
The heading "Press Release: May 1, 1995:" is centered on the line. Next, you want to align the paragraphs along the left and right margins.

3 Position the insertion point at the beginning of the second line before the word For, click **Format** on the menu bar, click **Justification**, then click **Full**
The change to full justification is applied to the entire paragraph and all subsequent text in the document. Notice the Full justification button on the Power Bar is depressed. The text is aligned with both the left and right margins, except for the last line You want to see if justification makes the section describing the prizes stand out more in the document.

4 Position the insertion point at the line beginning **Enter our great Technology Giveaway**, then click and drag to select the text up to and including the word prizes
Your screen should look like Figure 4-10.

5 Watch how the text placement changes as you slowly click **Justify Left** ▣, **Justify Center** ▣, **Justify Right** ▣, **Justify Full** ▣, and **Justify All** ▣
You decide that Justify Center is the best choice for this text.

6 Click ▣, then click outside the selected text
Each line of the selected text is centered between the left and right margins. Your screen should match Figure 4-11. To see how the alignment affects the text on paper, save, then print the document.

7 Click the **Save button** ▣, click the **Print button** ▣, then click **Print**

FIGURE 4-10:
Text selected for
justification change

FIGURE 4-11:
Text with justification
changes

Text full-justified

Text centered

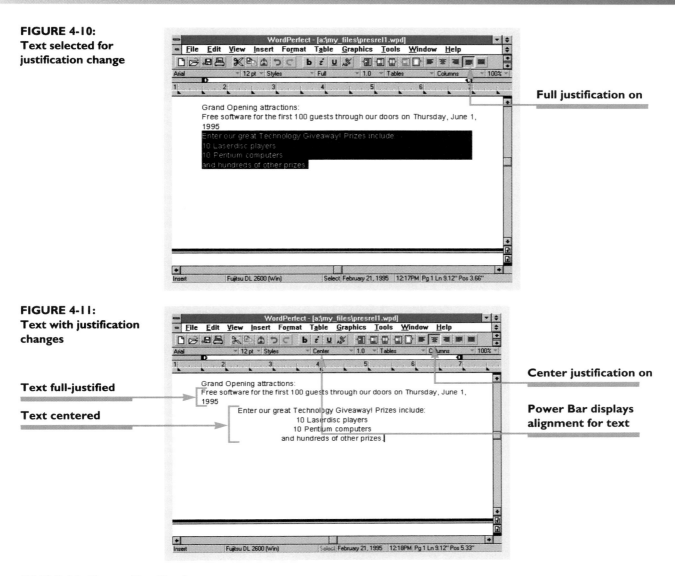

Full justification on

Center justification on

Power Bar displays
alignment for text

TABLE 4-3: Types of justification

JUSTIFICATION	BUTTON	DESCRIPTION
Left		Aligns text along the left margin, producing "ragged-right" margins
Right		Aligns text along the right margin, producing "ragged-left" margins
Center		Centers each line of text between the right and left margins
Full		Aligns text along the left and right margins, except for the last line of the paragraph
All		Aligns text along the left and right margins, including the last line of the paragraph

QUICK **TIP**

To undo an alignment
immediately after
applying it, click the
Undo button
on the Power Bar.■

Setting tabs

Another way to align text is to use tabs. **Tabs**, or tab stops, move text after the insertion point to the next tab stop, and are indicated by black triangles on the Ruler Bar. Only one line of text can be moved at a time. In WordPerfect, tabs are preset at every half inch, but you can reset these as needed. When you change the tab settings in a document, changes take effect from that paragraph on. Tabs are useful when you want to create columns of information and indent paragraphs for certain styles of business correspondence. Table 4-4 lists and defines commonly used tabs. ▶ Audiosyncracies wants to include a sample pricing list for their discounted televisions at the end of the press release. Use the following steps to add a paragraph and enter the three columns of information for the promotional description.

1   Press **[Ctrl][End]**, press **[Enter]**, type **To our valued customers!**, press **[Enter]** twice, then type
    Here is just a small sampling of the competitive pricing we offer at Audiosyncracies! During our opening week celebration, if you can find these televisions for less, we'll beat our competitors' pricing by giving you double the difference!

2   If the Ruler Bar does not appear, click **View** on the menu bar, then click **Ruler Bar**
    The Ruler Bar allows you to see tab stops and to set tabs quickly using the mouse. Your screen should look like Figure 4-12.

3   Position the insertion point at the beginning of the paragraph at the word **Here**, then press **[Tab]**
    This moves the first line of the paragraph over one tab, or .5" to the right.

4   Position the insertion point at the end of the paragraph, then press **[Enter]** twice
    A blank line is inserted in the document.

5   Click the **Tab Set button** 🔲 on the Power Bar
    The Tab Set dialog box opens, as shown in Figure 4-13. You can also open the Tab Set dialog box on the Format menu by clicking Line, then Tab Set. Now clear the preset tabs.

6   Click **Clear All**, then click **OK**
    This clears all the tabs on the Ruler Bar. See the continuation of this lesson to set tabs for the second and third columns.

FIGURE 4-12: New paragraph entered and Ruler Bar displayed

Tab Set button

Format Toolbar

Ruler Bar

Preset left tabs

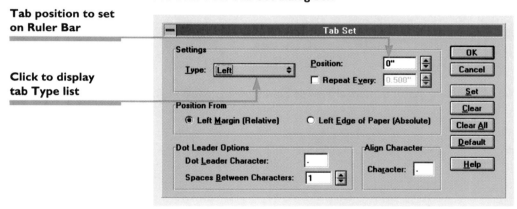

Everyday discounts:
Books - 10% off publisher's list for hardcover
Computer Software - 20% off list price
Computer Hardware - Our best buys on new technology

Audiosyncracies: 58 Emerald Wing - Washington Mall, Tarrytown, NY
Store hours: Monday-Saturday: 9am-10pm Sunday: 11am-5pm
Phone: 914-555-0101 FAX: 914-555-1010

To our valued customers!

Here is just a small sampling of the competitive pricing we offer at Audiosyncracies! During our opening week celebration, if you can find these televisions for less, we'll beat our competitor's pricing by giving you double the difference!

FIGURE 4-13: Tab Set dialog box

Tab position to set on Ruler Bar

Click to display tab Type list

TABLE 4-4: Tab types

TAB	EFFECT
Left	WordPerfect default tab; text moves to right of tab
Center	Text centers around the tab
Right	Text moves backward to the left of the tab
Decimal	Text you type before you insert the decimal point moves to the left of the tab, text entered after the decimal moves to the right of the tab, decimals are aligned
Dot leaders	Dot tabs include dot leaders (a row of dots between the insertion point and the next tab setting); use with left, right, center, or decimal tab

QUICK

To return to the default tab settings, click Default in the Tab Set dialog box.■

Setting tabs, continued

You are going to add pricing information for the list of television sets that Audiosyncracies is deeply discounting during the opening celebration. You want to align the first column of information with the left margin, the second column at the 3.5" mark, and the third column at the 5" mark. You will use the Ruler Bar to set tabs for the second and third columns.

7   Click directly below the **3.5" mark** on the Ruler Bar to set a left tab
A left tab marker appears at 3.5 on the Ruler Bar.

8   Click directly below the **5" mark** on the Ruler Bar, double-click the new **tab marker**, click the **Type list arrow** in the Tab Set dialog box, click **Decimal**, then click **OK**
A decimal tab appears at **5" mark** on the Ruler Bar to align the prices. For more information on how to use the Ruler Bar efficiently, see the related topic, "Ruler Bar QuickMenus and dialog boxes."

9   Type the following information, using the left margin to align the first column; press **[Tab]** between items you type; press **[Enter]** at the end of each line

Mfr/Model	Size	Price
Sony XBR2650	26 inches	249.00
Panasonic KM29	29 inches	309.00
Mitsubishi CS402R	40 inches	1999.00
Sony XBR4255	42 inches	2215.00

10 Compare your document with Figure 4-14, then save your work

FIGURE 4-14: Press release with added tabular information

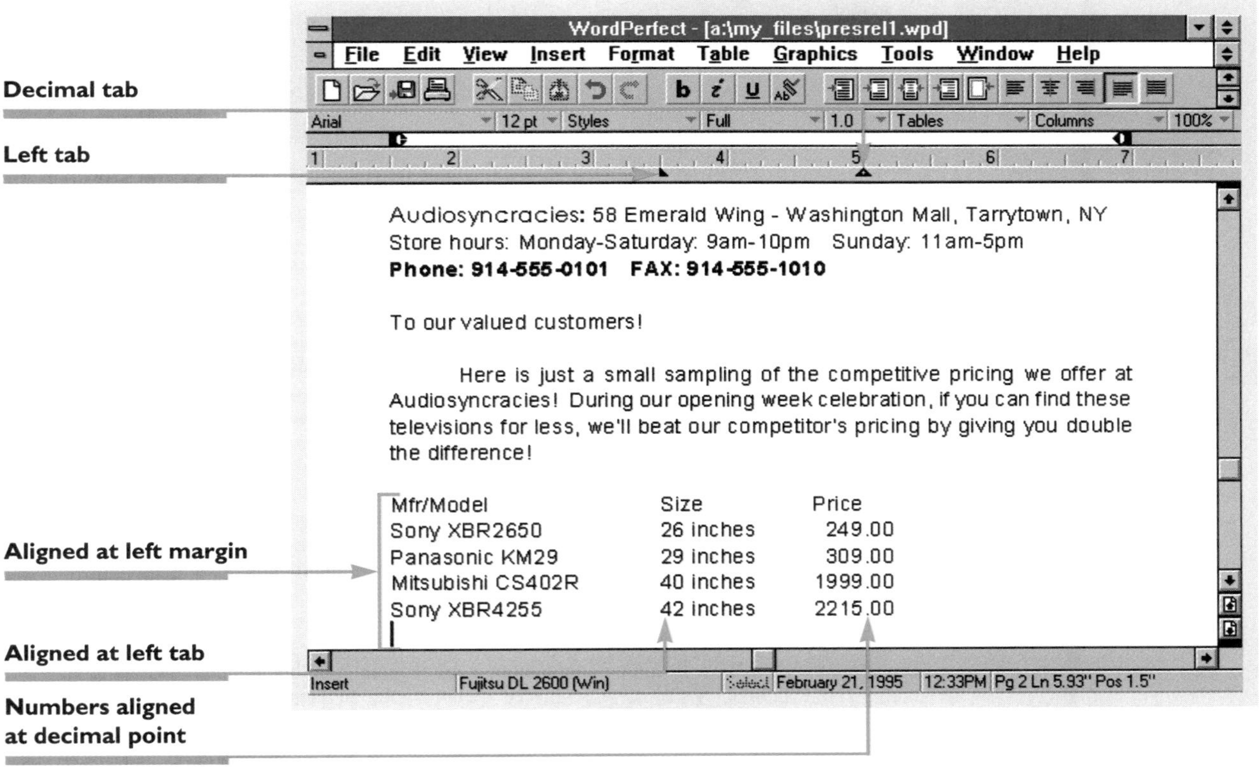

Decimal tab

Left tab

Aligned at left margin

Aligned at left tab

Numbers aligned at decimal point

Ruler Bar QuickMenus and dialog boxes

When you right-click on the Ruler Bar, you can quickly access Ruler Bar features, options, and preferences through a QuickMenu. Right-clicking in the tab area opens a QuickMenu for tabs. You can double-click markers or areas on the Ruler Bar to open dialog boxes for features that use the Ruler Bar. Double-click on the Tab marker to open the Tab Set dialog box for setting tabs.

TROUBLE?

If you need to move text back to the previous tab setting, press [Shift][Tab].■

Indenting paragraphs

Setting indents is yet another option for aligning text. While a tab moves just one line of text to the next tab stop, an **indent** moves all subsequent lines of text in the current paragraph to the next tab stop. Indents are canceled by pressing [Enter], and you need to reset the indent if you want another paragraph to be indented. Table 4-5 lists the different indent types available on the Format menu. ▶ Additional promotional text needs to be added to the end of the press release. Follow the steps below to indent the final paragraph.

I   **Position the insertion point at the end of the document, then press [Enter]**
This inserts a blank line and positions the insertion point for the new paragraph.

2   **Click Format on the menu bar, click Paragraph, then click Indent as in Figure 4-15**
The insertion point is repositioned to the temporary indent. Because you did not reset the tabs adding the price list, it moves to the tab stop to the current 3½" mark. You can also click the Indent button 🔲 on the Toolbar.

3   **Type the text below, pressing [Enter] twice at the end of the paragraph**
Audiosyncracies! Watch out for our next Audiosyncracies grand opening celebrations in Paramus on November 1, 1995 and in Manhattan on January 2, 1996!
The text automatically wraps to the new temporary left margin. Compare your completed paragraph with Figure 4-16. Remember to save your work.

4   **Click the Save button 🔲**
All your work is now saved in PRESRELI.WPD on your student disk.

TABLE 4-5: Indent types

INDENT TYPE	BUTTON	ACTION
Left indent	🔲	Indents entire paragraph to the right one tab stop
Double indent	🔲	Indents entire paragraph inward one tab stop from each margin
Hanging indent	🔲	Indents all but the first line of a paragraph one tab stop to the right

FIGURE 4-15: Format menu and Paragraph menu with Indent highlighted

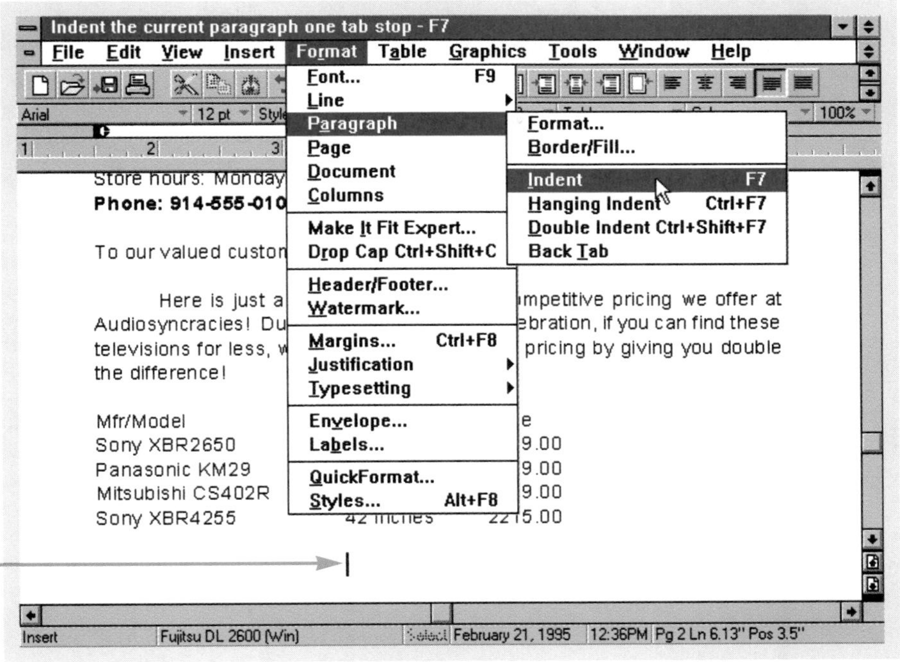

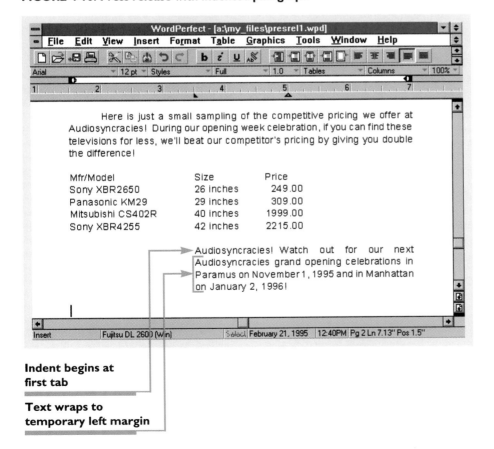

FIGURE 4-16: Press release with indented paragraph

Insertion point at indent

Indent begins at first tab

Text wraps to temporary left margin

QUICK TIP

You can indent an existing paragraph by placing the insertion point in front of the first character in the paragraph, then choosing the type of indent you want.■

TROUBLE?

If you need to remove an indent, position the insertion point at the beginning of the indented text and press [Backspace].■

Using QuickFormat

QuickFormat allows easy copying of fonts and alignment styles from one area of text to another. By placing the insertion point in the paragraph containing the format you want to copy, then clicking the QuickFormat button on the Toolbar, you can specify the formatting styles you want to copy by simply dragging over the text you want to reformat. To turn off QuickFormat, click the QuickFormat button again. ▶ After reviewing your document, you realize that when you added the new text at the end of the press release, you did not use the proper character format for the name of the store, "Audiosyncracies." Use QuickFormat to make this change throughout the document.

1 Press [↑] to display Audiosyncracies: 58 Emerald Wing - Washington Mall, Tarrytown, NY
Your screen should look like Figure 4-17. This is the last occurrence of the word "Audiosyncracies" that was formatted correctly.

2 Double-click the word **Audiosyncracies** in the first line
The store name with the correct character format, Century Gothic, 13 pt, is now selected. You need to copy this format to the remaining occurrences of the word in the document.

3 Click the **QuickFormat button** 🔲 on the Toolbar
The QuickFormat dialog box appears. The Characters option copies only the fonts and attributes of the current text.

4 Click the **Characters radio button**, if necessary, then click **OK**
The mouse pointer changes to I. With this special mouse pointer, drag over any text to which you want to apply the new format. Refer to Figure 4-18 to locate the next occurrence.

5 Double-click **Audiosyncracies**
QuickFormat changes the word from the document's default font to the QuickFormat font.

6 Scroll through the document, and select the next two occurrences of **Audiosyncracies**.

7 Save and print the document
Compare your document with Figure 4-19. You have completed the press release, and it is ready to send to the client. Close the document and exit WordPerfect.

8 Click **File** on the menu bar, then click **Exit**

FIGURE 4-17:
Beginning of added text to be changed

Formatted to Century Gothic 13pt

QuickFormat button

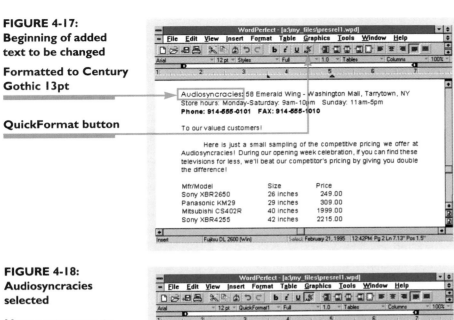

FIGURE 4-18:
Audiosyncracies selected

Next occurrence to be QuickFormatted

QuickFormat cursor

Select these words to format Century Gothic 13pt

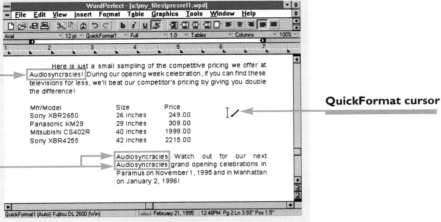

FIGURE 4-19:
Final document

Press Release: May 1, 1995:

For General Release:

Audiosyncracies blasts off in the Washington Mall! Come join the celebration!

Audiosyncracies, the electronics boutique for the 21st century, is opening a mega-superstore in the Emerald Wing of the Washington Mall, Tarrytown.

Audiosyncracies has it all! Computers, Software, Home Entertainment, and High Tech Toys. More than just another "computer store," this is the emporium to take you into the next millennium!

Try it before you buy it! The Computer Bank has 25 multi-media computers running all the latest games, home productivity, business productivity, and educational software. Experience CD ROM Entertainment, 3DO Interactive, SEGA, Super NES, and more!

Let your ears and eyes do the walkin'! Audiosyncracies' home-entertainment listening booths offer the latest in digital audio and video components! Experience laser disks, CDs, digital video and more! Enjoy a preview and relax in our lavish showroom.

Play and Play!!! Audiosyncracies The ToyROOM -- will make you a kid again! All the high-tech quality toys for you to play and experience. Be the first kid on your block to bring home the hottest in technotoys!

Take five! A Cup and a Byte, our way cool coffee bar is the place to meet and greet all your fellow techno buddies while enjoying a cafe latte, cappuccino, or espresso and a light healthy snack.

Grand Opening attractions:
Free software for the first 100 guests through our doors on Monday, June 1, 1995
Enter our great Technology Giveaway! Prizes include:
10 Laserdisc players
10 Pentium computers
and hundreds of other prizes.

Everyday discounts:
Books - 10% off publisher's list for hardcover
Computer Software - 20 % off list price
Computer Hardware - Our best buys on new technology

Audiosyncracies: 58 Emerald Wing - Washington Mall, Tarrytown, NY
Store hours: Monday-Saturday: 9am-10pm Sunday: 11am-5pm
Phone: 914-555-0101 FAX: 914-555-1010

To our valued customers!

Here is just a small sampling of the competitive pricing we offer at Audiosyncracies! During our opening week celebration, if you can find these televisions for less, we'll beat our competitor's pricing by giving you double the difference!

Mfr/Model	Size	Price
Sony XBR2650	26 inches	249.00
Panasonic KM29	29 inches	309.00
Mitsubishi CS402R	40 inches	1999.00
Sony XBR4255	42 inches	2215.00

Audisyncracies! Watch out for our next Audiosyncracies grand opening celebrations in Paramus on November 1, 1995 and in Manhattan on January 2, 1996!

CONCEPTSREVIEW

Label each element of the WordPerfect window shown in Figure 4-20.

1 _____

2 _____

3 _____

4 _____

5 _____

6 _____

7 _____

8 _____

9 _____

10 _____

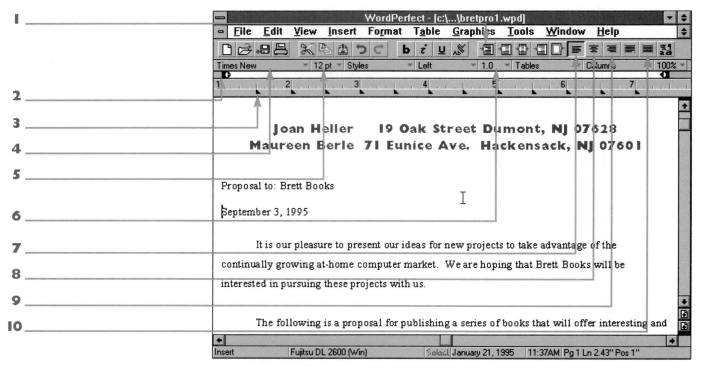

FIGURE 4-20

Match each statement with the format command it describes.

11 Specifies the amount of space between lines of text

12 Indents a single line of text or aligns columns of information

13 Makes text look thicker or darker

14 Aligns the entire paragraph at the tab stop

15 Specifies that text should be aligned along the left margin, right margin, or both

16 Creates a temporary boundary for text

a. Tab

b. Margin

c. Indent

d. Justification

e. Line spacing

f. Bold

Select the best answer from the list of choices.

17 Text aligned on both the left and right margins is what type of justification?

a. Right

b. Full

c. Left

d. Center

18 The easiest way to change line spacing is to

a. Click the Tab Set button on the Power Bar

b. Press [Enter] after each line

c. Click the Line Spacing button on the Power Bar

d. Increase the top and bottom margins

19 Which Power Bar button would you click to change the height of the font in your document?

   a. Font Size

   b. Font

   c. Tab Set

   d. Line Spacing

20 The easiest way to copy character formats is to use

   a. QuickSelect

   b. QuickFormat

   c. QuickCharacter

   d. QuickCopy

APPLICATIONS
REVIEW

1 Open a document and practice formatting.

   a. Open the document UNIT_4-2.WPD.

   b. Select the words "Creative Kitchens" in the first sentence of the letter.

   c. Click the Font Face button on the Power Bar, then click any font of your choice. The phrase appears in the new font. Try a few fonts until you find one of your liking.

   d. With "Creative Kitchens" still highlighted, click the Bold button on the Power Bar. The words appear in boldface.

   e. Click the Font Size button on the Power Bar, then click 14. The words appear in a larger font size.

   f. Click anywhere in the document to deselect the highlighted words.

   g. Repeat the steps above with the other occurrence of "Creative Kitchens" in the second paragraph of the body of the letter.

2 Using the same document, change the margins, justification, and line spacing.

   a. Move the insertion point to the beginning of the document, and save it as KITCHEN.WPD to your MY_FILES directory on your Student Disk.

   b. If the Ruler Bar isn't already visible, click Ruler Bar on the View menu.

   c. Click and drag the left margin marker on the Ruler Bar to the 1½" mark. Click and drag the right margin marker to the 6½" mark. Notice that there is now more white space on the left and right sides of the document.

   d. Click the Line Spacing button on the Power Bar and click 1.5. The lines are now spaced farther apart.

   e. Click the Justification button on the Power Bar and click Full. The lines of text are now aligned along both the right and left margins.

   f. Move the insertion point to the beginning of the second paragraph in the body of the letter.

   g. Repeat the steps above, but choose different margins, line spacing, and justification. Notice that the changes you make apply only to the text following the insertion point.

   h. Save the document, then close it.

3 Open a document and add indents and tabs to it.

   a. Open the document UNIT_4-3.WPD and save it as MEMO.WPD to your MY_FILES directory on your Student Disk.

   b. If the Ruler Bar isn't already visible, click Ruler Bar on the View menu.

   c. Move the insertion point immediately to the right of the colons (:) after "Date," "To," "From," and "RE," then press [Tab] once or twice as needed to align the information opposite the colons on the tab stop at 2".

   d. Move the insertion point to the beginning of the paragraph that starts "Accompanying this memo. . . ."

   e. Indent the paragraph by clicking the Indent button or by clicking Paragraph, then Indent on the Format menu. The entire paragraph moves to the first tab stop.

   f. Repeat the steps above to indent the other two paragraphs of the memo.

   g. Move the insertion point to the beginning of the document.

   h. Set a left tab by clicking directly below the 0.25 mark on the Ruler Bar. Notice that the three indented paragraphs move to the tab stop you have just set.

   i. Set another left tab by clicking directly below the 0.75 mark on the Ruler Bar. Notice that the location of the information in the heading of the memo moves to the tab stop you have just set.

   j. Save the document, then close it.

   k. Exit WordPerfect.

INDEPENDENT
CHALLENGE 1

You are a sales representative for Clearwater Valve Company. You have a list of prospective clients, one of whom is Mr. Ken Kikuchi of CryoTech Pharmaceuticals, 891 Avocado Avenue, Escondido, CA 92925.

As part of your job, you write letters to these prospective clients, introducing yourself as a sales representative for Clearwater Valve Company and explaining that Clearwater designs and manufactures the highest-quality valves in the industry. You explain that Clearwater can design valves to meet extreme conditions of temperature, pressure, and acidity.

To complete this independent challenge:

1 Write a short letter introducing yourself to Mr. Kikuchi, briefly explaining what your company does, and requesting the opportunity to visit him and others at CryoTech Pharmaceuticals.

2 Save the letter as VALVE1.WPD, then print it.

3 Now make the following changes in the format of the letter:

a. Move the left margin to 1.5. Move the right margin to 7.25.

b. Make the line spacing 2.0.

c. Change the font for every occurrence of "Clearwater Valve Company" to Swiss721 BlkEx BT font. If that font isn't available, choose one of your liking.

d. Make every occurrence of "Cryo" bold, and italicize every occurrence of "Tech" so that the company name is formatted as "**Cryo**_Tech_ Pharmaceuticals."

e. Set a left tab stop 0.4" from the left margin. Indent the first line of every paragraph to this tab stop.

4 Save the letter as VALVE2.WPD, then print it.

5 Submit the first and final drafts of the letter.

INDEPENDENT
CHALLENGE 2

Find the lyrics to one of your favorite songs. You can locate these on the outside of record albums or often inside the booklet that comes with compact discs. If you don't have access to CDs or record albums, go to your local library and get a song book. Find a book that has the lyrics for all verses of the song you choose. Try to find a song that has a repeating chorus.

To complete this independent challenge:

1 Create a document, typing all the lyrics. Be sure to end each line with [Enter] as required.

a. Proofread the document and correct any spelling errors.

b. Be sure to enter the song title and the lyricist (the person who wrote the song) at the top of the document.

c. Save the document as SONG1.WPD.

2 Now make the following changes in the format of the lyrics:

a. Move the left margin to 1.25. Move the right margin to 6.75.

b. Make the line spacing 1.5.

c. Change the font face and font size for every occurrence of the chorus so that it is different from the other verses. Choose a font and size of your liking. Use QuickFormat to complete this step.

d. Make every occurrence of the title of the song bold, both in the heading and throughout the lyrics.

e. Set a left tab stop 0.5" from the left margin. Use a hanging indent to this tab stop at the first line of every verse.

f. Italicize the lyricist's name.

g. Type your name and date at the bottom.

3 Save the song as SONG2.WPD, then print it.

4 Submit the first and final drafts of the song.

UNIT 5

OBJECTIVES

▶ Add page numbers

▶ Insert headers and footers

▶ Suppress a header

▶ Insert and edit footnotes and endnotes

▶ Insert a page break

▶ Keep text together

▶ Create a Table of Contents

▶ Convert text to columns

Working
WITH MULTIPLE PAGES

Most of the documents you've worked with so far are single-page documents. However, many of the documents you will create in the future will consist of multiple pages, presenting new word processing challenges. For example, you might want to keep track of the pages, include footnotes, and format the document determining specific page breaks. Several WordPerfect commands help you with these tasks. Some of these commands display **Feature Bars**. Feature Bars appear below the Power Bar and contain options appropriate to a particular command. ▶ Jennifer Laina just finished writing a company style guide to be used by the writers in the newly formed Catalogs Division. The document, Promotional Text Writing Guidelines, is a few pages long and includes the condensed version of the General Writing Style Guide. Jennifer asks you to review and organize this document before she distributes it to other writers. ▶

Adding page numbers

If a document includes more than one page, you will probably want to add page numbers. This task is easy in WordPerfect. You can choose the type of page numbers you want, any text to be included with the page numbers, and where you want to place them on the printed page. See the related topic, "Including text with the page number" for more information on how to customize page numbers. Page numbers can be included in a header or footer but can also stand alone on the page. You will learn about headers and footers in the next lesson. Table 5-1 shows different page number types and suggested uses for each. ▶ As a rule, writers at The Write Staff are requested to put page numbers in documents with more than one page. This helps to organize the document and helps to reorder pages that might have been placed out of order. Try adding page numbers to the style guide document.

1   **Open UNIT_5-1.WPD, then save it as GUIDE1.WPD to the MY_FILES directory on your Student Disk**
There are intentional errors in the document that you will correct in a later lesson.

2   **Press [↓] until a black and gray horizontal bar crosses your document window**
This is the page break. The second page of your document begins below this line; the first page ends above this line. Your screen should look like Figure 5-1.

3   **Position the insertion point at the beginning of the text on the second page of the document before the word "identify"**
The placement of the insertion point determines where page numbering will begin. You want the page numbers to start on Page 2 because it is one of The Write Staff's conventions to leave the first page of a document unnumbered.

4   **Click Format on the menu bar, click Page, then click Numbering**
The Page Numbering dialog box appears.

5   **Click the Position list arrow in the Placement box, then click Bottom Center**
Page numbers appear centered at the bottom of the Sample Facing Pages, as shown in Figure 5-2. Facing pages are left and right pages. If you wanted to change the type of numbers, or add text to accompany the page number, you would click Options. However, the default numbers are fine for this document.

6   **Click OK, then press [↓] to scroll to the bottom of Page 2**
Figure 5-3 shows the second page of GUIDE1.WPD after adding page numbers. Be sure to save your document.

7   **Click the Save button 🖫 to save your document**

TABLE 5-1: Types of page numbers

TYPE	EXAMPLE	SUGGESTED USES
Arabic numerals	1, 2, 3	WordPerfect's default setting; body of a document
Lowercase roman numerals or letters	i, ii, iii, a, b, c	Table of contents, acknowledgments
Uppercase roman numerals or letters	I, II, III, A, B, C	Table of contents, acknowledgments, appendices

FIGURE 5-1: Page break

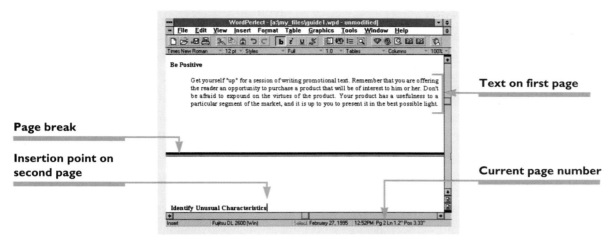

Text on first page

Page break

Insertion point on
second page

Current page number

FIGURE 5-2: Sample Facing Pages

Page numbering
position

Sample pages

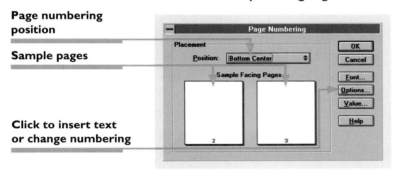

Click to insert text
or change numbering

FIGURE 5-3: Second page of GUIDEI.WPD

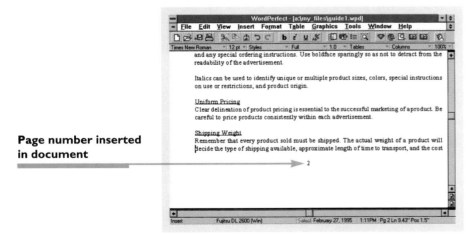

Page number inserted
in document

Including text with the page number

Unless you change them, page numbers appear in the same font as the text of a document. To change the font of page numbers, click Format, click Page, then click Numbering. In the Page Numbering dialog box, click Font. The Page Numbering Font dialog box opens, in which you can choose a font.

QUICK **TIP**

You have to be working in Page View to see the page numbers in your document.

Inserting headers and footers

A **header** is information that appears at the top of each page of a document, and a **footer** is information that appears at the bottom of each page. A header or footer might include your name, the company name, the page number, chapter headings, or titles. You can choose to have headers and footers appear on each page or on alternating pages. For additional information on changing headers or footers, read the related topic, "Editing a header or footer" in this lesson. ▶ You want to insert a header in the style guide document that includes the company name and the date the guide was last revised.

1 Press **[Ctrl][Home]**
The header will start on the page where the insertion point is located and will appear on every subsequent page. The insertion point is positioned at the beginning of the document.

2 Click **Format** on the menu bar, then click **Header/Footer**
The Headers/Footers dialog box appears, as shown in Figure 5-4. Header A is selected by default. You can create two headers and two footers for every document. If you wanted to create a footer, you would click either Footer A or Footer B, then continue with the following steps.

3 Click **Create** in the Headers and Footers dialog box
The insertion point moves to the upper-left corner of the page, and the Headers/Footers Feature Bar appears, as shown in Figure 5-5. Refer to Table 5-2 for a description of the Feature Bar buttons.

4 Click **Insert Line** on the Features Bar, type **The Write Staff**, press **[Tab]** eight times, type the date **October 17, 1995**
This places the company name against the left margin and the date against the right margin above a thin horizontal line.

5 Click **Close** on the Headers/Footers Feature Bar
Figure 5-6 shows a partial page with the new header.

6 Click the **Next Page button** 🔲 on the scroll bar to check that the header appears on the next page

7 Click the **Save button** 🔲 to save your work

TABLE 5-2: Headers/Footers Feature Bar buttons

BUTTON	ACTION
Number	Adds a page, chapter, volume number, or secondary number that allows for tracking a second set of page numbers in a document
Insert Line	Creates and adds a vertical or horizontal line
Pages	Specifies pages—odd, even, or every other page—on which the header information should appear
Distance	Specifies amount of space between text and the header or footer
Next	Moves to the next defined header or footer
Previous	Moves to the previously defined header or footer

FIGURE 5-4: Headers/Footers dialog box

Selected by default

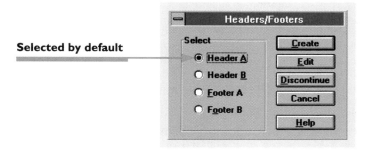

FIGURE 5-5: Headers/Footers Feature Bar

Click for help

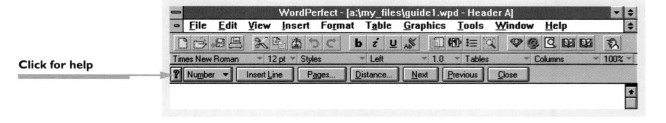

FIGURE 5-6: GUIDE1.WPD with header

Horizontal line as part of header

Header

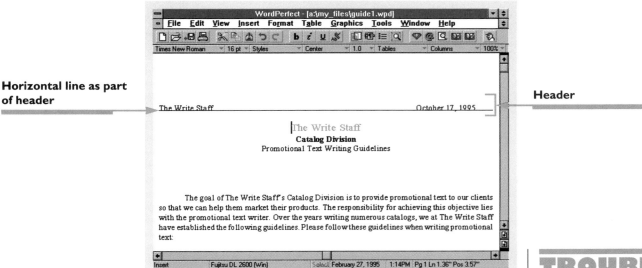

Editing a header or footer

Click anywhere inside the header or footer. Right-click, then click Feature Bar. Edit the header or footer text as you normally would, using any of the available WordPerfect formatting or editing options. After making changes, click anywhere outside the header or footer to return to your document.

TROUBLE?

If the header or footer doesn't appear after you close the Headers/Footers Feature Bar, check that you are in Page View. Headers and footers do not appear in Draft View.■

Suppressing a header

If you don't want a header, footer, or page number to appear on a specific page, such as on the title page of a document, you can use the Suppress option. **Suppress** allows you to skip the header, footer, or page number on a particular page without deleting it from any other pages. ▶ Jennifer tells you to follow the same convention for headers that you did for page numbers; the header you created should not appear on the first page of the style guide. Complete the following steps to suppress the header.

1   **Position the insertion point at the beginning of the document**
This places the insertion point on the page where you want to suppress the header.

2   **Click Format on the menu bar, click Page, then click Suppress**
The Suppress dialog box appears, as shown in Figure 5-7.

3   **Click Header A**
This tells WordPerfect what you want to suppress. The Suppress dialog box now has a check in the Header A check box. Note that you can also use this dialog box to suppress footers and page numbers. You can check as many check boxes as you like.

4   **Click OK**
The dialog box closes.

5   **Click the Save button** 🖫 **to save your changes, click the Print button** 🖨, **then click Print**
Header A does not appear or print on the first page of the style guide. See Figure 5-8.

FIGURE 5-7: Suppress dialog box

Click to suppress Header A

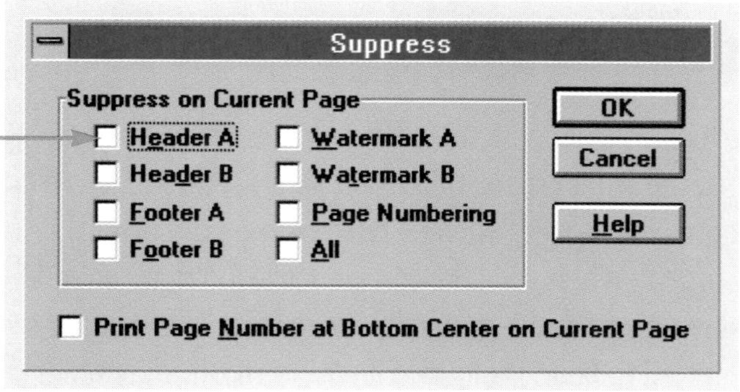

FIGURE 5-8: Page 1 of GUIDE1.WPD document without header

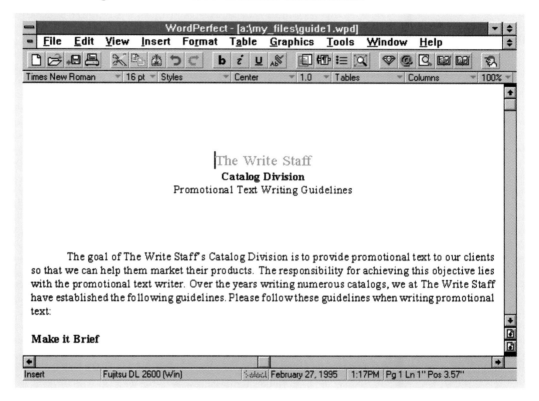

Inserting and editing footnotes and endnotes

Use footnotes or endnotes to list your sources in a research project or to provide additional information about items in your document. **Footnotes** appear at the bottom of any page, whereas **endnotes** are usually printed at the end of the document. When you add, edit, or delete footnotes or endnotes, they are renumbered and reformatted automatically. You can quickly edit any footnote or endnote with the insertion point positioned anywhere in the document or directly in the footnote or endnote. ▶ Emily Caitlin is responsible for overseeing the legal aspects of all the documents created at The Write Staff. Include a footnote in the style guide that states The Write Staff has the right to make changes to the document when necessary.

1 Position the insertion point after the word "text" at the end of the first paragraph on the first page
This is where you decide to place the footnote.

2 Click **Insert** on the menu bar, click **Footnote**, then click **Create**
The Footnote/Endnote Feature Bar appears. Table 5-3 explains these Feature Bar buttons. At the bottom of the page a dividing line appears, followed by a number, as shown in Figure 5-9. If you wanted to create an endnote, you would click Endnote on the Insert menu.

3 Type **The Write Staff reserves the right to make changes to this document when necessary.** Then click **Close** on the Footnote/Endnote Feature Bar
The footnote is inserted at the bottom of the first page of the document. After reviewing the guides, Emily suggests that you edit the footnote to make it clearer.

4 Click **Insert** on the menu bar, click **Footnote**, then click **Edit**
The Edit Footnote dialog box appears. Now you need to specify which footnote you want to edit. To edit an endnote, you would choose Endnote on the Insert menu.

5 Type **1**, if it is not already displayed, then click **OK**

6 Select the words "make changes to," then type **revise**
The phrase "make changes to" is replaced with the word "revise."

7 Click **Close** on the Footnote/Endnote Feature Bar
You've edited the footnote and now you return to the main text of the style guide.

8 Save and Print the document
Use the printout to compare the first page and the edited footnote with Figure 5-10.

TABLE 5-3: Footnote/Endnote Feature Bar buttons

BUTTON	ACTION	BUTTON	ACTION
Note Number	Reinserts the note number if you accidentally delete it	Previous	Moves to the previously defined footnote or endnote
Next	Moves to the next defined footnote or endnote	Close	Turns off the Footnote/Endnote Feature Bar and returns to the text of the document

FIGURE 5-9: Entering a footnote

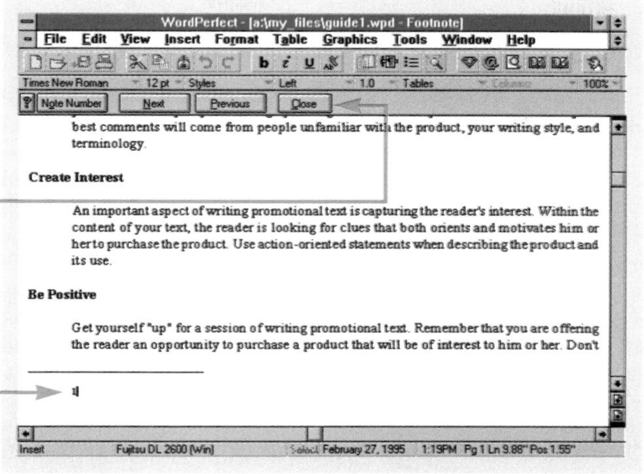

Footnote/Endnote Feature Bar

Footnote number in text

FIGURE 5-10: Page 1 of GUIDE.WPD with edited footnote

The Write Staff
Catalog Division
Promotional Text Writing Guidelines

The goal of The Write Staff's Catalog Division is to provide promotional text to our clients so that we can help them market their products. The responsibility for achieving this objective lies with the promotional text writer. Over the years writing numerous catalogs, we at The Write Staff have established the following guidelines. Please follow these guidelines when writing promotional text:[1]

Make it Brief

As a promotional text writer, you will play a critical part in the success or failure in the marketing of the product. You also face a series of challenges. In a glance, the reader is going to determine his or her level of interest in your product. At the same time, the client is concerned about the price of advertising based on the size of the advertisement. The more concise your text is, the closer we will come to meeting the target audience and satisfying the needs of the client.

Clarity

The message you are trying to convey is often lost in the text. A thorough review of your work is necessary. It is our experience that merely passing your text around the office for review has limitations. Staff may think they know what you mean, or may be less than critical because of your role (or theirs). While it may seem a little unusual, we suggest that you test the clarity of your writing by having friends or family read the text. Some of your best comments will come from people unfamiliar with the product, your writing style, and terminology.

Create Interest

An important aspect of writing promotional text is capturing the reader's interest. Within the content of your text, the reader is looking for clues that both orients and motivates him or her to purchase the product. Use action-oriented statements when describing the product and its use.

Be Positive

Get yourself "up" for a session of writing promotional text. Remember that you are offering

[1]The Write Staff reserves the right to revise this document when necessary.

QUICK **TIP**

When editing footnotes and endnotes, you can also change fonts and point sizes, and apply character formats such as bold and italics.

Inserting a page break

In multiple-page documents, page breaks are automatically set for you. However, you can insert a page break into a document anywhere you desire by inserting hard page breaks into the document yourself. A **hard page break** generates a new page at a specified point no matter how much text is on the page. By contrast, a **soft page break** is determined by the margins; pages are determined and often change, depending on the amount of text on the page. ▶ Jennifer has requested that the Condensed General Writing Style Report always begin on a new page. Right now, it starts in the middle of Page 3 in the Promotional Text Writing Guidelines. Use the following steps to break the document into separate pages.

1   Click **Find and Replace** on the Edit menu, type **Condensed General**, click **Find Next**, click **Close**, then click to the right of the word "feature" at the end of the previous paragraph
The insertion point is now positioned where you want the page to end. This is where you insert a hard page break, as shown in Figure 5-11.

2   Click **Insert** on the menu bar, then click **Page Break**
A bold line appears between the paragraphs at the insertion point. A hard page break has been inserted.

3   Press [↓] twice
The new page with the header is on your screen, as shown in Figure 5-12. Notice that "Pg 4" appears in the status bar.

4   Click the **Save button** 🖫 to save the document with its new page break

FIGURE 5-11: Position to insert a new page

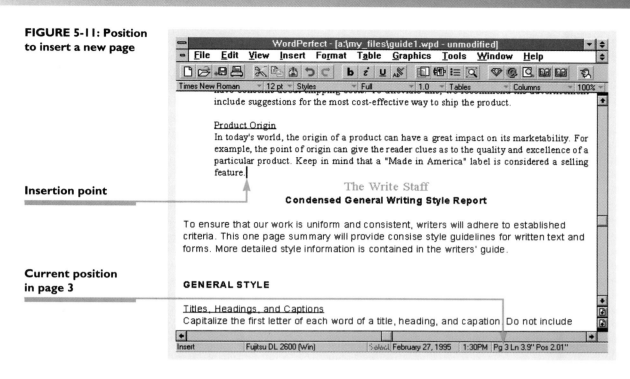

Insertion point

Current position in page 3

FIGURE 5-12: GUIDE1.WPD with inserted hard page break

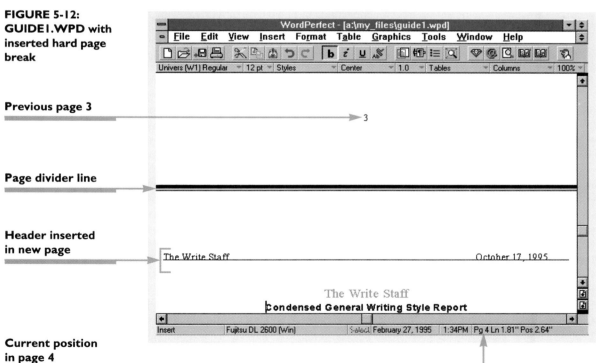

Previous page 3

Page divider line

Header inserted in new page

Current position in page 4

QUICK **TIP**

You can press [Ctrl][Enter] at any point in the document to generate a new page.■

Keeping text together

Sometimes, in multiple-page documents, paragraphs begin or end awkwardly, leaving one line of text alone at the bottom or the top of a page. A single line of text that appears alone at the bottom of a page is called an **orphan**; a single line of text at the top of a page is called a **widow**. You should make sure your documents read well by removing any widows or orphans. The Widow/Orphan control feature can help you avoid these. Similarly, with the Block Protect command, WordPerfect ensures that certain blocks of text are kept together on a page. This command is useful for keeping headings and text together. Read the related topic, "Keeping blocks of text together" for additional information on other ways to keep text together. ▶ You first check to see if the document contains any widows or orphans and then make sure that your section headings stay with their respective text blocks. Just to be sure that no widows or orphans appear in the future, regardless of the edits you make to this document, you set the Widow/Orphan control.

1 Scroll through the document looking for widows and orphans
   Note that a single line appears at the bottom of the first page of the document, as shown in Figure 5-13. To reposition it and any others, you turn on the Widow/Orphan control feature.

2 Position the insertion point at the beginning of the document
   The Widow/Orphan control will take effect from the insertion point through the end of the document.

3 Click **Format** on the menu bar, click **Page**, then click **Keep Text Together**
   The Keep Text Together dialog box appears, as shown in Figure 5-14.

4 Click the **Window/Orphan check box**, then click **OK**
   The text is adjusted so that there are at least two lines of text together at the bottom of a page and also two lines at the top of a page. The last line of text from the first page has been moved to the second page so that an orphan does not exist.

5 Press [↓] to scroll to the bottom of Page 1
   You notice that now the heading "Be Positive" is separated from the paragraph it refers to. Use Block Protect to correct this problem.

6 Click to begin selecting the words "Be Positive," and drag the mouse to select the following paragraph, up to and including the words "best possible light"

7 Click **Format** on the menu bar, click **Page**, then click **Keep Text Together**
   The Keep Text Together dialog box opens.

8 Click the **Block Protect check box**, click **OK**, then click outside the selected text
   The text "Be Positive" is now together on a page with the paragraph. See Figure 5-15.

9 Click the **Save button** 🖫
   Your changes are saved.

FIGURE 5-13:
Page 1 with orphan

Orphan

FIGURE 5-14:
Keep Text Together
dialog box

Click to prevent
widows or orphans

Click to keep a
selected block of text
together on a page

FIGURE 5-15: Text
together on one page

Protected block

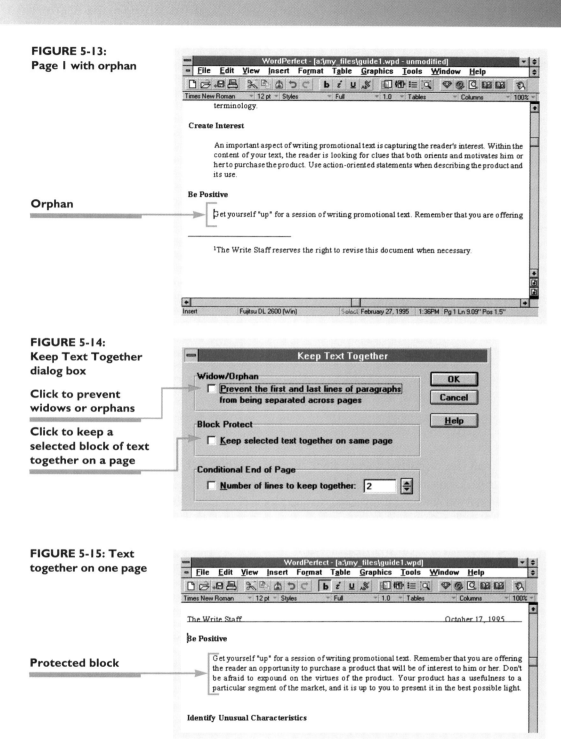

Keeping blocks of text together

Another way to keep blocks of text together on a single page is to use the
Conditional End of Page command in the Keep Text Together dialog box. You can
use this to prevent a paragraph from splitting between pages by setting the number
of lines to keep together. Click Format, click Page, click Keep Text Together then
choose Conditional End of Page.

Creating a Table of Contents

When working with multiple-page documents, it is often important to organize the information in a clear and logical way. Some types of documents like prose or letters can just flow, but technical documents or guides should be organized. You can organize your documents by including a list, an index, a table of contents, a cross-reference, or a table of authorities. Refer to Table 5-4 to learn more about these features. Any of these items are created in three basic steps: (1) mark the text you want to include, (2) define the way you want it to look and where you want it placed, and (3) generate the item. ▶ Jennifer is very pleased with the way the style guide is coming along. She thinks it would help the writers if the document had a list of all the major topics in the guide. Use WordPerfect's Table of Contents feature to create a table of contents.

1   Press **[Ctrl][Home]** to position the insertion point at the beginning of the document

2   Click **Tools** on the menu bar, then click **Table of Contents**
The Table of Contents Feature Bar, as shown in Figure 5-16, lets you define the **levels**, or headings, for your table. You have to select the text you want to appear as the entry in the table of contents.

3   Scroll the document and select the first boldface topic, **Make it Brief**
A table of contents can have up to five levels of headings and subheadings. You want two levels because you have underlined subtopics under some of your boldface main topics. First, mark the first level headings.

4   Click **Mark 1** on the Feature Bar
"Make it Brief" is now marked for a first level heading.

5   Repeat Steps 3 and 4 for each boldface topic in the document to mark level 1 headings for: **Clarity, Create Interest, Be Positive, Identify Unusual Characteristics, Use Proper English**, and **Standard Format**

6   Press **[↓]** to scroll the document; select **Boldface/Italic type**, click **Mark 2**; select **Uniform Pricing**, click **Mark 2**; select **Shipping Weight**, click **Mark 2**; and select **Product Origin**, click **Mark 2**

7   Press **[↓]** to scroll, select **Condensed General Writing Style Report**, click **Mark 1**; select **General Style**, click **Mark 1**; select **Titles, headings, and captions**, click **Mark 2**; then repeat this process for the remaining level 1 and level 2 headings in the document
All headings are marked. Continue in this lesson to finish creating the Table of Contents.

FIGURE 5-16: Table of Contents Feature Bar

Click Mark x where x is the level (1-5) of the entry

Click to specify number of levels and define the table of contents parameters

Click to create the table in the document

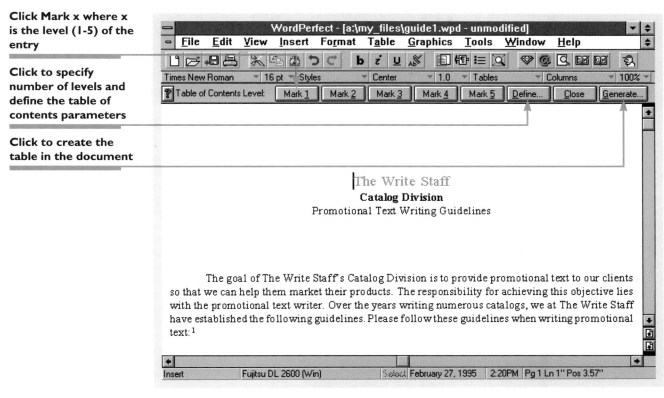

TABLE 5-4: Organizational features for large documents

FEATURE	USE
List	Lists items such as figures, illustrations, and tables in your document
Index	Lists page numbers for items that can be looked up in a printed document
Table of Contents	Lists titles and headings in the order in which they appear in a document
Cross-Reference	Refers your readers to other pages, figures, and notes, such as "see Page 12"
Table of Authorities	For legal purposes, lists where citations occur in a legal brief

QUICK **TIP**

The character formats of the selected text, such as bold, italics, or underlining, are retained in the table of contents.■

Creating a Table of Contents, continued

Once you have selected the text for the headings and subheadings, you must define where and how you want the table of contents to appear. You decide to place it at the beginning of the document, below the first paragraph.

8   **Press [Ctrl][Home], then press [↓] twelve times to position the insertion point along the left margin below the word "text"**

9   **Click Define on the Feature Bar**
The Define Table of Contents dialog box opens, as shown in Figure 5-17. Even though you have marked the levels, it is here that you need to *specify* the number of levels, the position for the page numbers for each level, and other options. You have two levels of headings.

10   **Type 2 in the Number of Levels box**
The defaults for page numbering and position are fine for now. Notice how the example of the Table of Contents style changed in the dialog box.

11   **Click OK**
The dialog box closes and a temporary marker is placed along the left margin, at the point where you placed the insertion point in Step 8. Be sure the marker is aligned with the left margin. The marker notes the location for the table of contents in your document. See Figure 5-18.

12   **Click Generate on the Feature Bar**
The Generate dialog box opens.

13   **Click OK**
A "Please Wait" message box appears on your screen as the table of contents is generated.

14   **Press [Ctrl][Home] then scroll the document**
Compare your document with Figure 5-19. In the table of contents, Level One headings are placed at the left margin, while Level Two headings are indented; the page numbers are flush right with dot leaders.

15   **Click Tools on the menu bar, then click Spell Check**
It's always a good idea to spell check every document before printing. When you have corrected all the words and closed the Spell Checker, you can save and print the guide.

16   **Click the Save button ⊞, click the Print button 🖨 on the Power Bar, then click Print**
The document is complete. Jennifer is very pleased with the way you used WordPerfect features to organize the document to make it useful for the other writers.

17   **Click File on the menu bar, then click Close**
The document closes and you are ready for your next writing assignment.

FIGURE 5-17: Define Table of Contents dialog box

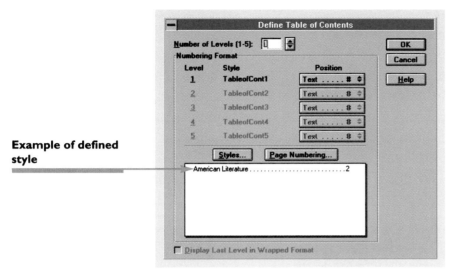

Example of defined style

FIGURE 5-18: Table of Contents marked and defined

Temporary marker for Table of Contents

> The goal of The Write Staff's Catalog Division is to provide promotional text to our clients so that we can help them market their products. The responsibility for achieving this objective lies with the promotional text writer. Over the years writing numerous catalogs, we at The Write Staff have established the following guidelines. Please follow these guidelines when writing promotional text:[1]
>
> << Table of Contents will generate here >>

Insert   Fujitsu DL 2600 (Win)   Select February 27, 1995   2:36PM Pg 1 Ln 3.4" Pos 3.9"

FIGURE 5-19: Table of Contents generated in GUIDE1.WPD

> The Write Staff
> **Catalog Division**
> Promotional Text Writing Guidelines
>
> The goal of The Write Staff's Catalog Division is to provide promotional text to our clients so that we can help them market their products. The responsibility for achieving this objective lies with the promotional text writer. Over the years writing numerous catalogs, we at The Write Staff have established the following guidelines. Please follow these guidelines when writing promotional text:[1]

Make it Brief 1

Clarity 2

Create Interest 2

Be Positive 2

Identify Unusual Characteristics 2

Use Proper English 3

Standard Format 3
    Boldface/Italic Type 3
    Uniform Pricing 3
    Shipping Weight 3
    Product Origin 3

Condensed General Writing Style Report 4

GENERAL STYLE 4
    Titles, Headings, and Captions 4
    Formatting - Boldface/Italics 4

WRITING GUIDELINES 4
    Introductory Text 4
    Pricing 4
    Origin of Product 4

---

[1]The Write Staff reserves the right to revise this document when necessary.

TROUBLE?

The table of contents picks up the character formats at the insertion point. If your table appears in a different font or alignment than expected, check and correct the format using the Toolbar or Power Bar buttons.

Converting text to columns

If you create documents such as newsletters, you might want to divide text vertically into columns on the page. By using the **Columns Define button** on the Power Bar, you can convert the document into newspaper-style columns. Text in newspaper-style columns flows down to the bottom of a page (or to where the columns break), then resumes at the top of the next column to the right. Table 5-5 shows all the types of columns you can use in WordPerfect. The related material, "Defining columns" discusses the various ways to set up columns in your document. ▶ Arianna, a staff writer, wrote the text for the latest company newsletter. She asks you to put the text into a two-column, newspaper-style format.

1   Open UNIT_5-2.WPD and save it as NEWSLTR1.WPD to the MY_FILES directory on your Student Disk
The Write Staff company newsletter appears, as shown in Figure 5-20.

2   Position the insertion point to the left of "For the record"
When creating columns, position the insertion point where you want the columns to begin.

3   Click the **Columns Define button** `Columns ▼` on the Power Bar, then click **2 columns**
The text is converted to two columns. Notice that the lines are left justified rather than full justified, as in most newspapers and magazines. Change the justification next.

4   Position the insertion point at the top of the first column

5   Click the **Justification button** `Left ▼` on the Power Bar, then click **Full**
Now the columns are full justified and look more professional. Be sure to check the spelling in your document.

6   Click **Tools** on the menu bar, then click **Spell Check**
When you have corrected all the words and closed the Spell Checker, preview the newsletter.

7   Click the **Zoom button** `100% ▼` on the Power Bar, then click **Page Full** to preview your document

8   Click the **Save button** 🖫, click the **Print Button** 🖨, then click **Print** to print the newsletter
Your document is saved and printed. Compare your printout with Figure 5-21.

9   Click **File** on the menu bar, then click **Close**
The document closes and you are ready for a new project.

TABLE 5-5: Types of columns

TYPE	DESCRIPTION
Newspaper	Text flows from one column to another
Balanced Newspaper	Adjusts text so that each column is equal in length
Parallel	Groups text in rows across the page
Parallel with Block Protect	Keeps all rows of the columns together; prevents separation of columns onto two pages

FIGURE 5-20: The Write Staff newsletter

> **The Write Staff**
>
> First quarter of 1995
>
> For the record
> Last year's fourth-quarter profits were at an all-time high. We increased our number of clients by 12%, and our gross revenues were up 9%. These figures surpass the goals we set a year ago. Increased numbers of clients and increased revenues also bring about increased numbers of writers and staff. I'm happy to report that we have hired two full-time writers and one new administrative assistant.
>
> New office plans
> We are planning to remodel our existing offices soon and we'll be adding on office space. We're looking to increase our total square footage by at least 50%. Remodeling construction is set to begin no later than late spring and should be completed by early fall. I think we'll all be glad to be able to wiggle our toes a little.
>
> Writer's Style Guide
> The Writer's Style Guide is being revised. As most of you know, we surveyed our clients on several issues over the past six months. From the results of the survey, we feel we need to make some minor changes to some of our promotional writing styles. A committee has been formed to review the existing style guide and make recommendations on changes suggested by the recent survey. Revised copies of the style guide should be distributed within the next month. Please read over the guide to familiarize yourself with the revisions.
>
> New employee recognition
> Because we have had the good fortune to hire three new people for The Write Staff, we are planning a New Employee Recognition Brunch to be held in the near future. We will let you know the details as soon as plans are finalized.
>
> Be good to yourself
> Our employee wellness program is in full swing for the new year. If you're interested in "Being Good to Yourself" call Erica at x2408 for information on how to get involved.
>
> Employee picnic
> The Spring Fling will be held in May. Employees and families are all invited to enjoy a day of good food, great company, softball, horseshoes, and the outdoors.

Left justified text

FIGURE 5-21: Newsletter converted to two columns

> **The Write Staff**
>
> First quarter of 1995
>
> For the record
> Last year's fourth-quarter profits were at an all-time high. We increased our number of clients by 12%, and our gross revenues were up 9%. These figures surpass the goals we set a year ago. Increased numbers of clients and increased revenues also bring about increased numbers of writers and staff. I'm happy to report that we have hired two full-time writers and one new administrative assistant.
>
> New office plans
> We are planning to remodel our existing offices soon and we'll be adding on office space. We're looking to increase our total square footage by at least 50%. Remodeling construction is set to begin no later than late spring and should be completed by early fall. I think we'll all be glad to be able to wiggle our toes a little.
>
> Writer's Style Guide
> The Writer's Style Guide is being revised. As most of you know, we surveyed our clients on several issues over the past six months. From the results of the survey, we feel we need to make some minor changes to some of our promotional writing styles. A committee has been formed to review the existing style guide and make recommendations on changes suggested by the recent survey. Revised copies of the style guide should be distributed within the next month. Please read over the guide to familiarize yourself with the revisions.
>
> New employee recognition
> Because we have had the good fortune to hire three new people for The Write Staff, we are planning a New Employee
>
> Recognition Brunch to be held in the near future. We will let you know the details as soon as plans are finalized.
>
> Be good to yourself
> Our employee wellness program is in full swing for the new year. If you're interested in "Being Good to Yourself" call Erica at x2408 for information on how to get involved.
>
> Employee picnic
> The Spring Fling will be held in May. Employees and families are all invited to enjoy a day of good food, great company, softball, horseshoes, and the outdoors.

Defining columns

You can make several choices, including the number and type of columns you want, the column spacing, and the column width. Click Format, click Columns, then click Define to set specific options for columns. The Columns dialog box appears, as shown in Figure 5-22. As you define the columns, you can preview the effect of your choices.

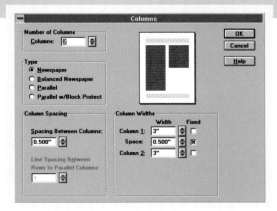

FIGURE 5-22: Columns dialog box

CONCEPTSREVIEW

Label each element of the WordPerfect document shown in Figure 5-23.

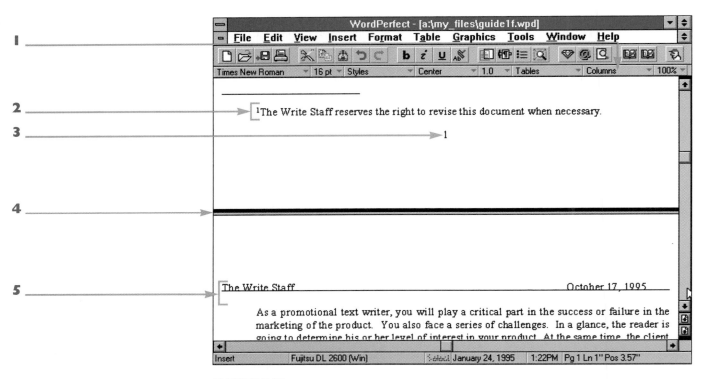

1 _____

2 _____

3 _____

4 _____

5 _____

FIGURE 5-23

Match each of the following WordPerfect commands or features with the phrase that describes its purpose.

6 Header

7 Footer

8 Column

9 Footnote

10 Table of Contents

a. Used to document sources of information

b. Information that appears at the top of each page

c. Information that appears at the bottom of each page

d. Divides text vertically on the page

e. Used to list topics and page numbers in a document

Select the best answer from the list of choices.

11 Which is NOT a Headers/Footers Feature Bar button?

  a. Distance

  b. Next

  c. Previous

  d. Position

12 What is a widow?

  a. A sentence that is split between two pages

  b. The line of text in the middle of a paragraph appearing at the bottom of a page

  c. The first line of a paragraph appearing alone at the bottom of a page

  d. The last line of a paragraph appearing alone at the top of a page

13 To change the text in a Footnote

a. You can't edit a Footnote once it is created

b. Just click on the Footnote number and enter new text

c. Click Edit on the menu bar, click Footnote, then click Edit

d. Click on the Footnote Feature Bar

14 To divide text on a page into vertical columns

a. Use the Ruler Bar to set tabs and create the columns

b. Click Window, click Split, then click Columns

c. Click Columns on the Power Bar, click desired option

d. You can't divide text vertically, only horizontally on a page

15 A Table of Contents

a. Lists all the tables in your document

b. Lists footnotes in the document

c. Displays page numbers for items that can be looked up in a printed document

d. Lists titles and headings in the order in which they appear in a document

APPLICATIONS
REVIEW

1 Set the page numbering.

a. Open Unit_5-3.WPD, then save it as FACTSHT.WPD.

b. Move the insertion point to the beginning of the document.

c. Click Format, click Page, then click Numbering. Position the number on the Bottom Right.

d. Click OK.

e. Scroll through the document. Notice that the page number appears at the bottom right of each page.

2 Insert a header.

a. Move the insertion point to the beginning of the document.

b. Click Format, then click Header/Footer.

c. Create Header A as "Investment Fund Fact Sheet."

d. Scroll through the document. Notice that the header appears at the top of every page.

3 Suppress a header.

a. Move the insertion point to the beginning of the document.

b. Click Format, click Page, then click Suppress

c. Click Header A.

d. Click OK.

e. Notice that the header no longer appears on the first page of the document but does appear on each subsequent page.

4 Insert a footnote.

a. Move the insertion point to the right of the phrase "Omaha Investors Group Plan Summary" in the first paragraph.

b. Click Insert, click Footnote, then click Create.

c. Type "Omaha Investors Group Plan Summary, February 1995," then click Close on the Footnote/Endnote Feature Bar.

d. Scroll to the bottom of the page to view the footnote.

5 Insert a page break.

a. Look through the document and see where you might want to insert a page break.

b. Find the heading "Fund Performance."

c. Insert a page break.

6 Use the Widow/Orphan control feature.

a. Move the insertion point to the beginning of the document.

b. Click Format, click Page, then click Keep Text Together.

c. Click the Widow/Orphan check box, then click OK.

d. Scroll through the document. Notice that no single, isolated lines of text appear at the top or bottom of the pages.

7 Add a Table of Contents.

a. Move the insertion point to the beginning of the document.

b. Click Tools, then click Table of Contents.

c. Mark two significant words of your choice as Mark 1 entries.

d. Position the insertion point at the beginning of the document.

e. Click Define and accept the defaults to define the table with one level.

f. Click Generate, then click Close.

g. Review the Table of Contents.

h. Add a page break at the end of the Table of Contents.

8 Convert text to columns.

a. Move the insertion point to the beginning of the page of the Table of Contents.

b. Click Format, click Columns, then click Define.

c. Set the number of columns to 3 and the type to Balanced Newspaper.

d. Spell check the document.

e. Add your name and current date to the bottom of the document.

f. Save the document.

g. Preview and print the document.

INDEPENDENT
CHALLENGE 1

Sell It! is a Seattle-based company that specializes in training sales representatives. As an employee of the company, you write training materials for your clients who attend seminars. You are currently preparing a pamphlet titled "How to Sell Anything" for an upcoming seminar. The pamphlet should provide tips on how to make a product more marketable, including advice about knowing your customer.

To complete this independent challenge:

1 Plan the pamphlet. Decide what tips you are going to give on how to be a good salesperson. You might include things like self-confidence, knowledge of the product, and understanding of competing products. You should include awareness of customer needs as a major tip.

2 Open a new document window in WordPerfect, then type a first draft of the pamphlet.

3 Prepare a title page at the beginning of the document.

4 Insert the following quote at an appropriate location within the document: "Knowing something about your customer is just as important as knowing everything about your product."

5 Create a footnote for the quote above. The text of the footnote is "Harvey Mackay, *Swim with the Sharks Without Being Eaten Alive*, Ivy Books: New York, 1988, p. 21."

6 Create a header with the title of the pamphlet, "How to Sell Anything."

7 Set the page numbering to print at the bottom center of each page.

8 On the title page, suppress the header and page numbering so that they appear only on the second and subsequent pages.

9 Convert the text to two columns.

10 Spell check, save the document as SELLANY.WPD, then print it.

11 Submit a printed copy of your document with your name and current date on it.

INDEPENDENT
CHALLENGE 2

Several of your friends and neighbors have requested that you write a newsletter for the community. The newsletter is a new project that is intended to keep everyone informed about newsworthy items, social events, political changes, and news updates.

Design the newsletter so that it has a few sections. These sections should have heads that are set apart in a different character format. "New and Noteworthy" should discuss any new projects or activities in your neighborhood. "Our Neighbors" should include any news about the people, births, weddings, engagements, and graduations. "The Social Scene" should discuss any parties, picnics, dance recitals, movie reviews, garage or tag sales. "Our Community" can cover the political scene. You can also include a "Classified" section.

To complete this independent challenge:

1 Plan the newsletter. Do some scouting, interviewing, and reporting. Take notes about what you want to include. Decide what items you are going to cover in the first edition.

2 Open a new document window in WordPerfect, then type a first draft of the newsletter.

3 Prepare a heading for the document. Some ideas include "The Neighborhood News," "Caryn's Chronicles," or "People's Press." Be sure to include a date in the heading.

4 Insert the following notes at appropriate locations within the document: "Leaf collection for the month of October has been scheduled for Tuesdays." and "The Bijou will be showing *Singin' in the Rain* on April 1st at 7:30."

5 Create footnotes for the notes above. The text of the first footnote is "The Department of Public Works reserves the right to change the date." For the second, include "Times subject to change without notice. Call the theater for exact show time on the day of the performance."

6 Create a header with the title of the newsletter.

7 Set the page numbering to print at the bottom center of each page.

8 On the title page, suppress the header and page numbering so that they appear only on the second and subsequent pages.

9 Convert the text to two columns.

10 Spell check, save the document as NEWSLTR2.WPD, then print it.

11 Submit a printed copy of your document with your name and current date on it.

UNIT 6

OBJECTIVES

▶ Plan a table

▶ Create a table

▶ Enter data in a table

▶ Insert and delete rows and columns

▶ Format a table

▶ Enter formulas in tables

Creating
TABLES

Using tables can help you organize information and enhance the appearance of your document. WordPerfect tables organize information into vertical columns and horizontal rows and let you calculate totals. You can use a table to quickly arrange columns of numbers, text, or even graphics. You can format tables just as you format the text in your document.

▶ The Chief Financial Officer (CFO), Emily Caitlin, has asked you to turn in an updated report of your monthly expenses to be charged to The Write Staff. Each writer is responsible for maintaining expense reports in order to be reimbursed for any expenses incurred as part of the job. Rather than creating a simple list document, you will use the WordPerfect Table tools to organize the information as a table of expenses to submit to Emily. ▶

Planning a table

To be effective, tables need to be planned. Table 6-1 lists some terms that you need to know when working with tables. When you plan a table, you determine the number of rows and columns you'll need, the information to be included, how to format cells, and whether you'll use numerical information or calculations. In some cases, you might not have enough information to fill a table. If so, there are other options; see the related topic, "Creating a bullet list" for more information.

▶ Your last assignment was writing a promotional brochure for the new Dinosaur Wing at the American Museum of Natural History in New York City. To complete the assignment, you traveled to visit the museum in Manhattan, bought three books and a video on dinosaurs and purchased a software package of dinosaur clipart images that you used in the brochure. Use the following steps as guidelines for planning a table.

1 **Determine the purpose of the table.**
You need to show the expenses you incurred while working for the client on this project.

2 **Make a list of the information to be included in the table.**
Your expenses include transportation, admission to the museum, lunch, three books, a video, and the software you purchased for this job.

3 **Determine how the table should look.**
You decide to use column headings and to show the total amount of the expenses. You want both the column headings and total expenses amount to appear in boldface; you want the description of the expenses left-justified in the cells, and all the numbers right-justified in the cells.

4 **Decide how many rows and columns the table will have.**
You want to organize the expenses in rows so you'll need eight rows: six rows for the six expenses, a row for the total, and a row for the column headings. You need two columns: one for the expense labels and one for the expense amounts.

5 **Determine the calculations, if any, you'll need.**
You need to add all the expenses to get one total amount.

6 **On paper, make a rough sketch that shows how you want the table to look.**
Figure 6-1 shows the sketch to use as a guide for creating the expense report using WordPerfect.

FIGURE 6-1: Rough sketch of expense table

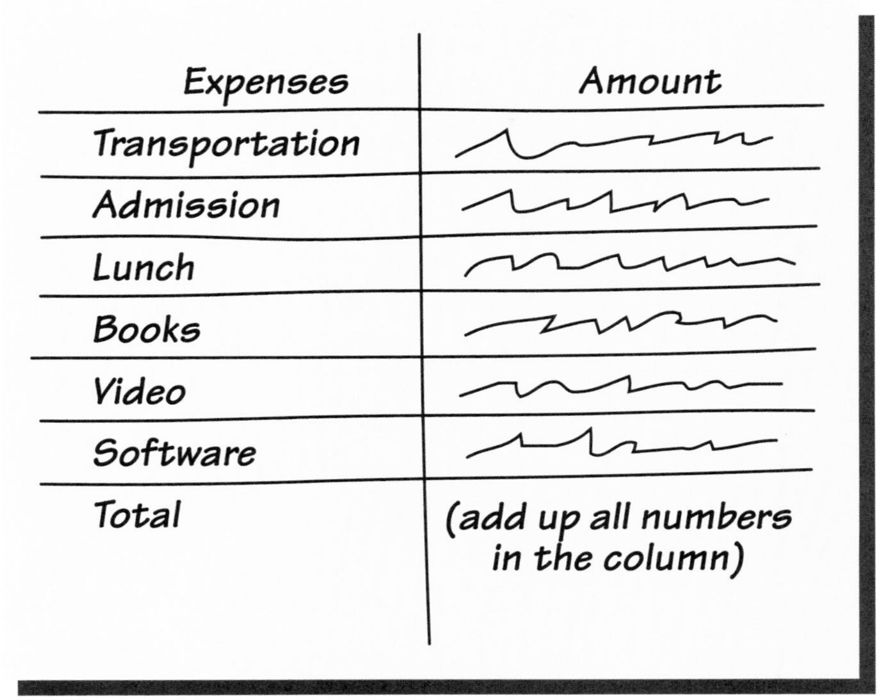

Creating a bullet list

You need at least two columns of data to create a table. If you don't have enough information to fill a table, but still want to organize the data in an itemized format, you can create a **bullet list**. Use the Bullet button on the Toolbar to turn existing text into a bullet list. First, select the text, click, then select a bullet or number style in the Bullets & Numbers dialog box. You can also insert bullets before you enter text.

TABLE 6-1: Table terms

TERM	DESCRIPTION
Columns	Run vertically; assigned letters, which appear in the status bar
Rows	Run horizontally; assigned numbers, which appear in the status bar
Cells	Intersection of a row and column; for example, A1, C3, etc.
Formula	Calculates totals and averages of numbers in a table
Formula Feature Bar	Creates formulas and functions in a table

Creating a table

A table consists of rows and columns that intersect to form cells. A cell might contain information such as text, numbers, or formulas. A **cell name**, or **cell address**, consists of a column letter and row number and identifies the cell's position in the table. Rows are identified numerically from the top row down, and columns are identified alphabetically from left to right. For example, cell A1 is in the upper-left corner of the table, and cell B3 is in the second column, third row. Within each cell, text wraps within margins, just as it does in a document window. The entire row increases its size to accommodate added text. ▶ Now that you have planned your expense table, you are ready to create it. You want the table to be included as part of an expense report memo. The memo will provide basic information about the specific expenses that are in the table.

1   Open **unit_6-1.wpd** and save it as **EXPENSE1.WPD** to the **MY_FILES** directory on your Student Disk
The memo EXPENSE1.WPD appears on the screen. You want Emily to know who the expenses are from (who to pay), which project and client they refer to, the date or span of dates that the costs were incurred, and what the expenses are for.

2   Read the memo, then position the insertion point before "type your name here"
The memo should include your name.

3   Select "type your name here," then type your name

4   Press **[Ctrl][End]**, then press **[Enter]** twice
This creates a blank line at the end of the paragraph between the text and the beginning of the table you will create.

5   Click **Table** on the menu bar, then click **Create**
The Create Table dialog box appears, as shown in Figure 6-2.

You can also create a table quickly; click the Table QuickCreate button on the Power Bar, then drag to select the number of rows and columns to include in a table. See Figure 6-3.

6   Type **2** in the Columns text box, press **[Tab]** and type **8** in the Rows text box, then click **OK**
This creates a table with two columns and eight rows and a single line around all the cells in the document. The width of the two columns is set automatically based on your page margins. You might need to scroll through the document to view the entire table, as shown in Figure 6-4.

Notice that the status bar indicates the position, or cell address, of the insertion point. The Tables Toolbar replaces the 6.1 WordPerfect default Toolbar. Table 6-2 lists other ways to move around in a table.

7   Click **File** on the menu bar, then click **Save**
Remember to always save your work.

FIGURE 6-2: Create Table dialog box

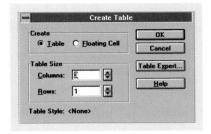

FIGURE 6-3: Table QuickCreate on the Power Bar

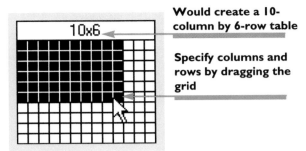

**FIGURE 6-4:
EXPENSE1.WPD
after creating table**

Insertion point

Location of insertion
point in the table

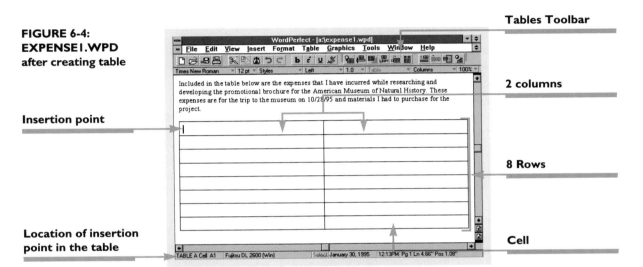

TABLE 6-2: Ways to move around in a table

TO MOVE	PRESS
One cell right	[Tab] or [→]
One cell left	[Shift][Tab] or [←]
One cell down	[Alt][↓] or [↓]
One cell up	[Alt][↑] or [↑]
First cell in row	[Home][Home]
Last cell in row	[End][End]
Top line of multi-line cell	[Alt][Home]
Bottom line of multi-line cell	[Alt][End]

Entering data in a table

Once you create a table, you need to enter data into it. You enter data into the cells of a table using the same techniques as entering text in a document. The boundaries of the cells become the left and right margins. You can think of cells as mini document windows. Table 6-3 lists the various ways to select rows, columns, or cells. You can apply text formatting options and use all editing commands as you would in any document; see the related topic, "Editing tables" in this lesson. ▶ Now you're ready to enter your expenses. Use the following steps to enter the data in the table.

1 Click cell **A1**

The insertion point is in the cell in the first column and first row of the table. The status bar displays the cell address where the insertion point is positioned.

2 Type **Expenses**, press **[Tab]**, then type **Amount**

"Expenses" and "Amount" appear in cells A1 and B1, respectively. They are the column headings for the table. It is a good idea to enter the column headings first, so you can align your information appropriately.

3 Click cell **A2**

4 Type **Transportation**, press **[Tab]**, type **30**, then press **[Tab]** again

Using the following data, enter the rest of the information in the table using the method described in Step 2. Enter the numbers as shown; you will learn how to format numbers as currency in a later lesson. Remember, if you make a typing error, you edit data in a table the same way you edit text in a document.

Enter in column A:	Enter in column B:
Lunch	**15**
Admission	**6.5**
Books	**62.75**
Video	**19**
Software	**29**
TOTAL	

Each cell of the table contains an entry, except cell B8. This cell will contain a formula for calculating the expense amounts. You will enter this formula in another lesson. Compare your table with Figure 6-5.

5 Click the **Save button**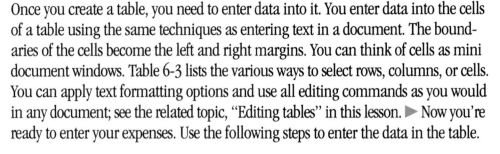

The table is saved in EXPENSE1.WPD.

FIGURE 6-5: EXPENSE1.WPD with data entered in table

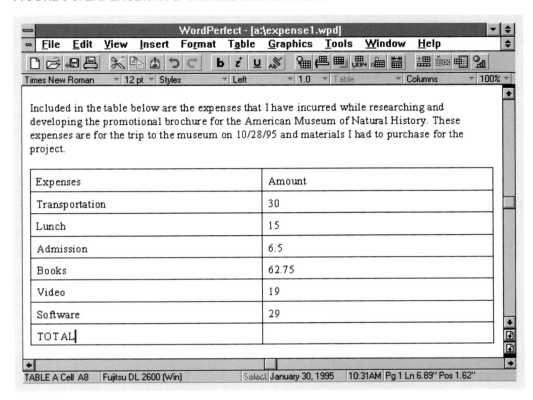

Editing tables

As you improve the appearance of your table, you might want to cut, copy, and paste data into cells. To cut, copy, and paste data into cells, select the cells, rows, columns, or text from your document, then click Cut ✂ or Copy 📋 on the Toolbar. You can also right-click in the table to display a QuickMenu, then click Cut or Copy; if you selected a row or column, the Cut/Copy dialog box appears. Make the appropriate selection, click OK, move the insertion point to the place where you want to paste or copy the cell, row, or column, then click the Paste button 📋 on the Toolbar.

TABLE 6-3: How to select various parts of a table

TO SELECT	DISPLAY	ACTION
Cell	⇧ or ⇦ in the cell	Click
Column	⇧ in the column	Double-click
Row	⇦ in the row	Double-click
Table	⇧ or ⇦ in any cell	Triple-click

TROUBLE?

If you press [Tab] after entering data in the last cell of a table, a new row of cells is added to the table. If you want to delete this new row, select the entire row, keep the cursor on the table and press [Delete].■

QUICK TIP

To keep a table from being divided by a page break, select the table, click Page on the Format menu, click Keep Text Together, then click Block Protect.■

Inserting and deleting rows and columns

If you create a table and it's the wrong size, you can delete or insert rows and columns. To insert or delete a row or column, position the insertion point where you want to make the change, then use the Table menu to Insert or Delete Columns or Rows. Specify the number of rows or columns you want to insert or delete, and whether you want to place the new row or column before or after the current insertion point position, then click OK. To learn about changing the width of columns, see the related topic, "Changing table column widths" in this lesson. ▶ You just remembered that during your meeting with the client, the museum director asked if you could pick up samples of a special paper to use for the brochure. You purchased these samples and need to include the cost in your expenses, so you need to add a row to your table.

1 Click cell **A7**
The insertion point is in the cell with the word "Software."

2 Move the cursor to the left-inside cell A7 to display the **row select arrow** ⇦, then double-click
Row 7 is selected. Your screen should look like Figure 6-6.

3 Click **Table** on the menu bar, then click **Insert**, or right-click to display the **Table QuickMenu**
The Insert Columns/Rows dialog box opens, as shown in Figure 6-7.

4 Click **Rows** in the Insert box, Type **1**, click **After** in the placement box, then click **OK**
A new blank row with the same formatting as the rest of the table is inserted below the Software cells. See Figure 6-8.

5 Make sure the insertion point is in cell A8, type **Sample paper**, press **[Tab]**, and type **10**
The new data is entered.

6 Click the **Save button** 🖫

Changing table column widths

Once you begin entering data in a cell, you might find that the column is too narrow or too wide for the entry. You can change the table column width using the mouse. Position the insertion point on the rule, the line separating the columns. When the mouse pointer changes to ╬, drag the rule to the left or right to increase or decrease the column width.

FIGURE 6-6:
Row 7 selected

Select arrow

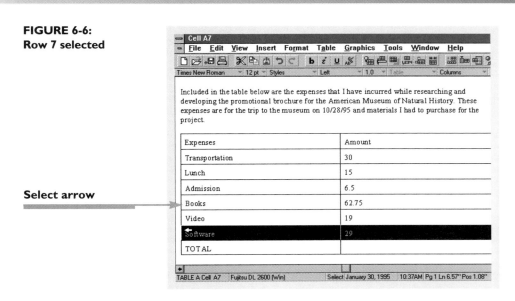

FIGURE 6-7:
Insert Columns/Rows dialog box

Specify the number of columns or rows to insert

Insertion point

Current configuration of table

Click to place new columns or rows before or after the current insertion point

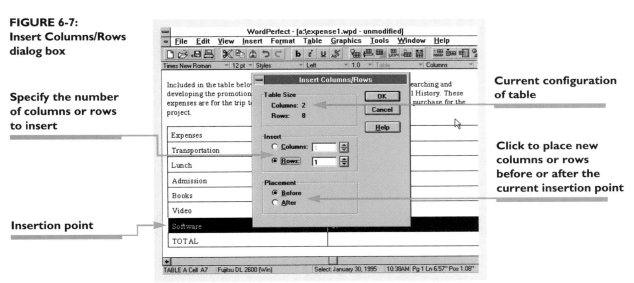

FIGURE 6-8: New row inserted in table

New cell A8

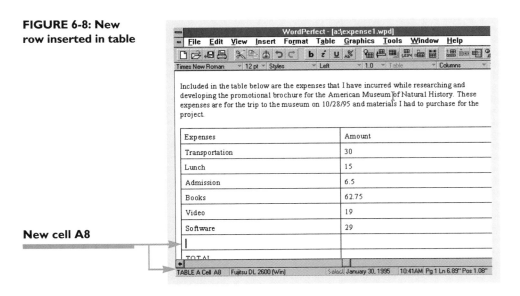

Formatting a table

Formatting, such as character formats, fonts, sizes, and alignment, enhances the appearance of your table. You can format a table while working in the document window or by using the Format dialog box from the Table menu. The Format dialog box lets you change the characteristics of a cell, column, row, or entire table. The **Table Expert**, as described in the related topic on the next page, provides a way to format a table quickly by selecting predefined formats or styles for your table.
▶ You want to show your colleagues that you can add style to any document, even an expense report. Format your table to make it more appealing, readable, and professional-looking.

1 Click cell **A1**, then drag across both headings in the first row to select them
The cells with the headings are highlighted.

2 Click **Table** on the menu bar, then click **Format**
The Format dialog box opens. You can also click the **Table Format button** 🖳 on the Toolbar or press [Ctrl][F12] to open the Format dialog box.

3 Click **Cell**
Boxes appear for setting the alignment, appearance, attributes, and size of the text in the selected cells, as shown in Figure 6-9.

4 Click the **Justification list arrows** in the Alignment box, click **Center**, click the **Bold check box** in the Appearance box, then click **OK**
The headings are now centered in the columns and appear in boldface.

5 Click cell **B2**, then drag down through cell **B9** to select cells B2 through B9
The numbers and the blank cell in the right column are highlighted.

6 Click **Table** on the menu bar, click **Format**, click **Right** in the Justification list in the Alignment box, then click **OK**
The numbers are now aligned on the right side of each cell.

7 Click **Table** on the menu bar, click **Number Type**, click **Currency** in the Number Type dialog box in the Available Types box, then click **OK**
The expenses now appear with decimal points and dollar signs.

8 Click cell **A9**, click **Table** on the menu bar, click **Format**, click the **Bold check box**, then click **OK**
"TOTAL" appears in bold.

9 Save your changes, then print your document
Compare your printed document with Figure 6-10, which shows all the formatting changes.

FIGURE 6-9: Format dialog box

Cells to format

Bold check box

Justification list arrows

Sample text with
selected formatting

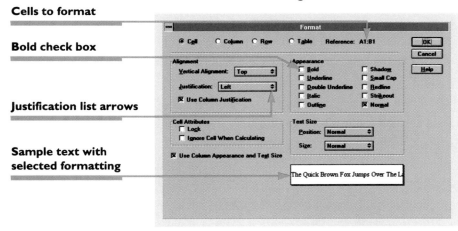

FIGURE 6-10: EXPENSE1.wpd with formatting changes

EXPENSE REPORT

TO: Emily Caitlin

FROM: Rachel Bunin

PROJECT: The American Museum of Natural History, New York City
JOB #: 1978

DATE: November 5, 1995

Included in the table below are the expenses that I have incurred while researching and developing
the promotional brochure for the American Museum of Natural History. These expenses are for
the trip to the museum on 10/28/95 and materials I had to purchase for the project.

Expenses	Amount
Transportation	$30.00
Lunch	$15.00
Admission	$6.50
Books	$62.75
Video	$19.00
Software	$29.00
Sample paper	$10.00
TOTAL	

Using the Table Expert

You can click Table Expert in the Create Table dialog box to set up your table using a preformatted design. You can also set up your columns and rows and then click Expert on the Table menu. Custom formatting a table with borders, lines, and patterns or colors in the cells can take time. If you want your table to have a certain style, the Table Expert dialog box lets you choose from a list of available styles and shows you how the style will be applied to your table. The Table Expert is particularly helpful when you want to create a certain style for all the tables in a document.

Entering formulas in tables

You can create and enter formulas in your table using the **Formula Feature Bar**. A **formula** uses cell addresses instead of numbers to perform calculations, such as adding the contents of cell B2 to the contents of cell C2 (B2 + C2). Formulas are very powerful in tables. They make your information dynamic rather than static. If you need the total for a column of numbers, you can add the numbers outside the document and simply type the number in the Total cell, or you can use a formula in the table. If the total is just a static number, it has to be recalculated manually and retyped in the document if any numbers change in the column. If the total is a formula, it will automatically change to reflect any new numbers in the column. Table 6-4 lists and explains the different symbols used in formulas, or calculations, you can create with WordPerfect. ▶ You need to add the amounts in column B to calculate the total cost of your expenses. By entering a formula in cell B9, you will complete the calculation and finish your expense report. Any changes to the list of expenses will automatically be reflected in the total amount.

1 Click cell **B9**

2 Click **Table** on the menu bar, then click **Formula Feature Bar**
The Table Formula Feature Bar appears, as shown in Figure 6-11. You will enter the formula to calculate the total expenses.

3 Click in the Formula Edit text box, then type
B2+B3+B4+B5+B6+B7+B8
The formula appears in the Formula Edit text box and "Formula Edit Mode is On" appears in the Feature Bar. Compare your screen to Figure 6-12, and check to make sure that your formula is correct. You can edit the formula as you would any cell entry.

4 Click ☑
The formula is inserted in cell B9, and Formula Edit Mode is turned off. The formula calculates your expenses, and the total ($172.25) appears in cell B9. If you want to cancel the changes you have made to the formula, you can click ☒ to turn off Formula Edit Mode and cancel the changes to the formula. See the continuation of this lesson to learn how to edit a formula.

FIGURE 6-11: Table Formula Feature Bar

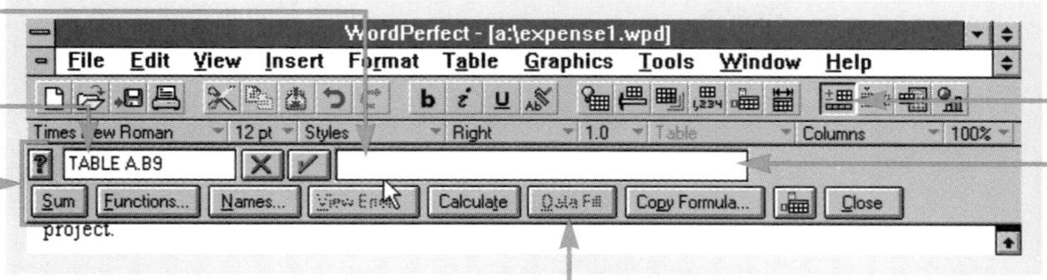
Formula Edit text box
Current location of insertion point
Feature Bar
Click Formula Bar button to toggle Formula Feature Bar on and off
Formula Edit text box
Fill in incrementing patterns such as numbers and days
WordPerfect - [a:\expense1.wpd]
TABLE A.B9
Sum
Functions...
Names...
Calculate
Data Fill
Copy Formula...
Close

FIGURE 6-12: Formula entered

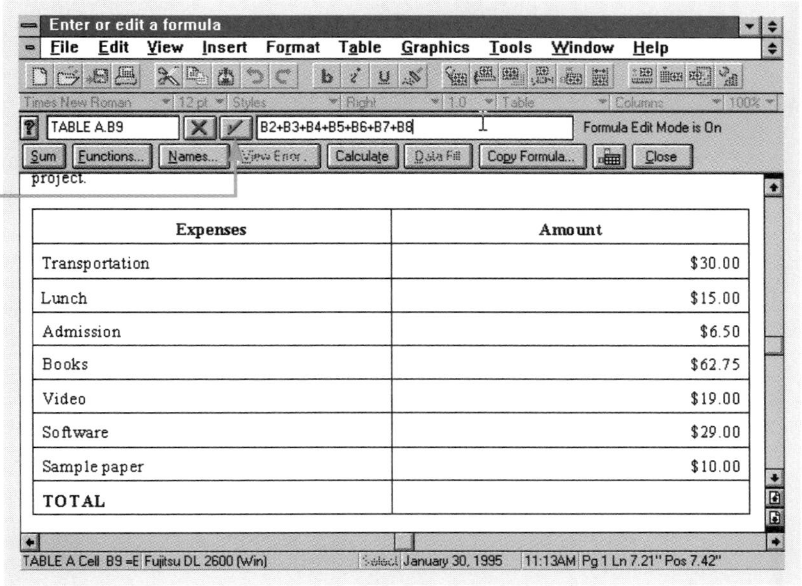
Click to accept a formula, insert it in the current cell, and turn off Formula Edit Mode
Enter or edit a formula
TABLE A.B9
B2+B3+B4+B5+B6+B7+B8
Formula Edit Mode is On
Expenses
Amount
Transportation
$30.00
Lunch
$15.00
Admission
$6.50
Books
$62.75
Video
$19.00
Software
$29.00
Sample paper
$10.00
TOTAL

QUICK TIP

There is a shortcut to typing a long formula into the Formula Edit text box. Simply position the insertion point in the cell that will contain the sum, then click Sum on the Table Formula Feature Bar. This adds the numbers in the cells directly above the insertion point and places the sum where the insertion point is.

TABLE 6-4: Symbols used in formulas

SYMBOL	WHAT IT DOES	EXAMPLE
+	Adds	B2+B3
–	Subtracts	B2–B3
*	Multiplies	B2*B3
/	Divides	B2/B3

Entering formulas in tables, continued

A final review of your receipts reveals that the software actually cost $39.00. Make this correction to your report.

5 Save your work

6 Click cell **B7**, then click to select **$29.00**
"$29.00" is selected.

7 Type **39**
"39" appears in the cell.

8 Click **Calculate** on the Table Formula Feature Bar
The change in cell B7 is reflected in the total. The new total in cell B9 is $182.25.

9 Click **Close** on the Formula Feature bar

10 Click the **Save button** 🖫, click the **Print button** 🖨, then click **Print**
You are very pleased with the way the expense report looks. Compare your printout with Figure 6-13.

11 Click **File** on the menu bar, then click **Close**
You submit your expenses to Emily for payment. Next time you have expenses to submit, you will use the same format and even suggest that your colleagues follow your format when they submit expenses. One way to reuse this form is to delete the contents and parts of the table. Refer to the related topic on the next page, "Deleting a table" to read about deleting tables and parts of tables.

FIGURE 6-13: Expense report with calculated total

EXPENSE REPORT

TO: Emily Caitlin

FROM: Rachel Bunin

PROJECT: The American Museum of Natural History, New York City
JOB #:   1978

DATE: November 5, 1995

Included in the table below are the expenses that I have incurred while researching and developing the promotional brochure for the American Museum of Natural History. These expenses are for the trip to the museum on 10/28/95 and materials I had to purchase for the project.

Expenses	Amount
Transportation	$30.00
Lunch	$15.00
Admission	$6.50
Books	$62.75
Video	$19.00
Software	$39.00
Sample paper	$10.00
TOTAL	$182.25

Deleting a table

There are times you need to delete an entire table or reuse the structure or contents of the table in your document. To accomplish this task, select the entire table, keep the cursor inside the table, click Table on the menu bar, then click Delete. The Delete Table dialog box opens. You can choose to delete an Entire Table, the Table Contents, the Formulas Only, or the Table Structure (leaving the text in the document). Specify the part of the table to delete, then click OK.

CONCEPTSREVIEW

Label each element of the WordPerfect window shown in Figure 6-14.

1 _____
2 _____
3 _____
4 _____
5 _____
6 _____

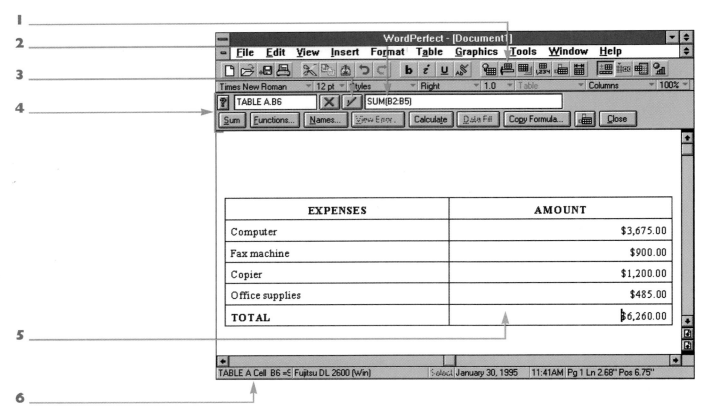

FIGURE 6-14

Match each of the following actions with the keystroke that produces it.

7 Moves the insertion point one cell to the left

8 Moves the insertion point one cell to the right

9 Opens the Table Format dialog box

10 Adds an extra line for text in a cell

11 Removes selected (highlighted) cells from the table

12 Opens the Create Table dialog box

a. [Enter]
b. [Tab]
c. [F12]
d. [Shift][Tab]
e. [Delete]
f. [Ctrl][F12]

Select the best answer from the list of choices.

13 In every table, the cell labeled A1
   a. Contains a graphics figure
   b. Cannot be used as part of a formula
   c. Is 2.49" wide
   d. Is the upper-left cell in the table

14 To create a table
   a. Select text in a document, click Tables on the Power Bar, then click Tabular columns
   b. With no selected text, click Tables on the Power Bar, then define the number of columns and rows in the grid
   c. Click Table on the menu bar, then click Create and specify the number of columns and rows
   d. All of the above

15 The formula A1+B2+C3

    a. Is not an acceptable table formula

    b. Adds the contents of cells in the first row

    c. Adds the contents of cells along a diagonal

    d. Adds the contents of cells in the first column

16 If you change a number in a cell that is referenced by a formula

    a. The formula recalculates the correct number

    b. You can't change numbers in cells

    c. You have to redo the math in your head and enter the correct answer

    d. None of the above

17 To insert a row in a table

    a. Select a row and click Table Insert Row

    b. Select a cell and click Edit Insert Table

    c. You can't insert a row

    d. Insert a column and press [Tab] twice

18 If a table has a cell labeled C4, it must also

    a. Contain a formula of the sum of cells C1 through C3

    b. Have a cell labeled C5

    c. Have a single-line border

    d. Have a cell labeled B3

APPLICATIONS REVIEW

1 Plan a table.

    a. On a notepad, write some notes for the purpose of creating the table in Figure 6-15.

    b. List the information in the table.

    c. Make some notes about how the table should look.

    d. Determine how many rows and columns are needed for the table.

    e. Jot down any calculations.

    f. Hand in the notes with your name on it.

State	Total Sales
New Mexico	4724.34
Nevada	3911.27
Texas	11086.67
Colorado	9413.09
TOTAL	

FIGURE 6-15

2 Create a table.

    a. Start with a blank document window.

    b. Open the Create Table dialog box.

    c. Choose 2 columns and 6 rows for the table size.

    d. Type the text from Figure 6-15 into the table.

3 Calculate a sum.

    a. Place the formula B2+B3+B4+B5 into cell B6.

    b. Select the numbers in the right column (including the total).

    c. Set Number Type (on the Table menu) to Currency.

4 Insert a row.

    a. Insert a row above the row for Nevada.

    b. Type New Jersey in the new cell in column A.

    c. Type 7653.86 in the new cell in column B.

    d. Recalculate the table so the total includes the new row.

5 Format the text.

    a. Center the text in the top row, and make it bold.

    b. Right-align the numbers in the right column.

    c. Make the word "TOTAL" bold.

6 Save the table.

    a. Save the document as STATESLS.WPD.

    b. Print the document.

    c. Close the document.

INDEPENDENT CHALLENGE 1

You are the movie critic for the *Daily Times*, a local newspaper. Your managing editor has asked you to write a feature article on the top-grossing movies of all time. You decide to use a table to rank the top five movies in order of income from box office receipts.

To complete this independent challenge:

1 Create a table and type in the following information:

Movie	Year	Income in millions
Jurassic Park	1993	330
E.T.	1982	229
Star Wars	1977	194
Return of the Jedi	1983	168
Batman	1989	151

2 Center the headings for each column, and make them bold.

3 Right-align the income figures and choose Currency for the number type.

4 Preview and print the completed table.

5 Save and submit your work.

INDEPENDENT CHALLENGE 2

After weeks of wondering about your food budget, you've decided to keep track of certain grocery items and the price you are paying for these items. Your "study" will be based on three trips to the store. You want to see if the cost of some key food purchases in your grocery bill are staying steady, rising, or falling over a period of three shopping trips. Select five key items that you always purchase (milk, coffee, orange juice, apples, soda, whatever). Keep the receipts for these items so you know what you've paid.

To complete this independent challenge:

1 Plan your table. Decide how you want to organize the information. You will have to make a table with four columns in your document, one column for the item name, then one column for each "shopping trip." You'll probably need six rows for each table. You might want more columns or rows, either to include notes about these items as part of the table, or to include more items. Submit a sketch of your plan.

2 Create the table in WordPerfect. Give the table a title in the document.

3 Give the columns headings. Use a character format to separate the headings from the data in the column. Center the headings for each column, and make them bold and italic.

4 Create the last row as a Total row. Format the label Total.

5 Right-align the income figures and choose Currency for the number type.

6 Create a formula to determine the total for each shopping trip.

7 Write a brief paragraph summarizing your findings at the bottom of the document.

8 Preview and print the completed table.

9 Save the document as SHOPSTDY.WPD and submit your work.

UNIT 7

OBJECTIVES

▶ Plan a graphic image

▶ Insert a graphic image

▶ Size and move a graphic image

▶ Format a paragraph with a drop cap

▶ Create a watermark

▶ Use TextArt

Working
WITH GRAPHICS IN DOCUMENTS

You can enhance the appearance of your document with graphic images, or graphics. **Graphics** can be used to create company letterheads, explain or enhance concepts, or just add decorative touches to your printed documents. ▶ The Write Staff was hired to write the announcement for the fundraising event, A weekend at the movies, sponsored by the village Library in Chatham. Michael Benjamin, the director of the Graphics department, wants you to enhance the text for the announcement. Although the text is well written, the document is rather dull. Graphics will make the document visually appealing and generate more interest. ▶

Planning a graphic image

You use graphic images to enhance the visual appeal of your documents. When you plan a graphic, you determine its purpose, the type of graphic to use, the placement of the graphic on the page, and the size of the graphic. Table 7-1 includes many terms that are useful to know when working with graphics. ▶ Michael asks you to begin enhancing the announcement by adding a graphic image to the document. First, you will need to plan the graphic.

1 **Determine the purpose of the graphic image.**
You'd like to use a graphic that adds to the message of the text and catches the reader's attention. You plan to use an eye-catching graphic that adds to the message "get here any way you can."

2 **Choose the type of graphic image to use.**
There are many types of graphics to choose from, such as pictures, logos, charts, or borders. **Clip art** is a collection of images or symbols stored on disk and available through your word processor. You select an image of hot air balloons to symbolize the magic and excitement that films bring to an audience as well as build on the message "get here any way you can."

3 **Decide where to insert the graphic image into the document.**
The placement of a graphic affects the way text appears in the document. You might need to move and resize the graphic after inserting it in the document. To start, you plan to place it near the top of the announcement.

4 **Determine what size you want the graphic image to be.**
You can enlarge or shrink graphics to suit the paper size or the amount of surrounding text. You don't want the image to overwhelm the text, yet you want it to be visible and significant in the document.

5 **Create a rough sketch of how you want the graphic image to look when it is placed in the document.**
Figure 7-1 shows a rough sketch of the graphic in the document.

FIGURE 7-1:
Rough sketch of the
document with graphic

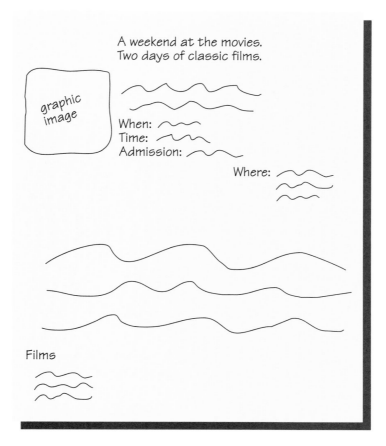

TABLE 7-1: Graphics terms

TERM	DESCRIPTION
Graphics figure	Clip art or an image that can be brought into a document; WordPerfect graphics figures are designated by the extension .WPG
Graphics box	A box that can contain a figure, an equation, or text. There are ten different predefined graphics box styles: Image, Text, Box, Equation, Figure, Table, User, Button, Watermark, or Inline Equation
Sizing handles	Small black squares that appear on the graphics box to indicate that the figure in the graphics box is selected and ready to be edited, sized, or moved
Graphics Box Feature Bar	A Feature Bar that appears when adding or editing a picture, equation, table, or other graphic in a document
Image	Charts, logos, and drawings created in the WordPerfect graphic format or another graphic format
Text	Quotes or other text information to be set off from the main document
Equations	Mathematical, scientific, or business formulas and expressions
Tables	Spreadsheets, statistical data, or text
Charts	Graphs, including bar charts, line charts, or pie charts, to represent numerical data

Inserting a graphic image

Once you determine the purpose of the graphic image, you can pick a graphic that suits your needs. You use the Graphics menu to **import**, or insert, clip art images, logos, or drawings into your document. There are several ways to add a graphic to a document. One method is to enable the feature Drag to Create on the Graphics menu to "draw" the graphics box directly into your document. This method gives you the most control over the initial size and location of the box on the page. Another method is to retrieve a clip art image, a chart, or a drawing directly into a document using the Image or Figure graphics box style. You can even add a caption to a graphic; read the related topic, "Adding captions." ▶ After planning the graphic, you have a clear image of how you would like the announcement to look. The text is interesting, and the character formatting helps, but the page doesn't really attract attention. You insert your graphic to give the announcement some life.

1 Open **unit_7-1.wpd**, then save it as **FILMS1.WPD** to the MY_FILES directory on your Student Disk
The text for the announcement is on your screen. Now you will retrieve the graphic for the announcement and insert it near the top of the document.

2 Press **[Ctrl][Home]**, then press **[↓]** four times
The insertion point is at the top of the document in the blank line above the word "When:." Because you plan to use standard clip art supplied with WordPerfect, you will import it directly using the Image command. When you retrieve an image, the graphic will be inserted in a graphics box at the insertion point.

3 Click **Graphics** on the menu bar, be sure there is *no* check mark next to Drag to Create on the menu, then click **Image**
The Insert Image dialog box opens, as shown in Figure 7-2; you might have different image filenames listed on your screen. You can also open the Insert Image dialog box by clicking the **Image button** ◆. A number of WordPerfect graphic images are listed in the Filename list box. WordPerfect graphics have a .WPG extension.

4 Scroll through the files in the Filename list box, click **hotair.wpg**, then click **OK**
Compare your screen with Figure 7-3. A picture of a landscape with multi-colored hot air balloons, inside a graphics box, is inserted to the left of the text in the document. The Graphics Feature Bar appears. The lines of text automatically align to the right of the image. Often when you insert an image, you need to adjust how the text wraps around the figure. Leave the text wrapping set to the default for now.

5 Click **Close** on the Graphics Feature Bar
The Graphics Feature Bar and the sizing handles on the graphics box no longer appear.

6 Save the document

FIGURE 7-2: Insert Image dialog box

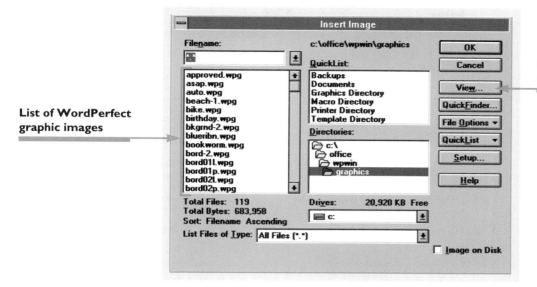

List of WordPerfect graphic images

Click to open a preview window

FIGURE 7-3: FILMS1.WPD with inserted image

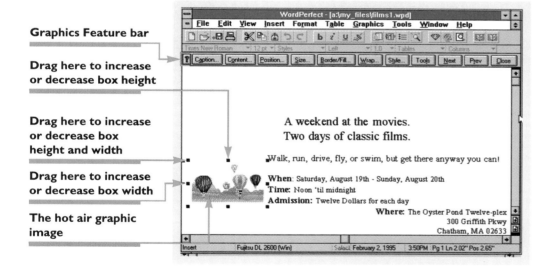

Graphics Feature bar

Drag here to increase or decrease box height

Drag here to increase or decrease box height and width

Drag here to increase or decrease box width

The hot air graphic image

TROUBLE?

If you can't find the list of WordPerfect graphic images, make sure you are looking on the correct drive. The .WPG files should be on the same drive as your WordPerfect program files. Click the Drives list arrow and select another drive, if necessary. You can also try clicking the Graphics Directory in the QuickList box of the Open Files dialog box.■

Adding captions

You might want to add a **caption**, text that describes a graphic image in a document. The Caption option on the Graphics Feature Bar enables you to add a caption to a graphic. When you choose the Caption option, a dialog box opens, giving options for the positioning and style of the captions. The option also automatically numbers each caption according to the location of the graphic within the document.

QUICK **TIP**

To see what each .WPG file looks like, click Preview in the Insert Image dialog box. As you highlight each file, a preview image appears in a window, giving you a preview before inserting the image in your file.■

Sizing and moving a graphic image

Graphics should be sized and placed in a document so they add to, rather than detract from, the message. A graphic that is too large overpowers the text, and a graphic that is badly placed draws the reader's attention away from the text. You can use the Graphics Feature Bar options or the drag and drop method to size and move graphics. To use drag and drop to position graphic images, click anywhere in the graphic to select it, then drag it to a new location. ▶ After reviewing the document, you decide that the image of the balloons sets the text off-center and that the image is too small. Michael gives you ideas for better sizing and placement. Resize and move the image per his specifications.

STEPS ▶

1 Click **Graphics** on the menu bar, then click **Edit Box**
   The hot air balloons graphic is selected, and sizing handles appear on all sides of the graphics box. The Graphics Feature Bar appears. You will use the Graphics Feature Bar to size the image and then move the box.

2 Click **Position** on the Feature Bar
   The Box Position dialog box opens as shown in Figure 7-4.

3 Type **.10** in the **Horizontal Place** text box, double-click in the **Vertical Place** text box, type **.799**, then click **OK**
   The graphic moves to the specified position from the top and is aligned .10" from the right margin. Next, resize the figure to make it wider and longer. Depending on which handle on the graphics box you drag, you can increase or decrease the height and/or width of the box.

4 Position the cursor on the handles to display the ⇔, then drag the handles up and to the left to resize the image as shown in Figure 7-5
   Next, Michael suggests that you place a drop shadow border around the image. This will give it the illusion of rising off the page and add to the feeling of flight.

5 Click **Border/Fill** on the Graphics Feature Bar, then click the **Border Style button** in the Border Options area
   The Border Options palette opens.

6 Click the **Shadow button** ⬜, then click **OK**.
   The border makes the image affect the text again. You need to move the graphic up a bit. Use drag and drop to reposition the text.

7 Position the insertion point inside the graphics box
   The pointer changes to ✛.

8 Drag the **graphics box** slowly up to align the top of the box with the top two lines of text, then release the left mouse button
   The image moves to the new location so your screen looks like Figure 7-6, and the lines of text adjust accordingly. Now that the balloons are positioned, you can deselect the graphic and close the Feature Bar.

9 Click to the left of the balloons to deselect the graphic, click **Close** on the Graphics Feature Bar, then click the **Save button** 🖬
   The sizing handles and the Graphics Feature Bar no longer appear. Depending on where you repositioned the graphic, your document might not match the figures in this book. Don't worry, as long as you think it looks attractive and professional.

FIGURE 7-4:
Box position dialog box

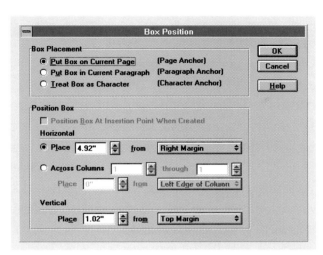

FIGURE 7-5:
Resizing the image

Drag here to increase or decrease box width

FIGURE 7-6:
FILMS1.WPD with resized and moved graphic

Drag cursor to reposition selected image

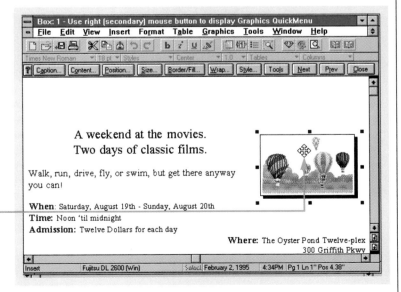

QUICK **TIP**

When moving a graphic, be careful not to click on one of the handles, or you will resize the box rather than reposition it.■

TROUBLE?

If you try to drag the graphic to an area where it won't fit, it automatically returns to the original location.■

Formatting a paragraph with a drop cap

A **drop cap** is a graphic element that adds style to the text in a document by creating a stylized character for the first letter in a paragraph. This letter is enlarged, placed to the left of the paragraph and "dropped" for a specified number of lines. The paragraph then wraps back to the left margin below the drop cap. There are 12 predefined styles for drop caps in WordPerfect, with various margin positionings, borders, and fills. To enhance the drop caps, see the related topic, "Adding borders and fills to drop caps." ▶ The first two paragraphs do not add any decorative elements to the announcement. Michael suggests that a drop cap would add an artistic element to the document and invite readers to read the paragraph. Use a drop cap to enhance the text in these two paragraphs.

1 Position the insertion point at the beginning of the first paragraph at the word "The"
You want to drop cap the letter "T" in the word.

2 Click **Format** on the menu bar, click **Drop Cap**, then scroll to display the paragraph
The Drop Cap Feature Bar opens, as shown in Figure 7-7. The "T" is now a drop cap. The drop cap formats the paragraph. If you change the text in this paragraph, no matter what the first word is, the first character or letter will always be a drop cap. You want the same style drop cap for the next paragraph. You could select borders to match the graphic but decide that would make the announcement too busy. When working with graphics in documents, you have to learn to use them sparingly, or else your documents end up looking too crowded.

3 Click the **Drop Cap Type button** on the Feature Bar
Samples of the 14 styles are shown. Refer to Figure 7-8 to select the same style for the next paragraph; the current style is indicated by a red border.

4 Position the insertion point at the beginning of the next paragraph at the word "We're," click, then click the style
The letter "W" is now a drop cap.

5 Click **Close** on the Drop Cap Feature Bar
Next, save and print the announcement to see how the graphics have affected the document.

6 Click the **Save Button**, then print your document
Compare your printed document with Figure 7-9.

FIGURE 7-7:
Drop Cap Feature Bar

FIGURE 7-8:
Fourteen predefined
Drop Cap Styles

Selected style

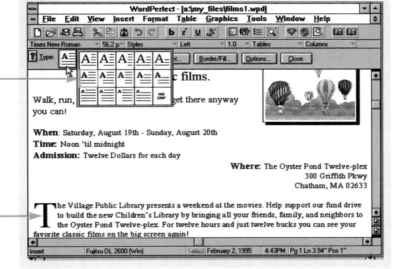

Paragraph formatted
with a drop cap

FIGURE 7-9:
FILMS1.WPD with
drop caps and graphic

Adding borders and fills to drop caps

You can add borders or fills to a drop cap, as with any graphic image in a document.
Click Border/Fill on the Drop Cap Feature Bar, and click on any border style or fill
style in the Border Options or Fill Options boxes for the drop cap.

Creating a watermark

A **watermark** is a drawing, logo, clip art image, or headline-sized text located behind the text in your document. For example, if you need to create a memo for the company picnic, you might want to include the company logo in the background of the memo. Watermarks function much the same as headers and footers; you can have one or two of them per section and edit them individually as well. To create a watermark, use the Watermark option on the Format menu. ▶ You decide that the Village Library logo would make a good watermark on the announcement. After all, you want the people to know that this is a fundraiser for the library. The library logo is a crane.

1 Click **Format** on the menu bar, then click **Watermark**
The Watermark dialog box opens.

2 Click **Watermark A**, then click **Create**
The Watermark Feature Bar appears, and your document is in full page preview, as shown in Figure 7-10.

3 Click **Image** on the Feature Bar
The Insert Image dialog box opens. This dialog box is very similar to the Insert Image dialog box you used to insert the graphic at the beginning of this unit.

4 Click **crane_j.wpg** in the graphic files list box, then click **OK**
The image of the crane appears on your screen in full page preview, and the Graphics Feature Bar opens. You work with a watermark as with any graphic. Your screen should look like Figure 7-11.

5 Click **Close** on the Graphics Feature Bar, click **Close** on the Watermark Feature Bar and return to your document
The watermark is inserted in your document. The image of the crane appears full-page behind the text. You can see the image as well as read the text.

6 Click the **Save button** 🖫, then click the **Print button** 🖨 and click **Print**
Compare your printed document with Figure 7-12.

FIGURE 7-10:
Watermark Feature
Bar and watermark
document in full page
preview

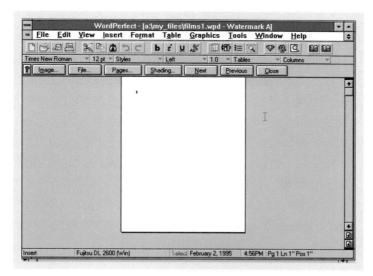

FIGURE 7-11:
Preview full page
with watermark

Feature Bar

Watermark

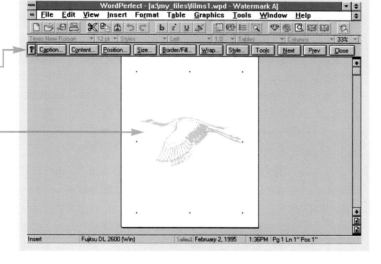

FIGURE 7-12:
Printed document
with watermark

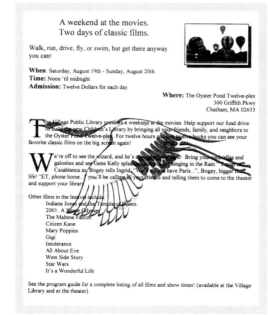

TROUBLE?

If the image of the
watermark overpowers
the text, click Shading
on the Watermark
Feature Bar and reduce
the value until the text
can be read easily.■

Using TextArt

Although character formats provide various fonts and styles that enhance the text, **TextArt** provides a way to create special text images from your words. You can shape the text as waves, pennants, circles, crescents, or bow ties. Text can be filled with colors and patterns, given borders and shadows of many colors, and sized within your document. To create text art, click TextArt on the Graphics menu, type the text you want, then select the font, style, and options for the text. You can also Cut or Copy text from the document to the Clipboard and then Paste it into the TextArt window. ▶ Michael reviews your work and thinks that the slogan "A weekend at the movies. Two days of classic films." is catchy but would be more effective if it were a TextArt image.

1   Press **[Ctrl][Home]**, drag the cursor to select the two lines **A weekend at the movies. Two days of classic films.**, then right-click, and click **Cut** on the QuickMenu

There is no need to retype this text; you can move it to the Clipboard and paste it in TextArt.

2   Click **Graphics** on the menu bar, and click **TextArt**

You may have to wait a moment while your computer loads the TextArt program. The buttons and menus in WordPerfect temporarily change to adopt the buttons and menus of the TextArt program. A TextArt image window opens in your document. Your screen looks like Figure 7-13.

3   Click the **Paste button** 🖼

The text is inserted in the edit box.

4   Click the **font list arrow**, click **Bauhaus 93** or, if that is unavailable, any other font that looks appealing, then click the **wave text shape** 🌊

Now that you have set the shape and font, you can have some fun and design the text. Step 5 includes some suggestions. You can design the text art to suit your personal style.

5   Click the **text fill pattern button** ▦, click the **text pattern foreground color button** ▣, click any green color, click **text pattern background color** ▢, click any yellow shade, click the **shadow button** ◻, then click any shadow style

When you are pleased with the way your TextArt is designed, you can return to the document.

6   Click anywhere outside the TextArt image

You are back in your document. The image, which is still selected, is placed too low on the page. It's interfering with your hot air balloon graphic, as well as the text at the top of the document. You need to move the TextArt image up and the balloon image down.

7   Place the cursor on the **TextArt image** so that the cursor changes to a ✥, drag the image up and to the left a little, then place the cursor on the **balloon image** and drag it down a little

Place the images so your screen looks similar to Figure 7-14.

8   Save and print **FILMS1.WPD**

The final printout should look similar to Figure 7-15.

9   Close the document and exit WordPerfect

Michael is sure that the Village Library will be pleased with the announcement. It will be posted around the town of Chatham and mailed to all library patrons.

FIGURE 7-13: TextArt program window

Type text here

Font list arrow

Font style arrow

TextArt image

Click rectangle shape for regular text

Click for more text shapes

Click for text shape

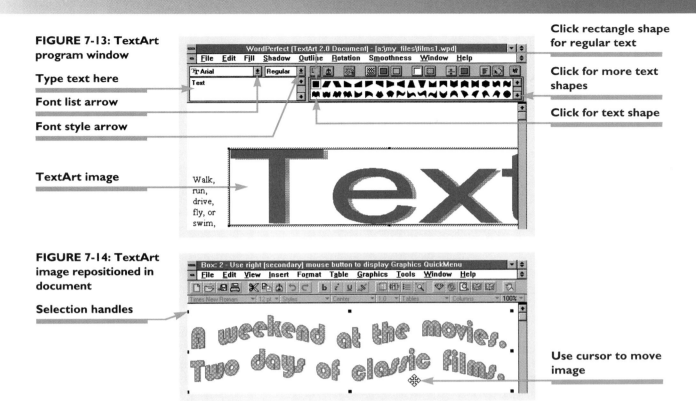

FIGURE 7-14: TextArt image repositioned in document

Selection handles

Use cursor to move image

FIGURE 7-15: Final printout of FILMS1.WPD

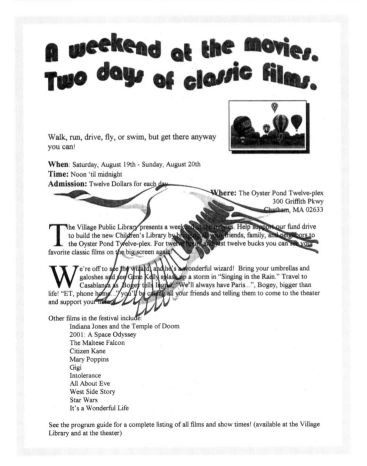

QUICK **TIP**

Double-click the TextArt image to open a QuickMenu where you can edit the content, font, and/or design elements.■

CONCEPTSREVIEW

Label each element of the WordPerfect window shown in Figure 7-16.

1 _____

2 _____

3 _____

4 _____

5 _____

6 _____

7 _____

8 _____

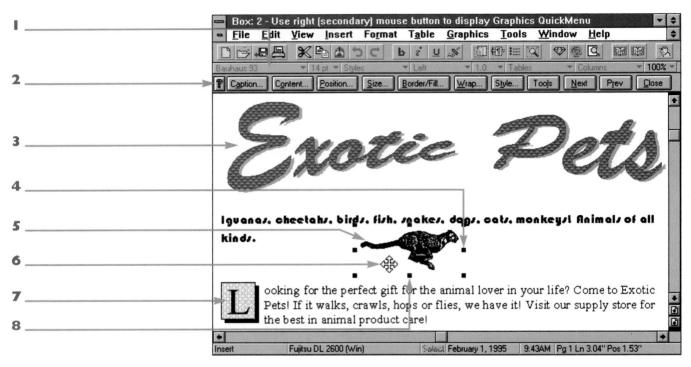

FIGURE 7-16

Match each of the following actions with its icon.

9 Image icon

10 Creates a drop cap

11 Creates a shadow border

12 Moves an image

13 Shapes TextArt

a. ▫

b. ♦

c. ◈

d. 🄰

e. ✥

Select the best answer from the list of choices.

14 A graphic image

  a. must be inserted at the top of a document

  b. must be inserted at the bottom of a document

  c. works like a footer and can be inserted at any time

  d. can be inserted anywhere in a document

15 Once a graphic image is in a document, use the handles to

  a. change the image to a new picture

  b. move and size the image

  c. name the image

  d. add text to the image

16 Clip art is stored on the hard disk

   a. in the graphics subdirectory as a .WPG file

   b. in the image subdirectory as a document file

   c. as an .IMG file in the MY_FILES directory

   d. it isn't on the hard disk

17 A watermark is

   a. an image that appears wet on the screen

   b. an image that is used to define where water can be placed in a document

   c. an image that is faint, with text flowing over it

   d. a special type of image file used in business applications

18 Which of these can't TextArt do?

   a. Make text stylized and into graphic elements in your document

   b. Add patterns and shadows to your text

   c. Create shapes from your words

   d. Create a faint image behind your document for text to flow over

19 Use a drop cap to

   a. enlarge the first word in a paragraph

   b. enlarge and stylize the first letter of the paragraph

   c. drop the first letter from each word

   d. capitalize the first letter of each word in a paragraph

APPLICATIONS
REVIEW

1 Plan a graphic image.

   a. Sketch a draft of an advertisement for a furniture shop.

   b. Identify the areas for text, TextArt, drop cap paragraphs, and images.

   c. The heading of the advertisement will be TextArt.

   d. Plan an image in the middle.

   e. Plan some descriptive text for the ad below the image.

2 Insert a graphic image.

   a. Open the file UNIT_7-2.WPD and save it as DESERT1.WPD to the MY_FILES directory.

   b. Insert the image HORSE_J.WPG in the document.

   c. Use the Box Position dialog box to center it on the page.

3 Size and move a graphic image.

   a. Use the sizing handles to make the image small enough to fit in the middle of the page.

   b. Use the move cursor to position it in the center of the page.

4 Format a paragraph with a drop cap.

   a. Format the paragraph with the word "Browse" as a drop cap.

   b. Style the drop cap to include a border.

   c. Style the drop cap to include a fill pattern.

5 Create a watermark.

   a. Southwest Furniture is looking to expand internationally, so create a watermark using the image WORLD.WPG.

   b. View your document.

   c. Make sure the watermark doesn't interfere with any text.

6 Use TextArt.

   a. Move the text "Desert Designs" to the Clipboard.

   b. Create a TextArt image from this text.

   c. Use a fill pattern for the TextArt.

   d. Use a text shape.

7 Save and print your document.

   a. Review the printout and determine any changes you feel would improve the cover.

   b. Edit the images as needed.

   c. Save and print the revised cover.

INDEPENDENT
CHALLENGE 1

You have just been elected to select five exciting clip art images for the Exotic Pets company. This company is expanding into a world-wide market. They offer exotic pets and are also a full-service organization: they are committed to animal conservation and protection as well as education.

To complete this independent challenge:

1 Open a new file and save it as EXOTIC1.WPD to the MY_FILES directory on the Student Disk.

2 Create a TextArt image using "Exotic Pets" as a heading for the document.

3 Use the View mode in the Insert Image dialog box to find and insert five images.

4 Use Border Options to place a border around each image.

5 Write a brief description below each image.

6 Format these descriptive paragraphs with drop caps.

7 Create a watermark on each page of the document, using the file CHEETAH.WPG.

8 Save and print the document.

INDEPENDENT
CHALLENGE 2

You have become part owner of a new greeting card company, CollegeCards. You have to design and create the first five cards. These prototypes will be marketed to university and junior college bookstores. If they buy the prototypes, you can go into mass production. You have to select one image for each card; use TextArt and drop caps to best establish CollegeCards as a premier greeting card company. The prototypes will be two-page documents: the first page will be the front of the card; the second page will represent the interior of the card.

To complete this independent challenge:

1 Select an image and create a card for Valentine's Day. Put your name at the top of the first page, design the two-page document, save it as VALDAY.WPD, then print the file.

2 Select an image and create a card for a general birthday. Put your name at the top of the first page, design the two-page document, save it as GBDAY.WPD, then print the file.

3 Select an image and create a card for a wedding anniversary. Put your name at the top of the first page, design the two-page document, save it as WANNIV.WPD, then print the file.

4 Select an image and create a card for Mother's Day. Put your name at the top of the first page, design the two-page document, save it as MOMDAY.WPD, then print the file.

5 Select an image and create a card for Father's Day. Put your name at the top of the first page, design the two-page document, save it as DADDAY.WPD, then print the file.

UNIT 8

OBJECTIVES

▶ Plan a merge

▶ Create a data file

▶ Enter data in
a data file

▶ Create a form file

▶ Enter fields in
a form file

▶ Merge data and
form files

▶ Edit data and
form files

Merging FILES

*I*f you write a letter and want to send it to more than one person, you can cut and paste the new name and address into the letter each time you print. Or, you can create one letter and one document with all the names and addresses, then merge the two files. You can use WordPerfect's merge feature to mass-produce letters, envelopes, mailing labels, contracts, phone lists, memos, and other documents. ▶ Jennifer Laina asks you to send each of your clients a letter reminding them that catalog season is just around the corner. In this unit, you will use WordPerfect's merge feature to complete this project. ▶

Planning a merge

Merging is a three-step process that requires careful planning. First, you create a data file, which contains the names and addresses of the people you want to send the letter to. Next, you create a form file, or form letter. Finally, you merge the data file and the form file to create a third file that contains all the personalized letters. See Figure 8-1 for a diagram of this process. ▶ In the past, a job like this would have taken hours. You would have had to write personalized letters for each client. But now you have the power of WordPerfect's Merge feature to complete this project in a short time. ▶ Use the following steps to plan the merged letters Jennifer asked you to create.

STEPS

1 **Determine the purpose of the merge.**
Jennifer wants you to send a reminder letter to each of your clients.

2 **Make a list of the information that needs to be included in the data file.**
The data file should include the clients' names and the companies' names and addresses.

3 **Decide what the form file will say.**
Jennifer wants to remind clients to submit new product information for the upcoming catalog season.

4 **Write a rough draft of the letter.**
Jennifer provides a rough draft of the letter, as shown in Figure 8-2.

FIGURE 8-1: Merging process

Create a data file

Create a form file

Merge the two files to create many personalized copies of original

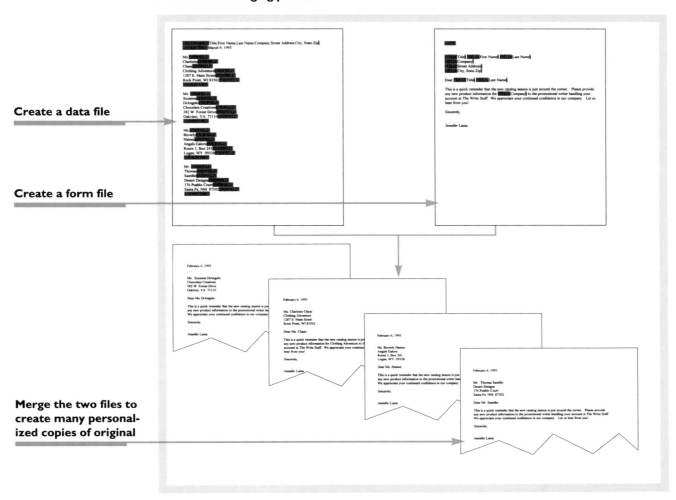

FIGURE 8-2: Draft of letter for merge

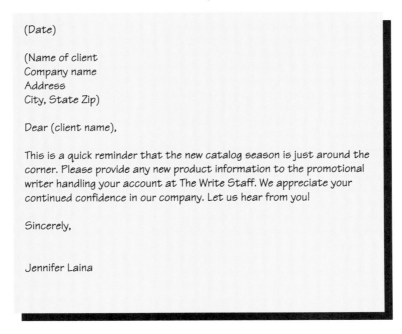

(Date)

(Name of client
Company name
Address
City, State Zip)

Dear (client name),

This is a quick reminder that the new catalog season is just around the corner. Please provide any new product information to the promotional writer handling your account at The Write Staff. We appreciate your continued confidence in our company. Let us hear from you!

Sincerely,

Jennifer Laina

Creating a data file

Data files contain the information, such as names and addresses, that is merged with a form file; this information is arranged into fields and records. A **field** is the smallest amount of information you can specify in a data file. For example, one field might contain a name, and another field might contain a zip code. A **record** is a collection of related fields. For example, one record might contain all the information about a person or a company. Data files can be in table or text format. To understand the difference between a data table file and a data text file, read the related topic, "Data text files vs. data table files," on the opposite page. ▶ You need to create a data file that contains records for all your clients. You can use this file to merge with the form letter Jennifer provided and any other correspondence you plan. You can also add records to this data file as your client list grows. The following steps will help you to set up your data file to include all the necessary fields.

1 Click the **New Blank Document button** 🗋
   This ensures that you will be working with a blank document window when you build the data file.

2 Click **Tools** on the menu bar, then click **Merge**
   The Merge dialog box opens, as shown in Figure 8-3.

3 Click **Data** in the Data File box
   The Create Data File dialog box appears on top of the Merge Feature Bar as shown in Figure 8-4. Now name and add the fields to be included in the data file.

4 Type **Title** in the Name a Field text box, then click **Add**
   "Title" appears in the Field Name List box.

5 Type each of the following fields in the Name a Field text box, one at a time, clicking **Add** after each field:
   First Name
   Last Name
   Company
   Street Address
   Each field name appears in the Field Name List box.

6 Type **City, State Zip** as one field name, click **Add**, then click **OK**
   The Quick Data Entry dialog box appears, as shown in Figure 8-5. You use this dialog box to enter information for each record. You will enter the data for each client in the next lesson.

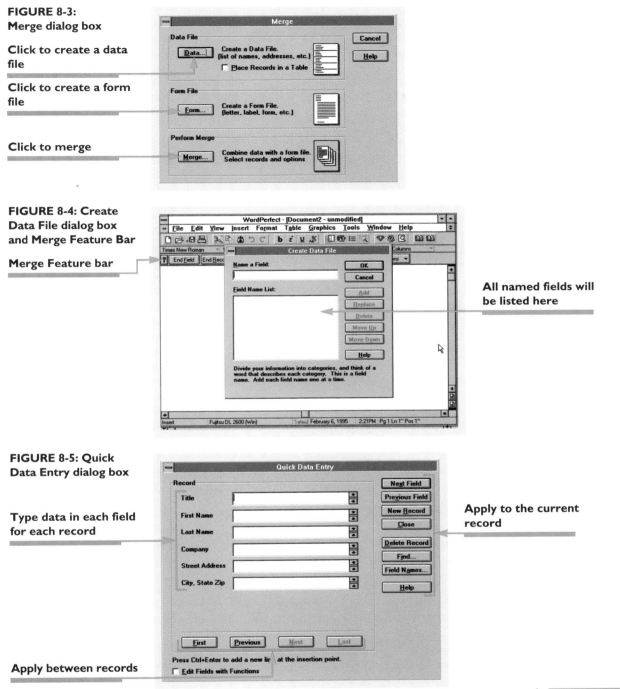

FIGURE 8-3: Merge dialog box

Click to create a data file

Click to create a form file

Click to merge

FIGURE 8-4: Create Data File dialog box and Merge Feature Bar

Merge Feature bar

All named fields will be listed here

FIGURE 8-5: Quick Data Entry dialog box

Type data in each field for each record

Apply to the current record

Apply between records

Data text files vs. data table files

There are two kinds of data files that can be used in a merge. A **data text file** is in text format, containing fields and records separated by merge codes. A **data table file** is in table format, where each column contains a field and each row contains a record. To create a data text file, choose Merge on the Tools menu, then click Data in the Merge dialog box. To create a data table, click the Place Records in a Table check box, then click Data.

QUICK **TIP**

The type of information in any field should always be the same from record to record. Don't insert a phone number, for example, in a zip code field.■

Entering data in a data file

Now that you've created your data file, you're ready to fill in the fields using the Quick Data Entry dialog box. Read the related topic, "Using other sources for data," for information on creating merge files with existing data files created in other programs. Merge codes are automatically inserted in your data file. **Merge codes** are used by WordPerfect to separate each field from the others and to end each record. Table 8-1 describes the merge codes WordPerfect uses. ▶ The catalog division is an expanding business for The Write Staff. Currently, you have four clients to whom you want to send the form letter. As you get more clients, you can add more records to this data file.

STEPS

1 Enter the following text, then click **Next Field** after each

Field Name Text box	You type
Title	**Ms.**
First Name	**Charlotte**
Last Name	**Chase**
Company	**Clothing Adventure**
Street Address	**1287 E. Main Street**
City, State Zip	**Rock Point, WI 83562**

2 Click **New Record**
You have entered the information for each of the fields in one record. The appropriate merge codes are automatically inserted, and the record is placed in the data file. You are now ready to enter the information for the other records.

3 Follow the procedure in Steps 1 and 2 to enter the next three records in the data file by typing the information below

Ms.	**Ms.**	**Mr.**
Suzanne	**Beverly**	**Thomas**
DiAngelo	**Haines**	**Santillo**
Chocolate Creations	**Angels Galore**	**Desert Designs**
382 W. Forest Drive	**Route 3, Box 241**	**376 Pueblo Court**
Oaktree, VA 73110	**Logan, WY 09328**	**Santa Fe, NM 87502**

4 Click **Close** after entering the last field name, then click **Yes** in the Save Changes to Disk dialog box
You need to save this file to disk. The Save Data File As dialog box opens. Name this file MERGE.DAT.

5 Type **MERGE.DAT** in the Filenames text box, save it to the MY_FILES directory on your Student Disk, then click **OK**
The .DAT file extension distinguishes the file from other WordPerfect files you have created.

6 Press **[Ctrl][Home]**
Compare your document with the partial MERGE.DAT document shown in Figure 8-6.
The records are separated by double lines.

FIGURE 8-6: Partial MERGE.DAT document

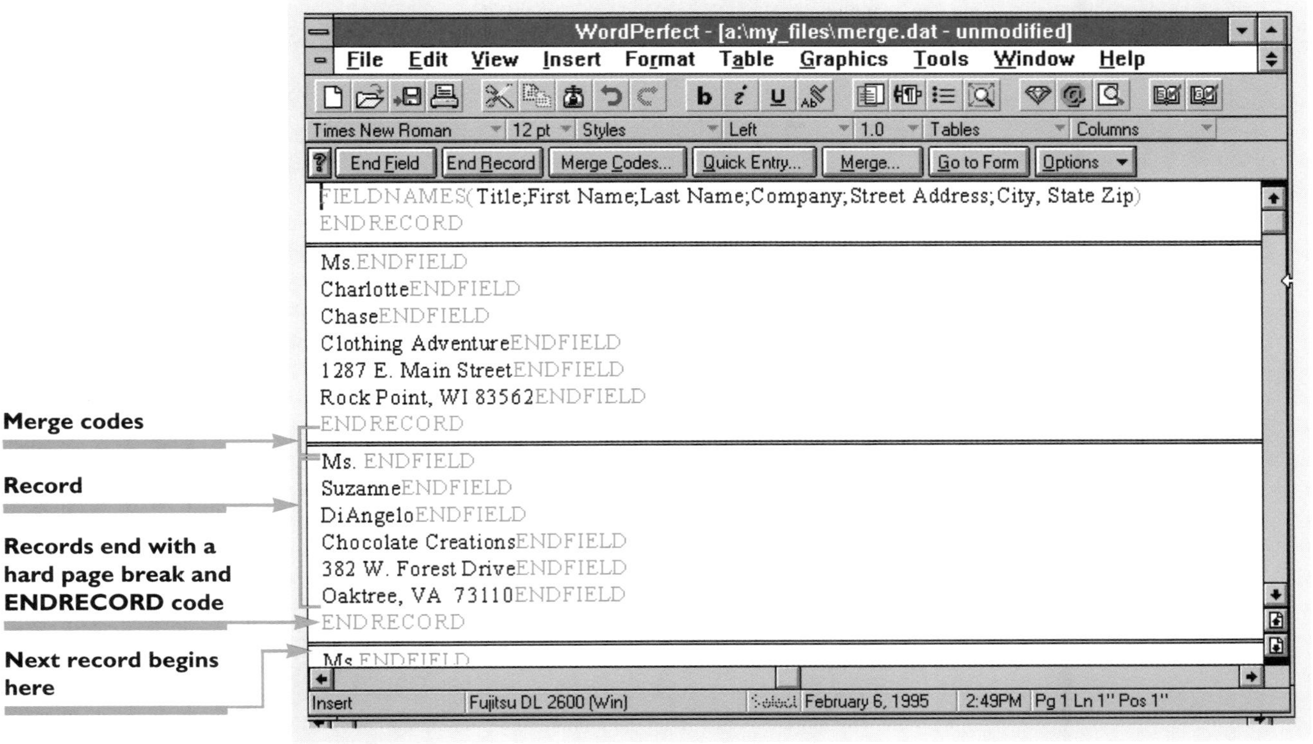

```
WordPerfect - [a:\my_files\merge.dat - unmodified]
File  Edit  View  Insert  Format  Table  Graphics  Tools  Window  Help

Times New Roman   12 pt  Styles      Left      1.0    Tables     Columns
End Field  End Record  Merge Codes...  Quick Entry...  Merge...  Go to Form  Options

FIELDNAMES(Title;First Name;Last Name;Company;Street Address;City, State Zip)
ENDRECORD

Ms.ENDFIELD
CharlotteENDFIELD
ChaseENDFIELD
Clothing AdventureENDFIELD
1287 E. Main StreetENDFIELD
Rock Point, WI 83562ENDFIELD
ENDRECORD

Ms. ENDFIELD
SuzanneENDFIELD
DiAngeloENDFIELD
Chocolate CreationsENDFIELD
382 W. Forest DriveENDFIELD
Oaktree, VA 73110ENDFIELD
ENDRECORD

Ms ENDFIELD

Insert    Fujitsu DL 2600 (Win)    Select  February 6, 1995  2:49PM  Pg 1 Ln 1" Pos 1"
```

Merge codes

Record

Records end with a hard page break and ENDRECORD code

Next record begins here

Using other sources for data

Rather than creating a WordPerfect data file, you can retrieve a data file from another source. For example, you can use a file you created in an earlier version of WordPerfect, or a database file created with another program such as Access, Paradox, or dBASE, or a spreadsheet file created with a program such as Quattro Pro or Lotus 1-2-3. To retrieve a file in another format, you must specify the file format so that it can be converted to WordPerfect format.

QUICK TIP

You can press [Enter] after entering each field rather than clicking the Next Field button. To begin a new record, you can press [Enter] at the end of a record rather than clicking the New Record button.

TABLE 8-1: Merge codes in a data file

CODE	USE
ENDFIELD	Indicates the end of the current field in a data file
ENDRECORD	Indicates the end of the current record in a data file

Creating a form file

The second step when merging is to create the form file. A **form file** is the base document that contains the text of your final document and merge codes. To create the form file, you need to open a new document, type or retrieve the letter you are going to use as the form letter, and then insert the field names that match the fields in the data file. You can associate the data file with the form file so that the two files are linked automatically. ▶ You will now create the form file as a new document and retrieve the form letter Jennifer created. You will associate this form file with the data file you created in the last lesson so that they will be linked for this project.

1 Click **Tools** on the menu bar, then click **Merge**
The Merge dialog box appears.

2 Click **Form** in the Form File box
The Create Merge File dialog box appears, as shown in Figure 8-7.

3 Click **New Document Window**, then click **OK**
The Create Form File dialog box appears, as shown in Figure 8-8. Notice that the Associate a Data File radio button is already on.

4 Type **MERGE.DAT** in the Associate a Data File text box, then click **OK**
MERGE.DAT is the data file you created in the last lesson. Associating a data file with a form file saves you the effort of having to type all of the field names into the form file; you just have to tell WordPerfect where to put them.

5 Click **Date** on the Merge Feature Bar, then press **[Enter]** four times
The date code is inserted at the top of the document and will print the current date on each letter. Now you are ready to insert the letter Jennifer created.

6 Click **Insert** on the menu bar, click **File**, then click **unit_8-1.wpd** in the Filename list box

7 Click **Insert**, and when a dialog box appears asking whether you want to insert the file into the current document, click **Yes**
The letter is added to your form file. Notice that the letter now consists of the date, the body of the letter, and the closing lines, as shown in Figure 8-9. In the next lesson you will insert the field names that form the address and greeting.

8 Save the document as **FORM.FRM** to the MY_FILES directory on your student disk
You can also save a form file with a .WPD filename extension, but the .FRM file extension identifies the document as a form file.

FIGURE 8-7: Create Merge File dialog box

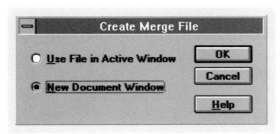

FIGURE 8-8: Create Form File dialog box

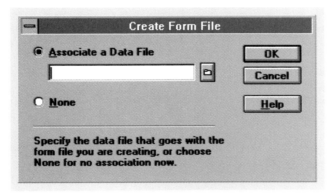

FIGURE 8-9: FORM. FRM document without field names

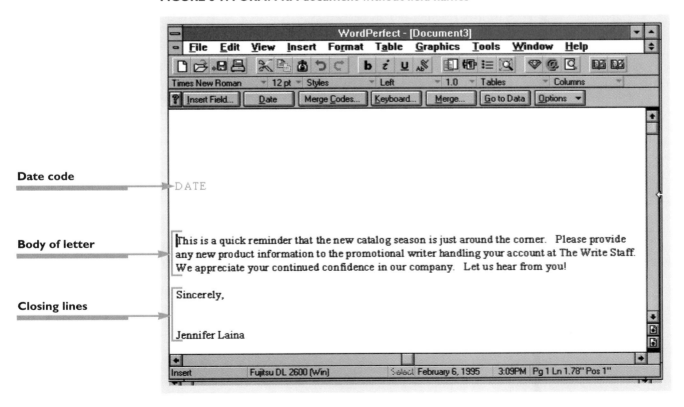

Date code

Body of letter

Closing lines

Entering fields in a form file

To complete the form file, you need to specify where you want the fields from the data file to be placed in the letter. You use the Insert Field button on the Merge Feature Bar to mark the place in the letter where information is to be inserted. This inserts codes at these locations to tell WordPerfect what information to insert. ▶ Now you are ready to insert the fields into the form file.

1 **Position the insertion point on the line above the first line of the body of the letter**
This is where you are going to start inserting the fields for the address.

2 **Click Insert Field on the Merge Feature Bar**
The Insert Field Name or Number dialog box appears, as shown in Figure 8-10. If this box is blocking any text in your letter you can move it by dragging its title bar to a better location.

3 **Click Title in the Field Name text box, click Insert, then press [Spacebar]**
This inserts a space between this field name and the next field name.

4 **Click First Name in the Field Name text box, click Insert, then press [Spacebar]**

5 **Insert the remaining fields listed below by clicking each field in the Field Name text box, clicking Insert, then pressing [Enter] after each**
Last Name
Company
Street Address
City, State Zip

6 **Press [Enter], type Dear, press [Spacebar], follow the procedure in Steps 3 and 4 to enter the Title and Last Name fields for the greeting, then type a colon (:)**
Make sure you don't type a comma after "Dear" and include a space between Title and Last Name. The greeting should look like:

Dear FIELD(Title) FIELD(Last Name):

7 **Click Close to close the Insert Field Name or Number dialog box**

8 **Press [Enter]**
This adds a blank line between the greeting and the body of the letter.

9 **Save and print your document**
It is very important to save your document before merging, as it is before any operation. Compare your document with Figure 8-11.

FIGURE 8-10: Insert Field Name or Number dialog box

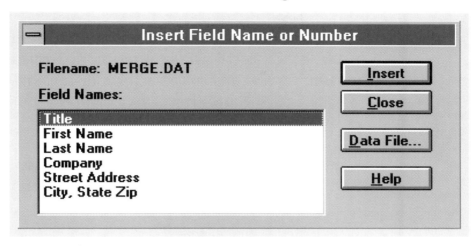

FIGURE 8-11: FORM.FRM document with field names

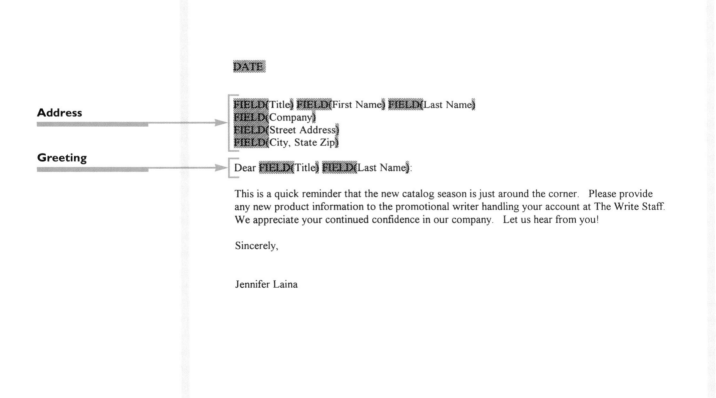

Address

Greeting

Merging data and form files

Once the data and form files are created, you are ready to merge the two documents. Table 8-2 lists the options in the Merge Data File Feature Bar. The two documents are merged into a third document. This is the document you will print. ▶ You're ready to merge the data file and form file you have created for The Write Staff.

1   Click **Window** on the menu bar, then make sure both the MERGE.DAT and FORM.FRM files are open
Make sure that FORM.FRM appears in your window. If the two filenames don't appear on the Window list, below the horizontal line, click File on the menu bar, then click Open and open the files.

2   Click **Merge** on the Merge Feature Bar
The Merge dialog box opens.

3   Click **Merge** in the Perform Merge box
The Perform Merge dialog box opens, as shown in Figure 8-12.

4   Check that the Form File text box displays <Current Document>, the Data File text box displays A:\ or B:\MY_FILES\MERGE.DAT, and the Output File text box displays <New Document>
The form file is the current document. MERGE.DAT is the data file from which the client address information will be extracted. The file named in the Output File text box is the new document to be created by the merge.

5   Click **OK**
The data file and the form file are merged in the current document window.

6   Use the **Previous Page button** 🔳 and **Next Page button** 🔳 to scroll through all four letters in the document
When the merge is complete, the document contains four letters separated by page breaks, one letter for each record in the data file. Figure 8-13 shows the merged document for Charlotte Chase, which is the first merged letter in this file.

You do not need to save the merged file because you have saved both the data file and form file; it is easy to merge these again if necessary. Merged files can take up a lot of space on your disk.

FIGURE 8-12: Perform Merge dialog box

FIGURE 8-13: Page 1 of the merged document

February 6, 1995

Ms. Charlotte Chase
Clothing Adventure
1287 E. Main Street
Rock Point, WI 83562

Dear Ms. Chase:

This is a quick reminder that the new catalog season is just around the corner. Please provide any new product information to the promotional writer handling your account at The Write Staff. We appreciate your continued confidence in our company. Let us hear from you!

Sincerely,

Jennifer Laina

TABLE 8-2: The Merge Data File Feature Bar

OPTION	USE IT TO
Row (table only)	Insert or delete a row (record)
Column (table only)	Insert or delete a column (field)
End Field (text only)	Insert an ENDFIELD code
End Record (text only)	Insert an ENDRECORD code
Merge Codes	Insert merge codes
Quick Entry	Edit data records
Merge	Perform the merge
Go to Form	Open or create associated form file
Options	Choose to display or hide codes, display codes as markers, remove the Merge Feature Bar, or sort records

QUICK **TIP**

If you are merging a large data file and you want to cancel a merge, press [Esc] or [Ctrl][Break].■

TROUBLE?

If data is missing after you merge the two files, go back and check that your data and form file field names and codes are included in both documents.■

Editing data and form files

After merging the files, you might need to make a change to the data file, form file, or both. Client lists, address books, or any data files are always in need of being updated: people and businesses are in a constant state of flux. To remain current with your data files, you must update them. Also, you want to be able to use a data file for various letters. You can often simply modify a form file slightly to be ready for your next mass mailing. Read the related topic "Creating a keyboard merge" for information on how to edit letters and make them more personalized at the point of printing. ▶ After reading through the letters, you spot a mistake in the city name of one of your clients. You also decide to include the company name in the body of the document to make the letter more personalized. Follow the next set of steps to edit the data file and form file, then merge the files again.

1 Click **Window** on the menu bar, then click **MERGE.DAT**
   The data file appears.

2 Position the insertion point to the left of "Oaktree, VA"
   The city should be Oakview. Because you want to use this data file for future mailings, it is important to edit the data file, rather than editing the merged file.

3 Press **[Insert]** to change to Typeover mode and type **Oakview**, then press **[Insert]** again
   The status bar indicates the field where the insertion point is placed. Notice also that the status bar displays "Typeover" while you make the change, and then automatically switches to display "Field: City, State Zip" again, as shown in Figure 8-14.

4 Click the **Save button** 🖫 on the Toolbar
   This saves the change you made to the data file. The second change you want to make is to add a field to the form file.

5 Click **Window**, then click **FORM.FRM**
   The form file appears.

6 Position the insertion point after "information" in the second line, press **[Spacebar]**, type **for**, then press **[Spacebar]** again
   This is where you want to insert the Company field name.

7 Click **Insert Field** on the Merge Feature Bar
   The Insert Field Name or Number dialog box appears.

8 Click **Company** in the Field Name list box, click **Insert**, then click **Close**
   The Company field appears in the text between the words "for" and "to," as shown in Figure 8-15. When the file is merged, the company name will appear here.

9 Click the **Save button** 🖫 to save the form file
   Continue with this lesson to generate your final output.

FIGURE 8-14: Editing a record in the data file

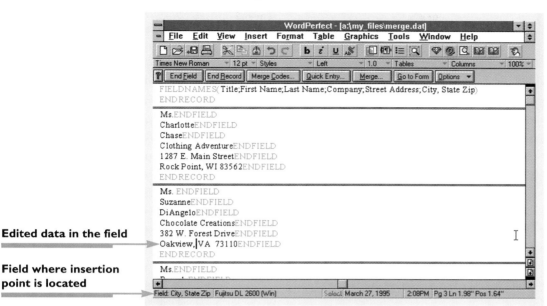

Edited data in the field

Field where insertion point is located

FIGURE 8-15: Company field added to form file

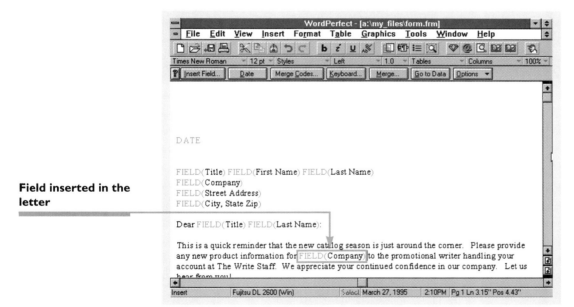

Field inserted in the letter

Creating a keyboard merge

If you have information in the form file that might change, such as a payment amount or appointment date, you can create a keyboard merge command in the form file. The merge will pause at the keyboard merge command and wait for you to type a response to the screen prompt. You can also skip to the next record, quit the merge, or stop the merge at the current position. To create a keyboard merge, click Keyboard on the Merge Feature Bar, type a prompt for the user to see, then click OK.

Editing data and form files, continued

Now that you have made the changes to the form file and the data file, you can merge the two files once again and print them.

10 Click **Window** on the menu bar, and make sure both the MERGE.DAT and FORM.FRM files are open
If the two filenames don't appear on the Window list click File on the menu bar, then click Open and open the files.

11 Click **Merge** on the Merge Feature Bar
The Merge dialog box opens.

12 Click **Merge** in the Perform Merge box
The Perform Merge dialog box opens.

13 Check that the Form File text box displays <Current Document>, the Data File text box displays A:\ or B:\MY_FILES\MERGE.DAT, and the Output File text box displays <New Document>

14 Click **OK**
The data file and the form file are merged for a second time in the current document window.

15 Click the **Print button** 🖫 on the Toolbar, then click **Print**
The letters are printed. Notice that each printed letter contains the current date and a different name, company name, and address. Compare your letter to Suzanne DiAngelo with the one in Figure 8-16. Proofread the letters one more time to make sure they are free of errors before you mail them.

16 Click the **Close All Files button** on the Merge Feature Bar to close all files, saving only FORM.FRM and MERGE.DAT when prompted
It is not necessary to save the merged file because you have both the data file and form file available to merge again if necessary.

As you have seen, the Merge function can create a large amount of personalized letters in a short amount of time. The letters will now arrive in plenty of time for your clients to update their catalogs.

FIGURE 8-16: Four merged documents with Thomas Santillo's on top

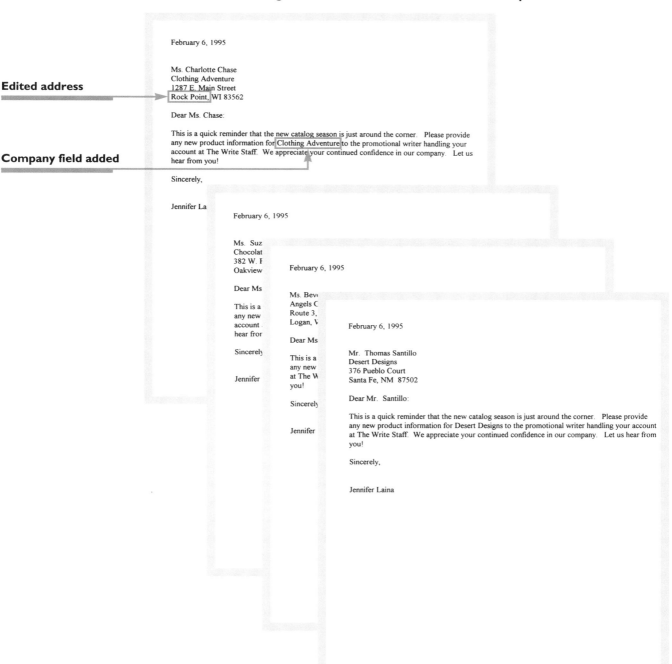

Edited address

Company field added

QUICK TIP

Preview your documents using the Zoom Full Page button to see how the letters fit on each page and to check for any errors.■

CONCEPTSREVIEW

Label each element of the WordPerfect window shown in Figure 8-17.

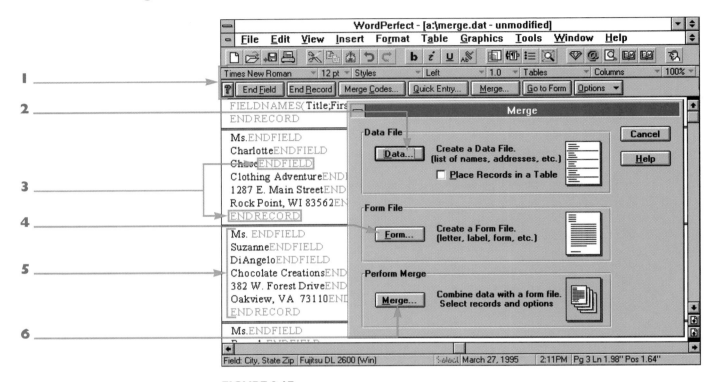

FIGURE 8-17

Match each of the following items with the phrase that best describes it.

7 Field

8 Record

9 Data file

10 Form file

a. Supplies variable data, such as name, address, and city

b. Is made up of the text and/or graphics you want in each document

c. Contains a group of related items in a data file

d. Each piece of information that you provide in a data file

Select the best answer from the list of choices.

11 Which of the following is the best reason to use the merge feature?

a. You want several exact copies of a file.

b. You want to send the same letter to several people, using each person's name and address.

c. You want to combine two memos into one long letter.

d. You want to copy several paragraphs from one letter to another.

12 When you use the merge feature, the resulting letters are in

a. The data file

b. The form file

c. The merged document

d. A merge code

13 Which of the following merge codes retrieves information from the data file into the form file during the merge?

a. FIELD

b. KEYBOARD

c. ENDRECORD

d. ENDFIELD

14 Which of the following merge codes signals the end of a single piece of information within the data file?

a. FIELD

b. KEYBOARD

c. ENDRECORD

d. ENDFIELD

15 To close all the files and save only those files that have changes, you can:

   a. Click Close on the File menu

   b. Click Save on the File menu

   c. Click the Close All documents button on the Utilities Toolbar

   d. Click the Save button on the WordPerfect default Toolbar

APPLICATIONS
REVIEW

1 Create a data file.

   a. Start with a blank document window.

   b. Create a data file with the following eight field names: Title, First Name, Last Name, Company, Street Address, City, State, Zip Code.

   c. Create the following three records in the data file:

Mr.	Ms.	Mr.
Patrick	Deanna	Edward
Angel	Schloss	Leach
Xerox	Ricoh	Canon
3452 Troy Rd.	742 N. Harris Ave.	3776 Birch Lane
Rochester	Detroit	Mountain View
NY	MI	CA
14604	49233	94042

   d. Save the data file as COPIERS.DAT, and close the document window.

2 Create a form file.

   a. Make sure a blank document window appears on the screen.

   b. Create a form file by clicking Tools on the menu bar, then Merge, then clicking the Form button in the Merge dialog box.

   c. In the Create Form File dialog box, type the name of the data file (COPIERS.DAT) that you created above.

   d. At the beginning of the form file, insert the DATE code by clicking Date on the Merge Feature Bar.

   e. Press [Enter] four times to leave space between the date and the inside address.

   f. Insert the FIELD merge codes for the inside address by clicking the Insert Field button on the Merge Feature Bar and choosing the appropriate field name. Format the FIELD codes and text so that the inside address appears as follows:

FIELD(Title) FIELD(First Name) FIELD(Last Name)
FIELD(Company)
FIELD(Street Address)
FIELD(City), FIELD(State) FIELD(Zip Code)

   g. Press [Enter] twice to insert a blank line below the inside address.

   h. For the greeting, type "Dear", press [Spacebar], then insert the FIELD code for the field names Title and Last Name.

   i. Press [Enter] twice to insert a blank line between the greeting and the body of the letter.

   j. Insert the body of the letter by clicking Insert on the menu bar, clicking File, typing UNIT_8-2.WPD in the Filename text box, clicking Insert, then clicking Yes. The body of the letter is inserted into the form file.

   k. In the last paragraph, immediately after the word "available" (and before the space to the left of the word "copiers"), insert a space and the FIELD code for the field name Company.

   l. Save the file as COPIERS.FRM.

3 Merge the data file and the form file.

   a. Click Merge on the Feature Bar. The Merge dialog box appears on the screen.

   b. Click the Merge button.

   c. Insert the name of the form file COPIERS.FRM into the Form File text box.

   d. Make sure the Data File text box has the name COPIERS.DAT, then click OK. The files are merged.

   e. Scroll through the document to make sure that it is formatted correctly.

4 Edit the data file and the form file.

   a. Click Window on the menu bar, then click COPIERS.FRM.

   b. Edit the letter.

   c. Click Window on the menu bar, then click COPIERS.DAT.

   d. Edit the data file to include another address and company name; use your name and address in the file, and make up a company name.

   e. Merge the data file and the form file again.

   f. Use the Spell Checker to proofread the document.

   g. Print all four letters.

   h. Close all documents using the Close All documents button on the Utilities Toolbar.

INDEPENDENT CHALLENGE 1

You have been asked to be the publicity chair for your upcoming high school class reunion. Using the WordPerfect Merge feature, create a personalized form letter to your classmates, informing them of the reunion.

To complete this independent challenge:

1 Create the data file.

a. You should include the following six field names: First Name, Last Name, Street, City, State, Zip Code.

b. Enter information for five classmates into the data file. Use fictitious names and addresses.

c. Save the file as CLASS.DAT.

2 Create the form file.

a. Type a letter with information about the reunion.

b. Include in the letter an inside address and a greeting. Remember to use the FIELD merge code instead of typing the information for each person.

c. In the body of the letter, state the type of event this is (a banquet or a dance, for instance) and who is invited (classmates and their partners, for example). Include the time, date, location, and cost for attending the reunion.

d. After the body of the letter, include a complimentary closing (for instance, "Sincerely yours,"), space for your signature, and your typed name.

e. Save the file as CLASS.FRM.

3 Merge the files.

a. Using the Merge command, merge the form file and the data file to create the personalized form letters.

b. After merging the files, examine the merged document to make sure it is correct.

c. Print two of the letters.

d. Submit a copy of the two letters.

INDEPENDENT CHALLENGE 2

Each year in December, just before the holiday season, you find yourself wishing you could contact all your friends and family around the country and tell them how you and your family spent the past year. December is a very busy time for everyone, and sitting down to write all those letters is a daunting task. Now that you have the Merge capability in WordPerfect, you can create one general letter and personalize it for each of your friends or family who live far away to update them on your doings.

To complete this independent challenge:

1 Create the data file.

a. You should include the following seven field names: First Name, Last Name, Street, City, State, Zip Code, Family.

b. Enter information for five or more friends into the data file. You may use names and addresses of people who live close by. For the Family field, list members of their immediate family.

c. Save the file as FAMFIL.DAT.

2 Create the form file.

a. Type a letter with information about how you spent the last year and any significant events in your family or neighborhood.

b. Include in the letter an inside address and a greeting. Remember to use the FIELD merge code instead of typing the information for each person.

c. In the body of the letter, include a personal note, such as "How are ..." and use the Family field name.

d. After the body of the letter, include a closing (for instance, "Wishing you a wonderful new year, with love,"), space for your signature, and your typed name.

e. Save the file as YRLYLTR.FRM.

3 Merge the files.

a. Using the Merge command, merge the form file and the data file to create the personalized form letters.

b. After merging the documents, examine the merged document to make sure it is correct.

c. Print two of the letters.

d. Submit a copy of the two letters.

UNIT 9

OBJECTIVES

▶ Plan a macro

▶ Record a macro

▶ Play a macro

▶ Edit a macro

▶ Use predefined macros

Creating
AND USING MACROS

*I*n this unit, you will work more efficiently with WordPerfect by using macros. If you find yourself entering the same information in many of your documents, such as your name, address, and phone number, or the company name, you can use a macro that enters this information for you. A **macro** is a series of prerecorded keystrokes or mouse clicks that perform a particular task. Once you record a macro, you can perform the task by pressing just one or two keys. You can record your own macros for individualized or highly specific tasks, or you can use WordPerfect's pre-defined macros that automate more generic, complex or repetitive tasks. You can explore these macros to find the ones that will help you with your work. ▶ As a writer at The Write Staff, you frequently write letters to clients. To speed up your work, you decide to create a macro that will enter the closing lines of a letter. ▶

Planning a macro

You can create a macro for any task. A good reason for creating a macro is to automate the writing tasks that you perform frequently. Table 9-1 lists some common uses for macros. To create a macro, you need to plan, record, and play it, then edit it, if necessary. Macros might seem complicated but they are really very simple, and there is an extensive on-line manual for macros in WordPerfect. To learn how to access this manual, read the related topic, "Macros on-line Help." ▶ You want to add the same closing lines to all your letters without having to type them each time you end a letter. Plan the macro using the following steps.

1 **Determine the task you want the macro to perform.**
You want to create a macro that will enter closing lines in a letter.

2 **Choose a name for your macro that you will remember.**
You decide to name this macro "MYCLOSE."

3 **Decide how to execute the commands you are recording.**
You decide to choose commands from the menu bar and to use the keyboard to type the text of the macro.

4 **Write down the actions you would use to perform the task.**
Because the order in which actions or instructions occur is important, you should verify the steps you'll use in a macro before recording it. Using an old letter as a model, enter the closing lines on screen, writing down every keystroke and mouse click, as shown in Figure 9-1.

TABLE 9-1: Common macro uses

CREATE A MACRO TO:
Print documents (entire document, certain pages, selected text, etc.)
Format documents (justification, indents, margins, character formats, etc.)
Change line spacing in documents (single, double, triple, etc.)
Add standard paragraphs to documents or letters (greeting, closing lines, etc.)

FIGURE 9-1: Notes taken while verifying the macro

Type Sincerely,
Press [Enter] four times
Type your name
Press [Enter]
Type Staff Writer

Macros on-line Help

An on-line macros manual is provided by WordPerfect. The manual must be installed as part of the custom installation. To use the manual, click Help on the menu bar, then click Macros. If it has been installed, the WP Online Macros Manual window opens, as shown in Figure 9-2. This on-line manual, which works like Help, contains information about macro commands and their syntax. It also includes additional instructions and examples for using macros.

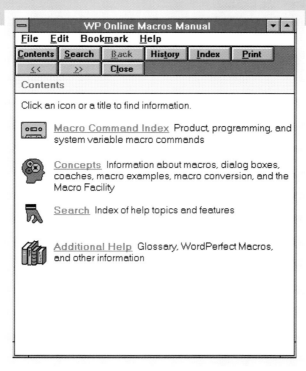

FIGURE 9-2: WP Online Macros Manual window

Recording a macro

Once you've planned a macro and verified that the actions and instructions to perform the task are correct, you are ready to record the macro. There are two ways to **record** a macro: you can have WordPerfect record the results of your keystrokes and mouse clicks as macro commands, or you can enter the macro commands yourself. Either way, you should understand the basics of macro commands. For example, **macro commands** require a specific syntax, or format, to function properly. If you need a macro for a specific task in only one document, you can create a temporary macro; read the related topic, "Recording a temporary macro," to find out more about this. ▶ Now you're ready to record the macro. You will have WordPerfect record the keystrokes and mouse clicks to create the MYCLOSE macro.

1 Click the **New Blank Document button** ⬜
A new file opens. You can also create a macro in an existing document.

2 Click **Tools** on the menu bar, click **Macro**, then click **Record**
The Record Macro dialog box appears, as shown in Figure 9-3.

3 Type **MYCLOSE**
This names the macro MYCLOSE. Macro names must follow the standard file naming conventions.

4 Click **Record**
The macro is saved to a macro directory already set up in WordPerfect and automatically assigned a .WCM filename extension to indicate that this file contains a macro. The Macro Feature Bar appears as in Figure 9-4. The mouse pointer changes to ⊘ when you record a macro. Every keystroke and most mouse clicks are recorded. While a macro is being recorded, you can't use the mouse to position the insertion point in the document; you must use the keyboard.

5 Perform the following keystrokes and actions carefully:
Type **Sincerely,**
Press **[Enter]** four times
Type your name, then press **[Enter]**
Type **Staff Writer**

6 Click the **Stop Record button** ⬛ on the Macros Feature Bar
Recording stops and the macro is saved to your disk.

7 Review the recorded macro
Compare your screen with Figure 9-5. Notice that the closing lines appear at the top of your document. When you play the macro, these closing lines will appear at the insertion point.

8 Close the document but do not save it
Because your macro is already saved as a .WCM file, you don't need to save this document.

FIGURE 9-3: Record Macro dialog box

Type macro name here

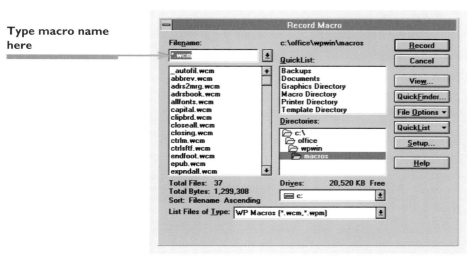

Pause while recording or playing

FIGURE 9-4: Macro Feature Bar

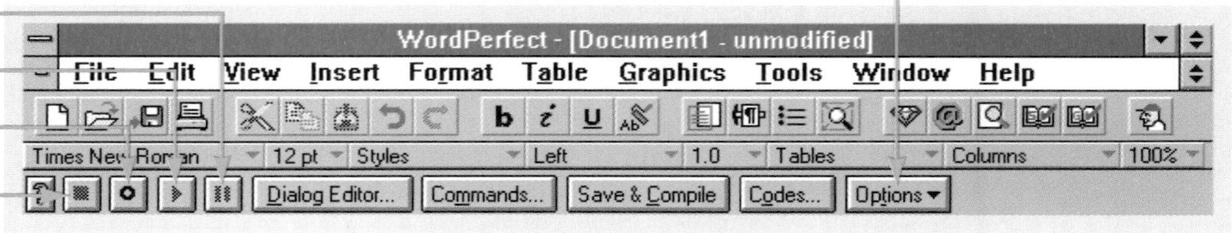

Click to close macro

Play the macro

Begin recording macro

Stop macro play or record

FIGURE 9-5: Recorded macro

Your name appears here

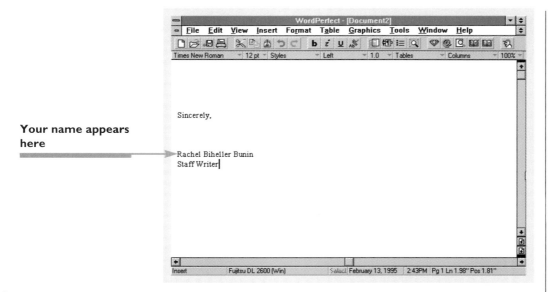

TROUBLE?

To make corrections while recording a macro, press [Backspace] to erase existing text, then retype the information on that line before moving to the next line.■

QUICK TIP

Press [Ctrl][F10] to name and start recording macro commands. Press [Ctrl][F10] again to stop recording the macro.■

Recording a temporary macro

Click Template Macro on the Tools menu. If you do not type a filename before recording a macro, a temporary macro is created. This temporary macro is deleted when you exit WordPerfect. You can play a temporary macro while working with the document, but it is not possible to save or name it.

Playing a macro

After recording a macro, you can play it using the Play command. When you **play** a macro, the macro repeats the actions that you recorded. If you choose to create a temporary macro and want to use it, read the related topic, "Playing a temporary macro," for instructions. ▶ You have a new client, Games International, and you just completed the first introductory letter to their president. Now is a good time to test your new macro. Use the following steps to play the macro that will insert the closing lines in a letter.

1   Open **unit_9-1.wpd**, then save it as **GAMES1** to the MY_FILES directory on your Student Disk

The document has no closing lines. You need to position the insertion point at the end of the last paragraph, where you want the closing to begin.

2   Press **[Ctrl][End]**

This places the insertion point after the blank line between the last paragraph of the letter and the closing lines to be entered by the macro. If you ever make changes to a document, remember to save it before playing a macro, just in case the macro doesn't play correctly.

3   Click **Tools** on the menu bar, click **Macro**, then click **Play**

The Play Macro dialog box appears, as shown in Figure 9-6.

4   Type **MYCLOSE**, which is the name of the saved macro, then click **Play**

The closing lines for the letter appear below the text of the letter, as shown in Figure 9-7. After playing the macro and seeing how it looks, you might notice errors or decide to make changes to the macro before storing it for repeated use. The next lesson covers how to edit a macro that you've created and saved.

5   Save the file to your student disk

FIGURE 9-6: Play Macro dialog box

Click to display list of recently used macros

Type name of saved macro here

List of macros

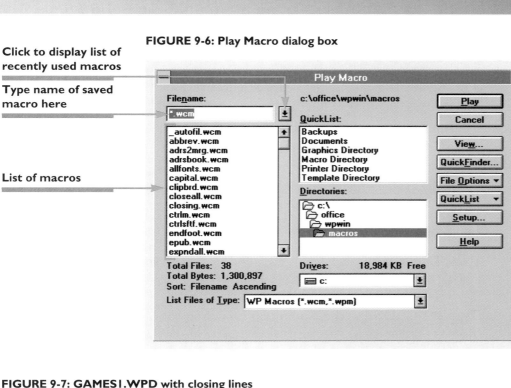

FIGURE 9-7: GAMES1.WPD with closing lines

Rachel Biheller Bunin
Staff Writer

Your name appears here

TROUBLE?

If you can't remember the name of your saved macro, click Tools on the menu bar, then click Macro. The last four macros you have played are displayed on the Macro menu. If that doesn't help, click the macro list arrows in the Play Macro dialog box to scroll through the list of available macros.■

QUICK TIP

Press [Alt][F10] to display the Play Macro dialog box and play a macro.■

Playing a temporary macro

To play a temporary macro, click Tools on the menu bar, click Template Macro, then click Play in the Play Macro dialog box without entering a name.

Editing a macro

After playing a macro, you might decide to include more information, or notice that it doesn't play properly. Either way, you need to edit the macro. When you edit a macro, a Macro Feature Bar appears, which provides options for inserting additional commands, checking for syntax errors and compiling the macro, and saving and closing the macro. A **macro compiler** is used to compile, or "translate," macros so that they can be played. ▶ The macro you created plays properly, but you would like to add a comma and the company name after your title. Edit the MYCLOSE macro to make this addition.

1 Click **Tools** on the menu bar, click **Macro**, then click **Edit**

The Edit Macro dialog box opens. It is very similar to both the Play Macro and Record Macro dialog boxes.

2 Type **MYCLOSE** in the Name text box, then click **Edit**

The Macro Feature Bar and the commands contained in the MYCLOSE macro appear. Each action included in the macro is listed on a separate line. Macro commands contain three parts: the command name, which indicates what action the command is making; the parameters, which are the variables used with a command to indicate a specific value or option; and the separators, which are the semicolons used to separate the parameters in a macro. Figure 9-8 shows the syntax of a recorded macro.

3 Position the insertion point between the last "r" in "Writer" and the following quotation mark (")

You are ready to add the comma and the company name.

4 Type **, The Write Staff**

Be careful not to delete any of the macro formatting characters; for example, the (or ". You cannot save or play a macro that has syntax errors. The Save & Compile button on the Macro Feature Bar makes sure the macro is error-free.

5 Click **Save & Compile** on the Macro Feature Bar

This performs a check for syntax errors. If you receive an error message, read the related topic, "What to do if you get an error when compiling a macro," then edit the macro. If no errors are found, the Save & Compile button appears dimmed, and you are ready to play the edited macro.

6 Click **Options** on the Macro Feature Bar, then click **Close Macro**

The macro closes and the Feature Bar no longer appears. GAMES1.WPD reappears on the screen.

7 Select *all* the closing lines (begin selecting with the "S" in Sincerely), then press **[Delete]**

The closing lines are deleted from the letter. Be sure there is a blank line between the last paragraph and the insertion point. Play the macro again.

8 Click **Tools** on the menu bar, click **Macro**, click **Play**, scroll the **Filename list box**, click **myclose**, then click **Play**

The edited macro plays and the closing lines, including the added company name, appear at the end of the letter.

9 Save and print the letter

Compare your final letter with Figure 9-9.

FIGURE 9-8: Syntax of recorded macro

Click to Save &
Compile or close
the macro

WordPerfect auto-
matically inserts the
Application command

Insertion point

Parameter

Separator

Command name

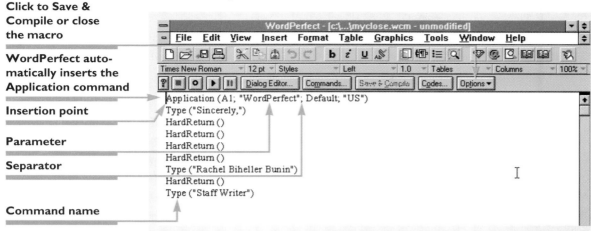

FIGURE 9-9: Letter with company name added to closing lines

Your name appears
here

What to do if you get an error when compiling a macro

A macro won't play if it has an error. If you receive an error message after clicking Save & Compile or Close Macro on the Macro Edit Feature Bar, you can choose Cancel Compilation or you can choose Continue Compilation and check for errors. After you correct all the errors, compile the macro so it will play.

QUICK **TIP**

To edit a macro quickly, retrieve it directly into a document window. Click File on the menu bar, click Open, then choose the name of the macro you want to edit. The Macro Feature Bar won't appear.■

Using predefined macros

A collection of predefined macros that perform many useful tasks comes with WordPerfect. You can find a list of all the macros supplied by WordPerfect by reviewing Additional Help, WordPerfect Macros in the on-line Macros Manual. Read the related topic, "Naming your macros," for tips on organizing your macros in the macro list. ▶ After reviewing the list of macros available, you decide to try the macro PGBORDER.WCM. This macro inserts a border of your choice around the document page. The border will make your document more attractive and professional as you try to get new clients.

1 Click **Tools** on the menu bar, click **Macro**, then click **Play**
The Play Macro dialog box opens.

2 Scroll the list box and click **PGBORDER.WCM**
The description of the macro in the dialog box tells you what the macro does. Refer to Figure 9-10.

3 Click **Play**
The Graphic Page Borders dialog box appears with border choices listed in the scroll box, as in Figure 9-11. You can preview these and then insert your border.

4 Click **Preview**
View the "Classic" choice. It doesn't seem to fit the style of a letter to a company that sells games.

5 Click **OK** in the Preview Border dialog box
You decided to choose "Confetti" after viewing the other borders because you are sending this letter to a toy company.

6 Click **Confetti**, then click **OK**
The border is inserted in your letter. Next, you want to view the border on the page.

7 Click the **Page/Zoom Full button** 🔍 on the Toolbar
Your screen looks similar to Figure 9-12. The Confetti border adds nicely to the letter for Games International.

8 Save and print the letter
The letter with its new border is ready to send out to your client.

9 Close the file and exit WordPerfect

FIGURE 9-10: Play Macro dialog box with PGBORDER.WCM selected

Selected macro

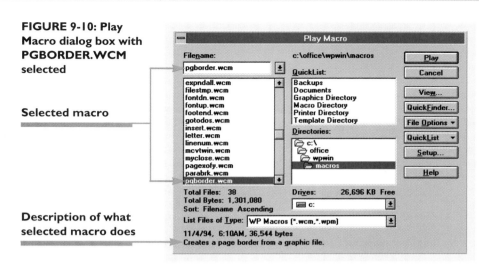

Description of what selected macro does

FIGURE 9-11: Graphic Page Borders dialog box

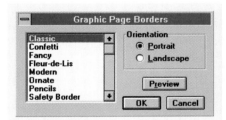

FIGURE 9-12: Result of PGBORDER macro

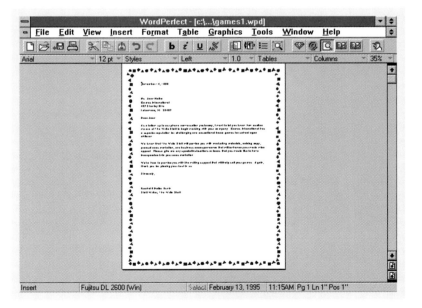

Naming your macros

Macros are listed in alphabetical order in the Play Macro and Record Macro dialog boxes. If you want your own macros to be easily identified among the macros supplied by WordPerfect, there are two ways to do so. First, you could create a new subdirectory called MYMACROS and save your macros there. Another method is to name all your macros beginning with a special character, such as *, so they appear together on the list.

CONCEPTSREVIEW

**Label each element of the WordPerfect
screen shown in Figure 9-13:**

1 _____

2 _____

3 _____

4 _____

5 _____

6 _____

7 _____

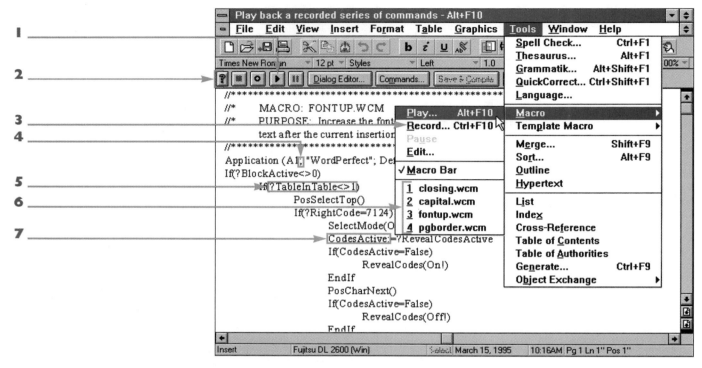

FIGURE 9-13

Select the best answer from the list of choices.

8 capital.wcm

9 pagexofy.wcm

10 saveall.wcm

11 watermrk.wcm

12 parabrk.wcm

a. Saves open documents

b. Capitalizes first letter of current word

c. Helps user create a watermark from a .WPG file or from text

d. Places x of y page number in specified location and format

e. Places a paragraph break at the end of the paragraph

13 What is a macro?

a. a keystroke command that takes the place of a pull-down menu command

b. a pull-down menu command that takes the place of a keystroke command

c. a short, user-created command that takes the place of several (or many) keystrokes or mouse operations

d. a series of keystrokes or commands that accomplishes a specific task

14 Which keystroke command plays a macro?

a. [Ctrl][F10]

b. [Ctrl][F9]

c. [Shift][F10]

d. [Alt][F10]

15 Which menu contains the Macro command to start recording a macro?

a. Edit

b. Insert

c. Tools

d. Help

16 Which keystroke command stops the recording of a macro?

a. [Ctrl][F10]

b. [Ctrl][F9]

c. [Shift][F10]

d. [Alt][F10]

17 Which of the following cannot be used as a macro name?

a. clearscreen

b. mymacro

c. altm

d. test

18 Which menu contains the on-line macros manual?

a. Format

b. Help

c. Tools

d. Edit

19 What do you think the predefined macro fontup.wcm does?

a. creates a new font

b. enters the word "font" in the document

c. increases font size by 2 points

d. decreases font size by 2 points

20 In order for a macro to be played, it must first be:

a. controlled

b. compiled

c. configured

d. closed

APPLICATIONS
REVIEW

In this section, you will create and edit a macro that formats a line of text so that it becomes a title. The macro centers the line of text and converts it to all uppercase letters.

1 Plan your macro.

a. Start with a blank document window.

b. Type the phrase "this is a test" so that you will have a line of text to work with when you record the macro.

c. Press [Enter] to mark the end of the title and to create a new blank line below the title.

d. Move the insertion point anywhere within the phrase or immediately to the right of the phrase.

2 Name and begin to record the macro.

a. Display the Record Macro dialog box by clicking Tools on the menu bar, clicking Macro, then clicking Record

b. Type the name "title" for your macro.

c. Click Record to begin recording.

3 Record and save the macro.

a. Select the phrase by clicking Edit on the menu bar, Select, then Paragraph.

For simplicity, you can treat the title as a paragraph.

b. Center the title by clicking Format on the menu bar, Justification, then Center.

c. Turn off Select by pressing [F8].

d. Stop recording the macro by clicking the Tools menu, then clicking Macro and Record, or by pressing [Ctrl][F10].

4 Play the macro.

a. Start with a blank document window.

b. Type "Applications Review Unit 9: *{your name}*" as a title.

c. Print the document.

d. Click Tools on the menu bar, click Macro, then click Play.

e. Type the name of the macro ("title"), then click Play.

f. Print the document.

5 Edit the macro.

    a. Display the Edit Macro dialog box by clicking Tools on the menu bar, clicking Macro, then clicking Edit.

    b. Type the name of the macro ("title").

    c. Click Edit.

    d. Insert the new line "ConvertCaseUppercase ( )" below the line "SelectParagraph ( )."

    e. Finish the editing session by clicking Save & Compile on the Macro Feature Bar, then click Options, then Close Macro.

    f. Play the newly edited macro and view the changes.

6 Use a predefined macro.

    a. Select the title "Applications Review Unit 9: *{your name}*.

    b. Open the Play Macro dialog box.

    c. Play the fontup.wcm macro.

    d. View the results.

    e. Print the document.

INDEPENDENT
CHALLENGE 1

As a promotional writer at The Write Staff, you are often required to write interoffice memos. You realize that you have to type the following text repeatedly.

Date:
To: The Write Staff Employees
From: *(your name)*
Subject:

You decide to record a macro that automatically creates this memo header.

To complete this independent challenge:

1 Decide which keystrokes you need to record and what you will name the macro.

2 Carefully record the macro.

3 Play back your macro to make sure that it works.

4 If necessary, edit the macro, and make sure to save and compile it.

5 Print the macro.

6 Submit a printed copy of the macro.

INDEPENDENT
CHALLENGE 2

You have often thought about having letterhead printed to use in personal correspondence. In your personal writing, you often include your name, address, and phone number at the top of the page, and the current date above the salutation. You can create a macro that will open a new document, insert the information you need, and even add a graphic element to make the page look attractive. You decide to record a macro that automatically creates this stationery.

To complete this independent challenge:

1 Decide which keystrokes you need to record and what you will name the macro.

    a. Be creative in designing your personal letterhead. Use some elegant fonts and increased font sizes for your name and address.

    b. Plan to include a watermark, or perhaps a graphic image, in the letterhead.

2 Carefully record the macro.

3 Play back your macro to make sure that it works.

4 If necessary, edit the macro, and make sure to save and compile it.

5 Print the macro.

6 Submit a printed copy of the macro.

Glossary

Alignment   Positioning of text between the left and right margins of a document; also known as justification.

Antonyms   Words found in the Thesaurus that have opposite meanings from the word being looked up.

Application   Software program; such as WordPerfect or Quattro Pro.

Application icon   Graphic representation of a Windows application.

Button   Located on the Power Bar, Toolbar, Feature Bars, and in dialog boxes; used to direct Windows to carry out a command.

Cancel button   Removes a dialog box without making any changes. Also represented by the X above the Table Formula Feature Bar, is used to cancel an entry.

Cell   Intersection of a row and a column in WordPerfect tables.

Cell name or cell address   A column letter and row number that identifies the cell's position in the table.

Check box   Controls options that can be turned on (containing an "X") or off (empty).

Clip art   Images or symbols stored on disk.

Clipboard   A temporary storage area.

Close   Puts a file away without exiting WordPerfect.

Codes   Determine how your document looks on the screen and when printed. You cannot see these codes in a normal document window.

Column   Divides text vertically on a page in a document.

Command   An instruction given to the computer to carry out an action

Confirm button   Represented by a check mark above the Table Formula Feature bar; used to accept an entry.

Control menu box   A box in the upper-left corner of a window used to close a window.

Copy   Copies the selected information and places it on the Clipboard.

Cross-reference   Refers your readers to other pages, figures and notes, such as "see page 12."

Cut   Removes the selected information from a document and places it on the Clipboard.

Data   Information that is entered into the cells of a WordPerfect table or the fields and records in a data file used in merging.

Data file   Contains records to be merged with a form file.

Default   A program's predetermined setting that takes effect unless changed.

Delete   Removes characters to the right of the insertion point.

Desktop   Where you do your work and arrange your files.

Dialog box   Provides a way to choose and implement options using radio buttons, check boxes, or text boxes, lists or buttons.

Directory   A section of the disk used to store files that you create and applications you use.

Directories dialog box   Provides the options to open, save, copy, delete, and work with many additional file options.

Documents   Files created with WordPerfect.

Document window   Where you type and create a document.

Drag and drop   To move or copy text or objects from one location in a document to another.

Drive   Part of the computer used for storing files and applications.

Drop cap   A graphic element that adds style to the text in a document by creating a stylized character from the first letter in a paragraph.

Edit   Changes or revises a document.

Endnotes   Printed at the end of the document. See also Footnotes.

Exit   Leaves the WordPerfect application.

Feature bars   These provide easy access to options related to a specific feature, such as the Formula or Macro Feature Bar.

Field   The smallest amount of information you can specify in a data file.

File   Information stored on a disk under a single name.

File extension   The three letters, numbers, or symbols following the period in a filename; WordPerfect automatically assigns ".wpd" for WordPerfect files.

Find   Searches for words and phrases in a document.

Find & Replace   Searches and allows you to replace words and phrases in a document.

Font   Style of letters, numbers, and symbols; described by name, appearance, and size, such as Times New Roman Regular 12 pt.

Footer   Information that appears at the bottom of each page of a document.

Footnotes   Use to list sources or provide additional information about items in your document. Footnotes appear at the bottom of any page whereas endnotes are usually printed at the end of the document.

Form file   Contains the text that remains the same in each letter when merged with a data file; also includes the field names that correspond to the fields in the data file.

Format   The appearance of information in a file.

Formula   Calculates data in a WordPerfect table.

Formula Bar   Formulas for calculating data are created in this bar.

Function keys   Keyboard shortcuts that provide quick access to certain features in an application.

Grammatik   To check for grammatical errors; provides corresponding grammar rules and lists alternatives.

Graphical user interface   A display (based on pictures and icons) of computer commands.

Graphics   Pictures or borders that can be inserted into a document to provide clarity, interest, or visual appeal.

Group window   Located within the Program Manager and contains additional groups or applications.

Group icon   The picture representing a group of related applications such as File Manager, Accessories, Main, or WordPerfect.

Hard page break   Generates a new page at that point no matter how much text is on the page. By contrast, a soft page break is determined by the margins and pages and often change depending on the amount of text on the page.

Header   Information that appears at the top of each page of a document.

Headword   A word that can be looked up in the Thesaurus.

Help   Provides an explanation and usually instructions for a specific feature, dialog box, or task.

Icon   Small pictures used to represent programs, files, or functions.

Import   Insert clip art images, logos, drawings or other files into your document.

Indent   Moves a line of text or paragraph to the right one tab setting and resets the margin at the tab setting until the next [Enter] is pressed.

Index   Use to display page numbers for items that can be looked up in a printed document.

Insert   Inserts new text at the insertion point while pushing existing text to the right as you type.

Insertion point   A blinking vertical bar where text will be inserted or deleted.

Justification   Aligns text on the right or left margins or centers text between the margins.

Launch   Start a software program.

Line spacing   Determines the amount of space between the lines of text in a document.

List   Use to display items such as figures, illustrations, and tables in your document.

Macro   Series of recorded keystrokes or mouse clicks that automatically performs a task or series of tasks.

Margins   The boundaries around the outside of a document.

Menu bar   Located just below the window's title bar and contains headings for lists or groups of commands, or options.

Merge   Combines the information and text from the data and form files into one file.

Merge codes   Use to separate each field from the others and to end each record in your data file.

Mouse   Hand-held input device that you roll on your desk to position the mouse pointer on the Windows desktop.

Mouse pointer   An arrow indicating the current location of the mouse on the desktop.

Open   Loads a file from a disk into the computer's memory, making the file available to you to work on.

Operating system   Manages the basics of the computer including recognizing keyboard and mouse input, copying files, and loading programs into the computer's memory.

Orphan   A single line of text that appears alone at the bottom of a page.

Page break The next page of your document begins below this point, the previous page ends above this point.

Page View Provides a full "what you see is what you get" (WYSIWYG) environment in which to work on documents.

Paste Copies or moves information on the Clipboard to a new location in a document.

Point size The size of a font.

Power Bar Provides easy access to the most frequently used text-editing and text layout features.

Preferences Provides options for changing the default document window.

Program Manager Main control program of Windows; all Windows applications are started from the Program Manager.

QuickFormat Quickly copies fonts and formatting, such as bold, from one area of text to another.

QuickMenu Lists a set of options for a particular feature.

QuickSelect Selects text by clicking. You can select a letter, a word or words, a sentence or several sentences, one or more paragraphs, or an entire document.

QuickTip The name of the button displayed in a little yellow text box below the button on the Power Bar, Toolbar, or Status Bar.

RAM (random access memory) A temporary storage space that is erased when the computer is turned off or whenever there is a fluctuation in power.

Record A collection of related fields.

Replace Use choose the word in the Replace With text box in the Spell Checker and continue looking for the next spelling error or repeated word.

Reveal codes Displays all the codes that are in the document.

Ruler Bar Use to quickly set and move tabs and margins, make paragraph adjustments and position columns.

Save Saves changes to a WordPerfect document in a file on a disk.

Save As Creates a duplicate WordPerfect document with a new name.

Scroll bars The bars on the right side and bottom of a window that help you move quickly through a document, vertically and horizontally.

Scroll box The box in the scroll bar that helps you move quickly through larger portions of a document than scroll bars.

Selecting text Highlights text that will be affected by the next chosen option such as copying, moving, or formatting.

Show¶ Command displays a limited number of key symbols like space, tab, and hard-return in the document window.

Sizing buttons Buttons in the upper-right corner of a window that can be used to minimize or maximize a window.

Sizing handles Small squares on a selected graphic used to size or move the graphic.

Soft page break Generates a new page. See also Hard page break.

Spell Checker To check for spelling errors, duplicate words, and irregular capitalization of words in a document.

Status bar The line at the bottom of the WordPerfect window that shows document status, page number, date and time, as well as the vertical and horizontal position of the insertion point.

Suppress Option that allows you to skip the header, footer, or page number on a particular page without deleting it from any other pages.

Synonyms Words in the Thesaurus that have similiar meanings to the headword being looked up.

Syntax Rules for organizing elements such as those found in macros.

Tab marker Displays on the Ruler Bar to indicate type and placement of a tab stop.

Tab stops Indicated by black triangles on the Ruler Bar. When you press [Tab], the insertion point moves to the next tab stop.

Table of Authorities For legal purposes lists where citations occur in a legal brief.

Table of Contents Use to list titles and headings in the order they appear in a document.

Tables Organizes information into columns and rows without using tabs.

Task List Alternative method for switching between applications when an application is taking up the entire screen.

TextArt A way to create graphic images from your text.

Thesaurus To look up synonyms or antonyms for words in a document.

Timed document backup Makes a backup of a document at specified intervals.

Title bar   An area directly below the window's top border that displays the window's name.

Toggle   A button or command that switches back and forth between two modes.

Toolbar   Provides quick access to frequently used features and to additional Toolbars.

Typeover   Types over existing text to replace it character for character.

Undelete   Restores up to the last three deletions made in a document.

Undo   Restores the last change or deletion in a document.

Watermark   A drawing, logo, clip art image, or headline-sized text located behind the text in your document.

Widow   A single line of text at the top of a page.

Window   A framed region on the screen.

Word processing   Software application that enables you to produce a variety of documents, including letters, memos, newsletters, and reports.

Word wrap   When you reach the end of a line, keep typing to move the text to the next line.

Zoom Full Page button   Displays the page as it will appear when printed including all page margins.

Index